ACCESS

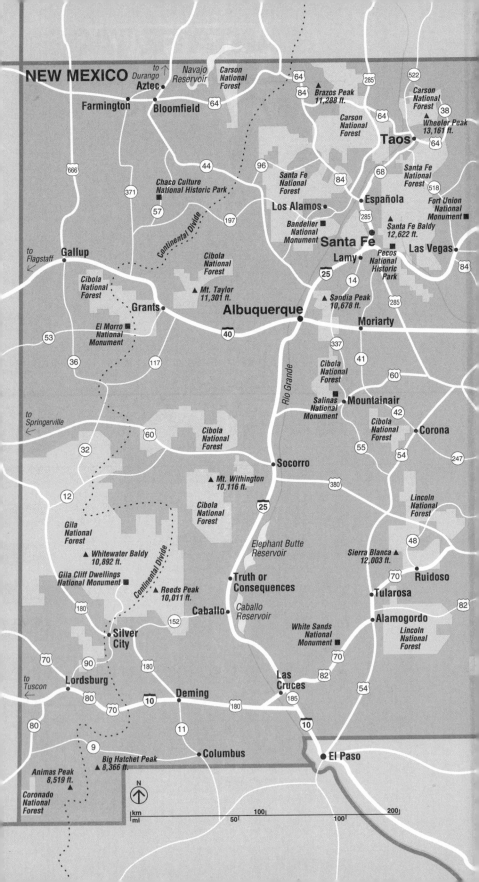

Orientation

Northern New Mexico is a region of the American continent that bypasses the mind and speaks directly to the unconscious, with a primitive attraction that many find irresistible. "Land of Enchantment" is the state motto, and it is more than a license plate slogan. Thousands of writers, artists, scientists, and celebrities, as well as countless unwary travelers, have been seduced by the land. Visitors to **Santa Fe**, in particular, have been known to begin house-hunting after their first hour in the city; others have moved there after seeing it in their dreams. Weary of Europe, writer D.H. Lawrence came here seeking new inspiration from "the aboriginal Indians and from the aboriginal air and land." Painter Georgia O'Keeffe, after visiting for one summer, could not rest easily until she had made the region her home and transformed it into O'Keeffe country. Physicist J. Robert Oppenheimer, exposed to the area in his boyhood, chose it as the perfect place to literally tamper with the elements by constructing an atomic bomb. And many film stars have turned their backs on the Hollywood nightmare to come live in the Santa Fe dreamscape, among them actress Greer Garson who settled in Santa Fe decades before it was chic, and actor Dennis Hopper who made **Taos** his home in the 1960s.

Once hostile and remote, Northern New Mexico today is a land of first-class hotels decorated with Indian and Hispanic motifs and crafts, well-publicized restaurants featuring Southwestern food (as well as most every cuisine in the world), down-home restaurants that offer blazing hot chile-based local food, art galleries displaying work ranging from regional folk artists to painters of international renown, plus excellent skiing, hiking, and fishing. But more than anything else, Northern New Mexico is a land of stark and powerful images. The first sight of a single twisted piñon tree clinging to life in the crevice of a barren rock can speak directly to the loneliness of the human condition. With familiarity, the same tree can come to symbolize the three very different cultures that coexist here. The piñon survives in the high desert against all odds, like the Indians of the 19 nearby pueblos, whose spirit has withstood centuries of material deprivation and hostile invasions. Its tenacious roots suggest the deep faith of the Hispanic population, whose ancestors carved villages and cities in a region where there was little commercial reason for either. And the needle-sharp green branches symbolize the prosperity brought in recent decades by Anglo expatriates. The symbolic here in New Mexico is visible in a thousand variations: in the bleached bones painted by O'Keeffe, in the black pottery of **San Ildefonso Pueblo**, in the folk art of Hispanic *santeros* (carvers and painters of religious icons).

At once as austere as a moonscape and brightly colored as a Mexican garden, this high-desert region is a striking blend of nature's grandeur and human humility. Mountain peaks as high as 13,000 feet rise into pristine blue skies, snowcapped in winter, studded with wildflowers in spring, alive with rushing streams in summer; in autumn whole mountainsides, especially above Santa Fe, turn a bright gold courtesy of enormous spreads of aspen trees. In the valleys, dry gullies (called arroyos) can suddenly metamorphose after a spring or summer downpour into rushing rivers hazardous to anything in their path. The first settlers, ancient Indians called Anasazi, made their homes high up in cliff dwellings that can still be visited at such historic sites as **Bandelier National Monument.** Their descendants, the Pueblo Indians, built flat-roofed villages of adobe (dried mud) that have remained inhabited for centuries. Spanish conquistadores and settlers who arrived in 1540 followed suit, and flat adobe construction, real or imitation, remains the norm today in Santa Fe, Taos, and the older sections of **Albuquerque.** Few structures are more than two stories high, and the colors run the full spectrum from beige to brown. A stroll through parts of Santa Fe in particular offers the illusion of

Taos Pueblo

being in a foreign land, so strong is the Spanish and Mexican influence and the devotion to human scale. Only in downtown Albuquerque, a modern metropolis of nearly a half-million people, have glass-and-steel skyscrapers been hurled into the face of the natural order.

Settled by the Indians more than one thousand years ago, the region was claimed by Spanish explorers in the 16th century and became part of New Spain, later called Mexico. Numerous mission churches are reminders of Catholic missionaries who came to convert the Indians. US troops conquered the area during the Mexican-American War in 1846, and for half a century it was the New Mexico Territory, a land of desperadoes such as Billy the Kid and unscrupulous lawyer-landgrabber-politicians like the Santa Fe Ring. Not until 1912 was the territory divided in half and given statehood as New Mexico and Arizona—the last two of the contiguous 48 states.

The most recent invaders of the region are the hordes of Anglos, many of them wealthy, who have built million-dollar homes in the hills, mostly near Santa Fe. In 20 years the majority population of Santa Fe has gone from 65 percent Hispanic to 51 percent Anglo. The presence of wealthy newcomers has induced the establishment of acclaimed upscale restaurants and high-priced boutiques. These changes have caused consternation among many locals, who long for the sleepier days of yore.

Santa Fe, the spiritual and artistic heart of the region, is the oldest state capital in the US. Here, in a city of only 60,000 residents, you can choose from among more than 4,000 rooms in large and small hotels and motels as well as in charming bed-and-breakfasts. Wandering through the narrow streets that once were burro paths or Indian trails reveals 200 restaurants offering a wide selection of tastes that ranges from the haute cuisine of **Santacafe** and **Coyote Cafe** to Frito pies at **Woolworth's;** more than 175 art galleries offering everything from traditional Western paintings to contemporary abstractions; and over 50 Indian jewelry shops laden with silver and turquoise bracelets

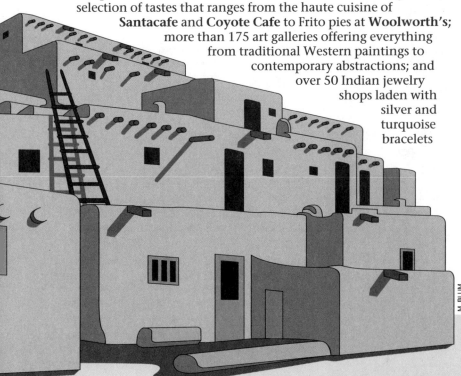

M. BLUM

and belts, with pottery, baskets, kachina dolls, and every other variety of Indian craft. Six museums display the best of the best in every art and craft, and in July and August the world-famous open-air **Santa Fe Opera** fills the night with music, as does the world-class Santa Fe Chamber Music Festival as well as the **Desert Chorale.**

Santa Fe is also a convenient jumping-off point for day trips. The red-and-yellow striated hills near **Abiquiu**—which O'Keeffe made famous—are not to be missed, and the **Santuario de Chimayó,** an old village church where miraculous healings have allegedly occurred, is also fascinating. The many Indian pueblos in the area offer an insight into another way of life.

For those who prefer similar attractions in a more compact package, Taos sits 70 miles to the north up a scenic drive through the canyon of the **Rio Grande.** Several dozen galleries offer a wide range of art, and a handful of restaurants, notably **Lambert's,** reach the level of Santa Fe's best. Two fine museums—the **Millicent Rogers Museum** and the **Harwood Foundation**—specialize in the works of the early Taos art colony. And the skiing at **Taos Ski Valley** is without argument the most challenging and spectacular in the state. More than 500 years old, **Taos Pueblo,** which sits just on the outskirts of town, is the oldest continuously inhabited apartment dwelling in the country. Five stories high in some places and all adobe, it is, along with **Acoma Pueblo,** among the most intriguing sights in the American West.

Nearly 300 years old, Albuquerque has its own historic attractions—from the buildings of **Old Town** to huge numbers of ancient Indian petroglyphs in the lava mesas to the west—although they have been overshadowed by the urban and commercial sprawl that has surrounded them. The city is better known, however, as the hot-air ballooning capital of the world; as the home of the **University of New Mexico;** and as a center for high-tech industries.

If possible, make the northerly 60-mile drive to Santa Fe in the late afternoon, when the setting sun lends an extra grace to the rolling hills dotted like leopard skins with piñon and juniper bushes, when the red earth blushes with delight, when the mountains turn a mysterious purple, when the fairies of enchantment come out to play. But if the place captures your soul—that is, if you don't want to go home again—don't say you were never warned.

How To Read This Guide

SANTA FE/TAOS/ALBUQUERQUE ACCESS® is arranged by neighborhood so you can see at a glance where you are and what is around you. The numbers next to the entries in the following chapters correspond to the numbers on the maps. The text is color-coded according to the kind of place described:

Restaurants/Clubs: Red   **Hotels:** Blue

Shops/🌿 Outdoors: Green   **Sights/Culture:** Black

Rating the Restaurants and Hotels

The restaurant star rating takes into account the quality of the food, service, atmosphere, and uniqueness of the restaurant. An expensive restaurant doesn't necessarily ensure an enjoyable evening; while a small, relatively unknown spot could have good food, professional service, and a lovely atmosphere. Therefore, on a purely subjective basis, stars are used to judge the overall dining value (see star ratings at right). Keep in mind that chefs and owners often change, which can drastically affect the quality of a restaurant, for better or for worse. The ratings in this guidebook are based on information available at press time.

The price ratings, as categorized at right, apply to restaurants and hotels. These figures describe general price-range relationships among other restaurants and hotels in the area. The restaurant price ratings are based on the average cost of an entrée for one person, excluding tax and tip. Hotel price ratings reflect the base price of a standard room for two people for one night during the peak season.

Restaurants

★	Good	
★★	Very Good	
★★★	Excellent	
★★★★	An Extraordinary Experience	
$	The Price Is Right	(less than $10)
$$	Reasonable	($10-$15)
$$$	Expensive	($15-$20)
$$$$	Big Bucks	($20 and up)

Hotels

$	The Price Is Right	(less than $50)
$$	Reasonable	($50-$80)
$$$	Expensive	($80-$140)
$$$$	Big Bucks	($140 and up)

Map Key

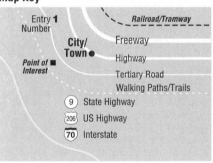

Area code 505 unless otherwise noted.

Getting to Northern New Mexico

Airports
Albuquerque International Airport (ABQ)

If you're flying on a commercial airline to Northern New Mexico, Albuquerque will be your first destination. **ABQ** is located on the south side of the city off I-25, and serves eight commercial airlines, a regional carrier (**Mesa Airlines**), and a commuter line (**Ross Aviation**). **Mesa Airlines** provides air-shuttle service between Albuquerque and Santa Fe up to seven times daily. In winter **Mesa** also offers service from Albuquerque to some New Mexico ski resorts, including **Angel Fire** and **Red River.**

Airport Emergencies 842.4004

Customs and Immigration 766.2621

Ground Transportation 842.4366

Information 842.4366

Lost and Found 842.4379

Paging 842.4379

Police 842.4379, 842.4366

Getting to and from Albuquerque International Airport
By Car

ABQ is about three miles from downtown Albuquerque. To get there, head north on I-25. To reach Santa Fe, continue north on I-25 for about 60 miles. For Taos, follow directions to Santa Fe, then continue north on US 285 approximately 15 miles to Española and then head east about 40 miles on NM 68 into Taos.

Renting a car is the perfect way to enjoy the spectacular scenery between Albuquerque, Santa Fe, and Taos. Car-rental companies at **ABQ** include:

Alamo............................842.4057, 800/327.9633

Avis................................842.4080, 800/331.1212

Budget 800/828.3438

Dollar 842.4224, 800/369.4226

Hertz 842.4235, 800/654.3131

National..........................842.4222, 800/227.7368

Payless 800/331.3271

Thrifty 842.8755, 800/367.2277

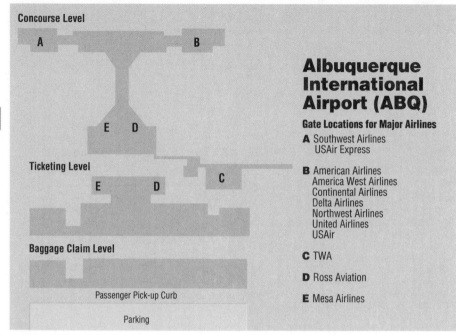

Concourse Level

A B

E D

Ticketing Level

E D C

Baggage Claim Level

Passenger Pick-up Curb

Parking

Albuquerque International Airport (ABQ)

Gate Locations for Major Airlines

A Southwest Airlines
USAir Express

B American Airlines
America West Airlines
Continental Airlines
Delta Airlines
Northwest Airlines
United Airlines
USAir

C TWA

D Ross Aviation

E Mesa Airlines

By Bus

Greyhound/Trailways (243.4435, 800/231.2222) and **Texas, New Mexico & Oklahoma Coaches (TNMO)** 243.4435 in Albuquerque, 471.0008 in Santa Fe, 758.1144 in Taos) provide regular service to Santa Fe (a 1.5-hour trip) and Taos (2.45 hours). **Shuttlejack** (243.3244 in Albuquerque, 982.4311 in Santa Fe, 800/452.2655) also offers daily service from **Albuquerque International Airport** to Santa Fe and Taos.

By Limousine

You can arrange to leave the airport in style by calling **American Limousine** (891.5466), **Lucky's Limousine Service** (836.4035), or **VIP Limousine Service** (883.4888).

By Taxi

There is a taxi zone on the airport's lower level where **Albuquerque Cab** (883.4888) and **Yellow Cab** (247.8888) cars are available to transport you to your destination.

Private Albuquerque Airports

For the real jet-setters (those wealthy enough to own their own planes), there are various private airports in Albuquerque that service single- and double-engine airplanes as well as small private jet airliners. Three such airports are: **Coronado Airport** (1000 Pan-American Fwy, 821.7777), **Double Eagle Airport** (7401 Paseo del Vulcan, 842.7007), and **Cutter Flying Service** (2502 Clark Carr Loop, 842.4184).

Santa Fe Municipal Airport

This small airport (473.7243), located approximately 15 miles south of downtown at the end of Airport Road, is used by private planes and shuttle lines.

Taos Airport

Approximately 12 miles west of Taos, off US 64, this airport (758.4995) services only private planes.

Airlines

American Airlines	800/433.7300
America West Airlines	247.0737, 800/247.5692
Continental Airlines	842.8220, 800/525.0280
Delta Airlines	243.2794, 800/221.1212
Mesa Airlines	842.4414, 800/637.2247
Ross Aviation	242.2811
Southwest Airlines	800/435.9792
TWA	842.4010, 800/221.2000
United Airlines	800/241.6522
USAir	842.4903, 800/428.4322

Getting Around Northern New Mexico

Bicycles

Santa Fe has numerous bike routes. The **Santa Fe Convention and Visitors Bureau** (201 W Marcy St, at Grant St, 984.6760, 800/777.2489) offers a bicycle map chock-full of information about riding in and out of town; you can also get the map by calling 988.RIDE. Rentals are available from **First Powder/Last Chance General Store** (Hyde Park, 982.0495), **Palace Bike Rentals** (409 E Palace Ave, at Delgado St, 984.2151), **Santa Fe Schwinn** (1611 St. Michael's Dr, between Llano St and Cerrillos Rd, 983.4473), and **Tees and Skis** (107 Washington Ave, at Palace Ave, 983.5637).

In Taos, rentals and information are available at **Gear Up Bicycle Shop** (129 Paseo del Pueblo Sur, at Kit Carson Rd, 751.0365).

Albuquerque also has a large network of bicycle paths. For a free map, call the **Office of Cultural Recreational Services** (768.3550). Rentals are available from **Rio Mountain Sport** (1210 Rio Grande Blvd NW, between Floral and Indian School Rds, 766.9970) and **REI (Recreational Equipment Inc.**; 1905 Mountain Rd NW, at Rio Grande Blvd E, 247.1191).

Buses

Santa Fe Trails (984.6730), the city's public bus system that covers most of Santa Fe, began service in 1993. Park at the **De Vargas Mall** (Guadalupe St, at Paseo de Peralta) and ride to the congested downtown plaza area in less than five minutes.

Taos has no bus system.

In Albuquerque, the **Sun Tran** (843.9200) buses cover the entire city, but only during daylight hours. There is regular service from 6AM to 7PM weekdays and from 6AM to 6PM on weekends. Buses run less frequently to the more remote parts of town and on weekends. The bus stops are well marked with the company's sunburst logo.

Driving

Navigating a vehicle through New Mexico can be an adventure. Year after year the state ranks among the worst three in automobile deaths per capita. It is also always near the top in alcohol-related auto accidents. Many New Mexicans have an ornery streak: They hate to stop at red lights, and they refuse to use directional signals. Drive defensively, and expect the drivers around you to do the unexpected at any time. Pedestrians have the right-of-way by law, and in Santa Fe and Taos people take full advantage of it.

Drivers in Taos, perhaps because of the narrow streets, tend to drive slowly and with courtesy, and they follow the rules.

Limousines

If you prefer to avoid parking and driving hassles and want someone else to navigate, several limousine companies in Northern New Mexico are ready to serve you.

Santa Fe:

American Limousine 891.5466

Limotion 471.1265

Santa Fe Hotelimo 438.0202

Albuquerque:

American Limousine 891.5466

At Last the Past (antique limo service) 298.9944

Classic Limousine 247.4000

Dream Limousine 884.6464

Lucky's Limousine Service 836.4035

VIP Limousine Service 883.4888

Parking

In June, July, and August, parking is a serious problem in downtown Santa Fe and Taos. There are municipal parking lots at 216 West San Francisco Street and 102 East Water Street in Santa Fe and on Padre Martinez Lane (between Don Fernando St and Ranchitos Rd) in Taos, but the crush of visitors tends to fill them up by around 10AM. If possible, leave your car at your hotel.

Parking in Albuquerque is abundant, except for the Old Town and **University of New Mexico** areas, which can be horrendous. There are municipal lots on Mountain Road NW (at San Felipe St) and on Central Avenue (between Romero and San Felipe Sts). Parking meters are in effect in some places in all three cities (these spots get taken quickly), except after 6PM and on Sunday and holidays.

Taxis

There are no cabs cruising the streets of Santa Fe, Taos, and Albuquerque. The following companies offer pick-up service:

Santa Fe:

Capital City Cab 438.0000

Taos:

Faust's Transportation 758.3410

Albuquerque:

Albuquerque Cab 883.4888

Checker Cab 243.7777

Yellow Cab 247.8888

Tours

Walking and vehicular tours in Santa Fe, rafting tours on the Rio Grande (departures from Santa Fe or Taos), and bus tours to such outlying areas as the Indian pueblos are offered by several tour companies. Contact the **Santa Fe Convention and Visitors Bureau** (984.6760, 800/777.2489), the **Santa Fe Chamber of Commerce** (510 N Guadalupe St, in the **De Vargas Center North** shopping mall annex, 988.3279), or the lobby desks of most hotels for information about specific operators and schedules. The **Taos Chamber of Commerce** (1139 Paseo del Pueblo Sur, between Paseo del Cañon and Salazar St, 758.3873, 800/732.8267) has details about white-water rafting trips.

Riding and walking tours are available in Albuquerque through **Rio Grande Super Tours** (242.1325), **Gray Line of Albuquerque** (242.3880, 800/256.8991), and **Okupin Tours** (867.3817). Ballooning is a popular pastime as well, and the city is home to a number of companies that will take you up, up, and away. Try **Hot Alternatives Etcetera Inc.** (269.1174, 800/322.2262), **Braden's Balloons Aloft** (281.2714, 800/367.6625), or **Hot Air Extraord-in-air** (266.9744). All will pick you up at your hotel or at other convenient locations.

Trains

Amtrak's (842.9650 in Albuquerque, 988.4511 in Santa Fe, 800/872.7245) *Southwest Chief*, which runs between Chicago and Los Angeles, stops in Albuquerque daily. The train arrives at First Street and Silver Avenue and continues northeast to the town of **Lamy,** where the **Lamy Shuttle Service** (982.8829) is available by reservation to take travelers 19 miles farther north to Santa Fe. There is no railway service to Taos.

Walking and Hiking

Downtown Santa Fe is best seen on foot. The maze of narrow old streets is as pleasurable to stroll as it is frustrating to maneuver in a car. This is also true of Santa Fe's **Canyon Road,** Albuquerque's Old Town District, and the entire town of Taos.

For more ambitious walks, in addition to the many miles of trails in national forest areas near all three cities, both Santa Fe and Albuquerque offer excellent hiking opportunities within minutes of downtown. In Santa Fe, the favorite is the **Atalaya Trail,** which starts at the **St. John's College** parking lot (the entrance to the college is at the intersection of Camino Cabra and Camino de Cruz Blanca) and climbs gradually to the summit of the 9,000-foot **Atalaya Peak** overlooking the city. In Albuquerque, a paved walking, jogging, and biking trail accessible from the **Rio Grande Nature Center** (entrance on Candeleria St, W of Rio Grande Blvd) runs the full length of the city through the cottonwood forest on the banks of the Rio Grande.

In the **Sangre de Cristo Mountains** is the **Pecos Wilderness** (a broad expanse located in the **Carson** and **Santa Fe National Forests**). Its most popular trailhead is the **East Portal** near the parking lot of the **Santa Fe Ski Basin,** 17 miles west of town on **Hyde Park/Ski Basin Road.** From here, the 20-mile **Windsor Trail** leads to the **South Portal** at the upper end of the **Pecos River Canyon** and provides access to the other trails through the wilderness. There are two other trailheads for the Pecos Wilderness—at **Santa Barbara Campground** near Peñasco (southeast of Taos) and at **El Porvenir** (west of Las Vegas).

The **Carson National Forest Service** (1139 Paseo del Pueblo Sur, between Paseo del Cañon and Salazar St, 758.6200) provides information on hiking in the forests.

FYI

Accommodations

Make hotel reservations ahead of time in all three cities. Santa Fe and Taos are jammed with tourists in summer and skiers in winter. Summer weekends in those two cities are the busiest; show up without a reservation on a Saturday and your chances of finding a room are not good, despite the fact that booming Santa Fe now has about 4,000 hotel rooms. Santa Fe's **Indian Market,** the third weekend in August, draws buyers and browsers from all over the country, and some downtown hotels get booked for that event up to a year in advance. Even the cheapest motels fill up early, and without a reservation you might have to stay in Albuquerque, 60 miles to the south, or Española, 24 miles to the north.

Albuquerque has 8,500 hotel rooms, but many are often booked by conventions. This city is most crowded during the New Mexico State Fair in

September and during the Albuquerque International Balloon Fiesta in October.

Bed-and-breakfasts proliferate throughout Santa Fe, Taos, and Albuquerque. For information, call one of the following:

Albuquerque Bed & Breakfast Association ....
  PO Box 7262, Albuquerque, NM 87504, no phone
  (promotional materials only)

Bed & Breakfast Inns of Taos 758.4747,
  ....800/876.7857

Bed & Breakfast of New Mexico..................982.3332

New Mexico Central Reservations 766.9770,
  ....800/466.7829

Santa Fe Central Reservations 983.8200,
  ....800/776.7669

Santa Fe Reservation and Lodging Service 989.3799

Taos Central Reservations 776.2233, 800/776.1111

Altitude

Albuquerque is perched a mile above sea level, and Santa Fe and Taos are even higher at 7,000 feet. The air is rarefied at these heights, which means your lungs take in less oxygen with every breath. Some people are unaffected by this; others find that they tire easily at first. It's good to follow a relaxed schedule the first day or two to give the body time to adjust. Those with heart problems should check with their doctors first to see if travel at these altitudes is advisable.

Climate

Northern New Mexico has four distinct seasons, and winter is definitely one of them. However, the sun shines more than 300 days a year, and rainfall is usually limited to scattered afternoon thunderstorms, mostly in spring (when the wind kicks up) and summer; normally there are not more than a handful of rainy days each year. Albuquerque gets a few light snowfalls in winter, while Santa Fe and Taos have been known to experience six or eight substantial storms. The low humidity throughout the area makes hot summer days much more bearable than at lower altitudes.

Average Temperatures (°F)

	Month	High	Low
Santa Fe	January	40	18
	April	59	35
	July	82	56
	October	62	38
Taos	January	40	10
	April	53	21
	July	87	50
	October	67	32
Albuquerque	January	46	24
	April	69	42
	July	91	64
	October	71	44

Drinking

New Mexico's legal drinking age is 21. Bars close at 2AM Monday through Saturday and at midnight on Sunday. Package sales, available in both liquor stores and most supermarkets, are banned on Sunday.

Money

Most banks in Albuquerque, **The Bank of Santa Fe** (241 Washington Ave, at Paseo de Peralta, 984.0500) in downtown Santa Fe, and the currency exchange counter at the **Albuquerque International Airport** (no phone) will exchange Mexican and Western European currencies. **Sunwest Bank of Albuquerque** (303 Roma Ave NW, at Third St, Albuquerque, 765.2205) and **United New Mexico Bank** (200 Lomas Blvd NE, between Second and Third Sts, 765.5000) will change all foreign monies. Banks are generally open Monday through Friday from 9AM to 3PM; drive-ups usually remain open later. Traveler's checks are accepted virtually everywhere.

Museum Passes

New Mexico's four state-run museums are the **Palace of the Governors**, the **Museum of Fine Arts**, the **Museum of International Folk Art**, and the **Museum of Indian Arts and Culture**. A three-day pass to all four costs $5.25.

Personal Safety

Santa Fe, Taos, and Albuquerque are quite safe, but it's a good idea not to wander around alone after dark in Albuquerque's downtown or East Central areas. In Santa Fe and Taos, many people don't even lock their doors.

Publications

Santa Fe's daily newspaper since 1849, the *New Mexican,* publishes a small calendar of events every day, and a more inclusive weeklong list appears every Friday in the arts section, *Pasatiempo.* The free, weekly *Santa Fe Reporter,* which has won a slew of national awards, publishes a complete calendar of art openings, and theater, music, and other events on Wednesday. The weekly *Taos News* does the same for Taos each Thursday. The daily *Albuquerque Journal,* the state's largest newspaper, and the *Albuquerque Tribune,* the afternoon daily, both publish weekend arts sections with a calendar of events on Thursday.

Radio Stations
AM:

KSWV (Spanish) 810
KVSF (news/talk)..............................1260
KTRC (easy listening) 1400

FM:

KSFR (classical) 90.7
KNYN (country and western)................95
KHFM (classical) 96.3
KBAC (eclectic) 98.1
KTMN (rock) 98.5
KTAO (eclectic/New Age) 101.5
KIOT (eclectic)..............102.3 in Santa Fe,
............................102.5 in Albuquerque

KOLT (country) 106
KBOM (oldies)..................................106.7
KBOM (rock) 107

Restaurants

Reservations are strongly suggested at the upscale restaurants in all three cities. Most inexpensive restaurants do not take reservations, and you may have to wait for a table, especially on Friday and Saturday nights. Casual dress is acceptable in almost all dining spots.

When a server in a New Mexican restaurant asks "Red or green?" he or she wants to know if you want red chile or green chile on your food. Green is usually more popular; red can be harder for some people to digest. Either can be hotter than the other on any given day. If you want half and half, say "Christmas." If your lips, tongue, and throat feel like they're burning, drinking water is *not* the way to dowse the fire. Instead, eat something sweet. Most New Mexican dishes come with sopaipillas, a local delicacy that is served instead of bread; put some honey on it and take a bite to reduce the chile heat.

Shopping

The best gift and souvenir shopping in Santa Fe is in the Plaza, Canyon Road, and Guadalupe Street districts, as well as at **Jackalope Pottery** (2820 Cerrillos Rd, between Camino Carlos Rey and Clark St, 471.8539) and **Trader Jack's Flea Market** (Hwy 84-285, eight miles north of Santa Fe). On the west end of town is **Villa Linda Mall** (Cerrillos and Rodeo Rds), the city's major shopping mall; and **Santa Fe Factory Stores** (at Cerrillos Rd and I-25), a large factory outlet mall with upscale shopping.

The historic district of Taos—the **Plaza, Kit Carson Road**, and **Bent Street**—and the **Taos Pueblo** have the best gift and souvenir shopping. **Paseo del Pueblo Sur** (from Kit Carson Road to Rancho de Taos) offers everything from supermarkets to discount department stores.

In Albuquerque, **Old Town** and the **Nob Hill** areas offer the best gift and souvenir shopping; major shopping malls are the **Coronado Center** (San Pedro Blvd, north of I-40) and nearby **Winrock Center** (Louisiana Blvd, just north of I-40).

Smoking

No-smoking sections exist in most restaurants in Northern New Mexico. In Albuquerque, a city ordinance prohibits smoking in such public areas as the airport and shopping malls. It's okay to smoke in malls in Santa Fe. Smoking is banned in some of Taos's public buildings.

Street Plan

Visitors can easily get lost in Santa Fe's narrow, winding thoroughfares. Not only are the streets a maze, but addresses are often not consecutive or just don't make sense. Either follow a map or ask a friendly local for directions. Taos's small size makes navigating easy—there really is only one main street. Albuquerque is laid out on a grid pattern and all addresses are designated by quadrant (NE, NW, SE, SW), with First Street and Central Avenue downtown as the dividing points.

Orientation

Taxes
The three cities have a sales tax—known technically as a gross receipts tax—that varies from 5.8 percent in Albuquerque, to 6.25 percent in Santa Fe, to 6.3 percent in Taos County, to 6.8 percent in the city of Taos. This tax is levied on all goods and services, and applies not only to hotel and restaurant bills, but to all purchases, including food bought at supermarkets. Medicine and doctor and dental bills are not exempt from the tax. Hotels also tack on a lodgers' tax—four percent in Santa Fe, three and a half percent in the city of Taos, three percent in Taos County, and five percent in Albuquerque—to room charges.

Telephone
The area code for the state of New Mexico is 505. Local calls from pay phones cost 25¢.

Tickets
Tickets for rock concerts and other national events can be purchased through **Ticketron** outlets at most record stores. For local cultural events, buy tickets at most of the larger hotels and at **Galisteo News** (202 Galisteo St, at W Water St, 984.1316). Tickets to the **Santa Fe Opera** can be purchased by mail or phone (PO Box 2408, Santa Fe, NM 87504, 986.5900, 986.5955).

Tipping
In restaurants the standard tip is 15 to 20 percent of the bill. Some eateries add a service charge of 15 to 18 percent for parties of five or more. Taxi drivers normally get 10 to 15 percent depending on the quality of the service, and tips for maids and porters are discretionary.

Visitors' Information Offices
The **Santa Fe Convention and Visitors Bureau** (201 W Marcy St, at Grant St, 984.6760, 800/777.2489) is open Monday through Friday. The **Taos Chamber of Commerce** (1139 Paseo del Pueblo Sur, between Paseo del Cañon and Salazar St, 758.3873, 800/732.8267) is open daily. The **Albuquerque Convention and Visitors Bureau** (121 Tijeras Ave NE, between Second and Commercial Sts, 243.3696, 800/284.2282) is open Monday through Friday.

The **State of New Mexico Welcome Center** (daily; 491 Old Santa Fe Trail, at Paseo del Peralta, 827.7400), the **Santa Fe Chamber of Commerce Information Center** (M-F; 510 N Guadalupe St, in the De Vargas Center North shopping mall annex, 988.3279), and the **Albuquerque Convention and Visitors Bureau**'s walk-in center (daily; 303 Romero St, between Mountain Rd and Rio Grande Blvd, no phone) also supply information on New Mexico.

Phone Book

Emergencies
Ambulance/Fire/Police 911
AAA Emergency Road Service
  Santa Fe and Taos 800/726.4222
  Albuquerque 291.6600
Dental Society Referrals, Albuquerque 242.0345
Handicapped Transportation Services
  Albuquerque 764.1550

Hospitals
  Santa Fe: St. Vincent Hospital..................983.3361
  Taos: Holy Cross Hospital 758.8883
  Albuquerque:
    Presbyterian Hospital 841.1234
    University of New Mexico Hospital 843.2411
24-Hour Pharmacies
  Santa Fe: Walgreen Drug Store.................982.4643
  Albuquerque: Walgreen Drug Store..........881.5210
Poison Control 800/432.6866
Police (nonemergency)
  Santa Fe 827.9126
  Taos 758.4656
  Albuquerque 768.1986
Rape Crisis Center
  Santa Fe 473.7818
  Taos 758.2910
  Albuquerque 266.7711
Visitor Information
Amtrak 800/872.7245
Greyhound/Trailways 243.4435, 800/231.2222
Passport Information
  Santa Fe 988.6351
  Albuquerque 848.3895
Sante Fe Trails 984.6730
Shuttle Jack 243.3244
Sun Tran 843.9200
Time and Temperature
  Santa Fe 473.2211
  Albuquerque 247.1611
24-hour Albuquerque Events Line 243.3696,
....800/284.2282
Weather and Road Conditions.............800/432.4269

The color blue has magical properties in both Pueblo Indian and Spanish traditions. The Indians not only value turquoise stone for its healing properties but also grow only blue corn, which they believe to be sacred. The Spanish tradition of painting window and door frames blue stems from a folk belief that it keeps evil spirits from entering the house.

Santa Fe has one of the largest Tibetan refugee communities in the US. In 1992 the Dalai Lama made a rare speaking appearance in Santa Fe. He was drawn to the Southwest, he said, by a vision of unity between Tibetan Buddhists and the native Hopi people.

The Main Events

New Mexicans love fiestas of every description, and from the beginning of May through Christmas there is rarely a slow day on the special-events calendar. Whether the occasion is a solemn religious procession by candlelight or a wild citywide street party, a world-renowned classical music festival or a spectacular hot-air balloon competition, New Mexicans observe it with boundless enthusiasm. Here are some of the most popular celebrations in Santa Fe, Taos, and Albuquerque:

January
Three Kings Day
All Indian pueblos observe 6 January, the traditional end of the Christmas season. This is the day every year when the governor and other tribal officers of each pueblo take office, and it is marked by sacred animal dances. To ensure successful hunting, men dressed as bears and buffalos, for example, dance for hours to achieve harmony with wild game. Although dance times are not prescheduled, they usually get going in the late morning. These events are free, but most pueblos charge for parking. Contact the individual pueblos for more information.

February
Celebrity Ski Classic
Scheduled during the otherwise uneventful off-season, film and television stars come to **Santa Fe** to raise funds for charity by competing against local skiers in this highly publicized ski race. For more information, call 983.5615.

March
Rio Grande Arts and Crafts Festival
During the second weekend in March, the **New Mexico State Fairgrounds** in Albuquerque is the venue for one of the year's best arts-and-crafts shows. It is especially noteworthy because it takes place when there are few other special events in the Southwest, and thus attracts many of New Mexico's best artisans. Call 292.7457 for more information.

April
Pilgrimage to Chimayó
On Good Friday thousands of Catholics from all over New Mexico make a pilgrimage on foot to **Santuario de Chimayó,** a small sanctuary in the hills between Santa Fe and Taos where it is believed that miracles occur. Pilgrims, walking on their knees and making the journey in wheelchairs—some carrying large wooden crosses—line US 285 north of Santa Fe for more than 30 miles. For more information, call 753.2831.

Gathering of Nations Powwow
The largest American Indian powwow in the United States is held in **Albuquerque.** Elaborate costumes and competition dancing for big cash prizes highlight the traditional ceremony, which climaxes in **American Indian Week,** the third week of the month. Admission is charged. For more information, call 836.2810.

Albuquerque Founder's Day
This commemoration, usually held concurrently with the **Gathering of Nations Powwow,** focuses on Albuquerque's Spanish Colonial heritage. **Old Town Plaza** is the site for cultural and historical celebrations, food vendors, and live entertainment. The festivities are free. Call 243.3696 for more information.

May
Cinco de Mayo Celebration
Mexico's Independence Day is observed with a huge celebration on the Sunday preceding 5 May at Albuquerque's **Civic Plaza.** The city's residents from all walks of life join this free, colorful extravaganza of Mexican food and dancing in the streets to live music. The festivities last from late morning through the evening. For more information, call 265.8331.

Taos Spring Arts Festival
The whole community of **Taos** collaborates to produce this exhibition of the arts that marks the beginning of the tourist season. Spanning the last two weeks of May, events include an arts-and-crafts show, artists' receptions at most galleries, literary readings, and musical performances. Most events are free. For more information, call 732.8267.

June
Spring Festival at El Rancho de las Golondrinas
In early June volunteers dress in Spanish Colonial garb and demonstrate traditional crafts, skills, and chores at this large Spanish hacienda near Santa Fe. Visitors get a feel for 18th-century frontier life. Admission is charged. For more information, call 471.2261.

Pedal the Peaks Bicycle Tour
During the third week of June, seven days of bicycle races attract cyclists from around the world to a varied, challenging series of courses on mountainous roads around Santa Fe, Taos, Albuquerque, Las Vegas, and Los Alamos. Call 800/795.0898 for more information.

July
Nambe Waterfall Ceremony
Virtually every New Mexico community has its own Fourth of July celebration, but the most unique happening is held at an idyllic creekside site below **Nambe Falls** on the reservation land of **Nambe Pueblo** between Santa Fe and Taos. Groups from various pueblos gather to perform bow-and-arrow, buffalo, corn, harvest, and snake dances throughout the day. Admission is charged. Some pueblo arts and crafts are offered for sale. Call 455.2036 for more information.

Rodeo de Santa Fe
The one major event of the summer season that is attended by more locals than tourists, this four-day rodeo, held during the first week of July, features calf roping, bucking broncos, bull riders, rodeo clowns, and lots of pageantry. It kicks off with a

parade and pancake breakfast on **Santa Fe Plaza.**
The rodeo is held at the **Rodeo Grounds** on Rodeo
Road, near Richards Avenue, at the southern edge
of Santa Fe. Admission is charged. For more
information, call 984.6760.

Taos Indian Pueblo Powwow

This American Indian powwow continues a tradition
that began as an annual diplomatic meeting and
peace celebration between Plains tribes and Pueblo
Indians long before the first Europeans reached
New Mexico. Held the second week of July in a large
temporary dance *ramada* (framework on poles
holding up a roof) constructed entirely of pine
boughs and branches, the powwow features
brightly costumed dancers from tribes throughout
the United States and Canada competing for cash
prizes. Admission is charged. Call 758.8626 for
more information.

Santa Fe Chamber Music Festival

During the second and third weeks of July, classical
works are performed by ensembles of some of
America's finest musicians in the **New Mexico Fine
Arts Museum**'s lofty, pseudorustic **St. Francis
Auditorium.** The festival also features world
premieres of new works by serious composers. Call
983.2075 for more information.

Opening Night at the Santa Fe Opera

The start of the six-week opera season is marked by
an elegant "tailgate party," where opera-goers—
men in black tie and women in exclusive designer
gowns—enjoy dinners individually catered by Santa
Fe's leading restaurants. Everything is set up
outdoors on folding tables in the opera parking lot.
There is no charge to sneak a peek at the haute-
cuisine picnickers, though opening night tickets for
the opera are expensive and must be reserved as
much as a year in advance. Call 982.3851 for more
information.

Eight Northern Pueblos Arts and Crafts Fair

Begun as an Indian pueblo-operated alternative to
Santa Fe's famous **Indian Market** (see below), this
fair features more than 1,100 vendors exhibiting
traditional and contemporary handmade American
Indian arts and crafts. The two-day event during the
third week of July also features dance performances, American Indian fashion shows, and other
activities. The larger pueblos north of Santa Fe,
including **San Ildefonso, Santa Clara, San Juan,**
and **Taos Pueblos,** take turns hosting the fair on
successive years. For more information, call
852.4265.

Spanish Market

This market fills Santa Fe Plaza the last weekend of
July with more than 200 vendors of handmade,
traditional Spanish arts and crafts such as tinwork,
woven goods, quilts, and wood carvings. Long a
minor-league stepchild of the **Santa Fe Indian
Market** (see below), in recent years the **Spanish
Market** has begun attracting more viewers and
buyers. But it has a long way to go before it draws a
crowd as sizable as the **Indian Market.** Call
983.4038 for more information.

August

Fiesta de Santo Domingo

Corn dances (sometimes called "rain dances") are
held at all New Mexico Indian pueblos during the
summer months to insure successful crops. On
4 August the largest corn dance of all takes place at
the **Santo Domingo Pueblo.** Thousands of dancers
in identical ceremonial dress take part in a
procession through the streets of this very
traditional pueblo located between Santa Fe and
Albuquerque. For more information on this free
event, call 843.7270.

Santa Fe Indian Market

The largest of all American Indian arts-and-crafts
markets fills the downtown plaza and radiates into
side streets for blocks around. More than 2,000
juried artisans show their work and more than
100,000 people from all over the world come to see
what's offered. Most participating Indian artists and
craftspeople sell more of their work this weekend
(the third of the month) than the rest of the year.
Serious buyers line up hours before the show
opens, and the best pieces are sold first thing in the
morning. This is the busiest tourist weekend of the
year in Santa Fe. Hotels are booked up at least four
or five months in advance, including lodging in
Albuquerque and Los Alamos. Call 984.6760 for
more information.

September

New Mexico Wine & Vine Festival

Samples from New Mexico's wineries are the central
attraction at the popular community festival in
Bernalillo, north of Albuquerque. Live music and
dancing round out the festival in early September.
Admission is charged. Call 867.3311 for more
information.

Santa Fe Fiesta

Santa Fe's community fiesta—the only large event
in town that is mainly for locals rather than
tourists—is unique. Part religious and historical
observance, part citywide block party, and part
drunken orgy, **Fiesta** starts at dark on Friday
evening the first weekend after Labor Day with the
burning of Zozobra. This 40-foot-high papier-mâché
marionette represents "Old Man Gloom" who has
been burned at the stake each year since the
ceremony was created in 1926 by early Santa Fe
painter Will Shuster. As Zozobra hurls curses and
verbal abuse over the loudspeakers at the onlookers
packing **Old Fort Marcy Park** (near the Cross of the
Martyrs), fire dancers taunt him and finally put him
to the torch, igniting the cache of fireworks in his
head. The crowd then spills out onto the plaza for
all-night street dancing. Other fiesta weekend events
include religious processions, a historical/hysterical
parade, and a pet parade. Call 984.6760 for more
information.

Taos Fall Arts Festival and San Geronimo Feast Day

A mirror image of the **Taos Spring Arts Festival**
(see page 13), this end-of-the-season blowout

during the last two weeks of September features a kaleidoscope of visual and performing arts. The closing days of the arts festival coincide with the feast day for **Taos Pueblo**'s patron saint, San Geronimo. The events are celebrated with all-day and evening dances, foot races, pole climbs, and an arts-and-crafts market at the Pueblo. Call 758.3873 or 800/732.8267 for more information.

New Mexico State Fair and Rodeo
One of the largest in the nation, this state fair lasts for most of the month of September and features livestock contests, arts-and-crafts shows, a carnival, nightly country and western concerts, replicas of old Indian and Spanish villages, and a Professional Rodeo Cowboy Association rodeo. Admission is charged. Call 265.1791 for more information.

Old Taos Trade Fair
Held at the historic **Martinez Hacienda** during the third weekend of September, this fair reenacts the early days when Taos was a trading center for Pueblo and Plains Indians, Spanish settlers, and Anglo mountain men. Costumes and lifestyle demonstrations are featured. Admission is charged. Call 758.0505 for more information.

October
Harvest Festival at El Rancho de las Golondrinas
This historical re-creation, at the historic Spanish Colonial hacienda southwest of Santa Fe, features as many as 200 volunteers in period costume. The staff at **El Rancho de las Golondrinas** raise crops using 18th-century farming methods, and this festival coincides with the harvesting of fields of blue maize. Lifestyle demonstrations include dying and spinning wool and grinding flour at the old waterwheel mill. Folk dancing rounds out the weekend program. Admission is charged. This celebration takes place the first weekend in October, coinciding with the **Albuquerque Balloon Fiesta.** For more information, call 471.2261.

Albuquerque Balloon Fiesta
Since 1972, when this event got its start as a 13-balloon race from an Albuquerque shopping mall parking lot, it has grown to become the largest event in New Mexico, with about 1.4 million spectators—four times the entire population of Albuquerque—and nearly 700 hot-air balloons from all over the United States and a dozen foreign countries. Held at the **Balloon Fiesta Park,** a hot-air balloon airport specially built for the event on the north edge of the city, the events take place the first two weeks of October and feature races, contests, balloon rides, and such dramatic events as mass ascensions (when all participating balloons lift off at once) and a "balloon glow," in which illuminated, tethered balloons light up the night sky. Because of the tremendous crowds and the fact that ballooning conditions are best soon after dawn, attending the spectacular mass ascensions means getting up at 3AM to wait in a very long line of cars. Admission is charged. Call 821.1000 for more information.

November
Dixon Arts Association Studio Tour
Of the many annual fall studio tours that enliven Northern New Mexico's village artists communities, the one at **Dixon** (a few miles off NM 68 south of Taos) was the first and is still the best. About two dozen local artists and craftspeople open their homes and studios to the public the first weekend in November, while others show their works at booths in the village community center. For more information, call 753.2831.

Southeast Arts and Crafts Festival
The state's most prestigious arts-and-crafts fair, a juried invitational event featuring works by the finest artisans of New Mexico, Texas, Colorado, and Arizona, is held in mid-November at the **New Mexico State Fairgrounds** in Albuquerque. Call 262.2488 for more information.

Indian National Finals Rodeo
Prize winners from the many rodeos held on American Indian reservations around the United States and Canada come to Albuquerque during the third week in November to compete for the title of National Indian Rodeo Champion in this four-day extravaganza of roping, racing, and bronco and bull riding at **Tingley Coliseum**, south of the **University of New Mexico,** near the airport. Admission is charged. Call 265.1791 for more information.

December
Christmas
Christmas is particularly beautiful in Santa Fe, Taos, and several areas of Albuquerque, especially in Old Town. Most of the adobe-style buildings in the historic districts, the plaza walkways, and many residential areas of all three communities are lined with lanterns called *farolitos* (in Santa Fe and Taos) or *luminarias* (in Albuquerque), made from altar candles set in sand inside brown paper bags. The lanterns are in place from the first week of December until New Year's Day. Conventional Christmas decorations such as colored lights and plastic Santas are rarely seen around Santa Fe and Taos. Instead, the plazas and other public areas are hung with fresh evergreen boughs and adorned with large wooden plaques hand-painted in Christmas designs. For decorating Christmas trees, the hot item is "chile lights"—blinking red lights in the shape of chile peppers. On Christmas Eve, Santa Fe residents by the thousands stroll along **Canyon Road,** stopping to warm themselves by bonfires and sing Christmas carols, while local businesses provide hot cider and other refreshments along the way. With piñon logs burning in many fireplaces, the air is filled with a crisp fragrance that signifies the winter season.

The New Mexico state flower is the yucca, the state tree is the piñon, the state bird is the roadrunner, the state cookie is the shortbread-like *bizcochito,* and the state motto is "it grows as it goes" (what that means is anyone's guess).

Santa Fe

Santa Fe is a city with a split personality that works to the delight of the visitor. One persona of Santa Fe is that of a Spanish *tía*, a warm and embracing old aunt, somber and religious. That is the Santa Fe of history: muted colors, ancient places of worship such as the **Santuario de Guadalupe** and the **San Miguel Mission**, narrow and twisting streets lined with old adobes, and the part of arty **Canyon Road** where the pavement ends and you can continue walking into a simpler world resembling a quiet corner of Mexico or Spain. It is a city of inexpensive New Mexican restaurants that include **Tia Sophia's** or **Diego's Cafe**, where the bean and the tortilla still reign and the chile comes in three hallowed flavors—hot, hotter, and why-can't-I-feel-my-tongue? It is a metropolis that was built by the old Spanish-speaking men who sit in the sun on white wrought-iron benches in the centuries-old **Plaza,** and where the smell of piñon smoke from a thousand Indian-style fireplaces fills the evening air in fall and winter. It is the place where Indians from the nearby pueblos sell silver and turquoise jewelry on blankets in front of the **Palace of the Governors,** which was built when Santa Fe was founded in 1610. It is the city of the traditional Western art of Frederic Remington and Charles Russell, and of the painters who came at the turn of the century and turned the remote village into a budding art colony (their work is prominently displayed in the **Jamison Galleries, Fenn Galleries**, and others). It is the location of the **Ríos Wood Yard**, where three generations of local men still chop and sell wood a few steps from where the **Gerald Peters Gallery** is selling O'Keeffe paintings for a half-million dollars.

The newer Santa Fe offers a different fulfillment, but it, too, is a sensual joy. This is a city where you'll discover excellent Italian food at **Ristorante La Traviata** and **Babbo Ganzo Trattoria** and first-rate East Indian food at the **India Palace;** mythical contemporary art at the **Peyton-Wright Gallery**, whimsical art at **Lightside**, and classic American paintings at the **Wyeth Hurd Gallery;** and people rocking the night away (in this once sleepy town) at such dance clubs as **Edge** and **Luna**. It is a city where mineral water and champagne are rapidly surpassing Coors as the drink of choice, where a contemporary art gallery has replaced an abandoned Spanish Baptist church, the huge and expensive **Eldorado Hotel** has displaced the Big Jo Lumber Company, and nationally known

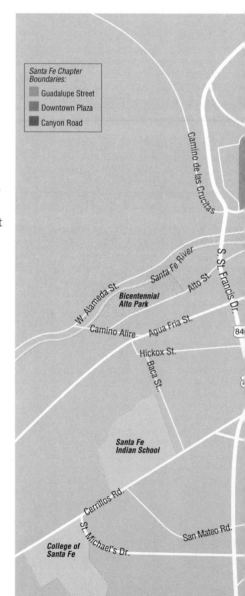

Santa Fe Chapter Boundaries:

Guadalupe Street

Downtown Plaza

Canyon Road

designer ice cream parlors have taken over local drugstores. These changes, made in the name of progress and tourism, irritate many residents who liked things the way they were, but who also realize that the local economy thrives on tourists.

The best part is that the two personae are not geographically separate. There is no "Old Town" here: the old and the new are intermingled in the same neighborhoods, on the same blocks—BMWs are parked right beside low-riders, new restaurants waft their enticing smells across the entryways to ancient churches. This is true in each of the three areas you'll want to explore on foot—the **Downtown Plaza, Canyon Road**, and **Guadalupe Street**.

Santuario de Guadalupe

ANTONIO COCILOVO

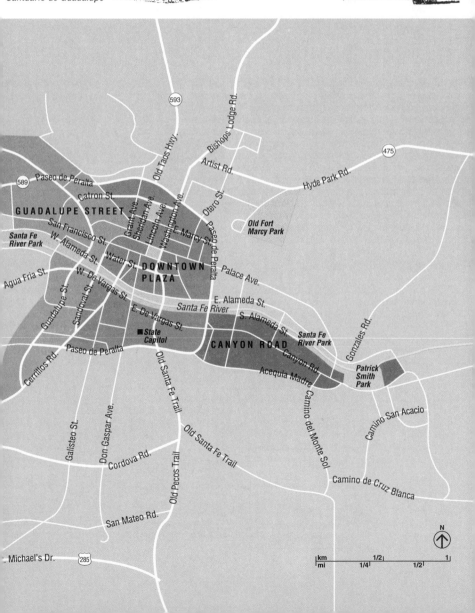

The best approach is to put on your walking shoes, leave all preconceptions behind, and pause for as long as you like in any church, museum, shop, or gallery that interests you. And try to forget you're still in the United States.

Allot at least a full day to walking the downtown area. (Serious shoppers and museumgoers can easily spend three days here.) The wall-to-wall art galleries of Canyon Road—a mixed bag of every kind of art and craft—will fill another day, and Guadalupe Street several more hours, not counting a hearty lunch at **Guadalupe Cafe** or **Zia Diner**, and dinner at the fine **Pranzo Italian Grill** or the exquisite (and pricey) **Encore Provence.** If you have time and transportation, don't miss the *Girard Collection* of thousands of folk-art toys, dolls, and masks at the **Museum of International Folk Art,** about 1.5 miles from the Plaza. Also take at least one day trip, which could include hiking in **Bandelier National Monument,** where Anasazi cliff dwellers lived; sight-seeing at **San Ildefonso Pueblo,** a contemporary Indian pueblo; and breathing the air of the past at **Chimayó,** a traditional Hispanic village whose ancient **Santuario de Chimayó** is venerated, a place where style and chic have not yet found their way, and where the atmosphere still speaks—regardless of your faith—of a more spiritual time.

San Miguel Mission

ANTONIO COCILOV

Downtown Plaza

What Times Square is to New York City, what home plate is to baseball, what "Go" is to Monopoly, the Plaza is to Santa Fe. It is the place where the game begins, the spot you are likely to pass again and again in your wanderings, and it's at the heart of Santa Fe's changing mentality, its commerce, and its controversy.

Laid out when the city was built in 1610, the Plaza is a square block of trees, grass, and walkways, fronted on four sides by museums, art galleries, Indian jewelry shops, an old hotel, and restaurants. For three centuries, just like the plaza of an old Mexican village, this was the place where the locals came to gossip, buy shoes, party, or just sit quietly and watch the passing parade of neighbors. And for decades it was the block that teenagers cruised around in their low-riders in the evenings. But in the past 20 years most of that has changed. Rising downtown rents have driven the local shops to malls at either end of town, and, apart from one cherished down-home remnant—**F.W. Woolworth**—the Plaza has become the focus of the tourist trade; automobile traffic is even banned on two of the four sides during the summer to create the feel of a visitor-friendly shopping arcade. Teenagers now meet their friends across from **Häagen-Dazs,** but most local residents have little reason to come here anymore. No change in Santa Fe has caused more bad feeling among the natives than the loss of their Plaza as a locally held treasure.

The Plaza is the literal center of the downtown area, a cultural and credit-card bazaar that radiates in four directions and encompasses about 30 square blocks of restaurants, galleries, shops, churches, hotels, and bed-and-breakfasts, all crammed side by side. Park your car in one of the downtown lots—or leave it at your hotel if possible—and explore this area on foot; there is no other way. And if you want to make friends with the locals, always call this "the Plaza"—not, as many visitors do, "the square."

1 Plaza Tree-shaded grassy areas criss-crossed by walkways make up the center of Santa Fe's downtown Plaza. For centuries locals congregated here to visit and promenade with strolling musicians on Saturday nights. During the 19th century, horse-drawn wagons that had been laden with goods in Missouri and had traveled over the Santa Fe Trail would come roaring into the Plaza at breakneck speed, circling round and round, scaring every dog and chicken in sight, as the drivers showed their pleasure at reaching the end of a long journey. Merchants would gather to see what was available to buy, while prostitutes loitered around and offered their own wares.

Today, except for a few old men and in-line skating teens, the Plaza is largely a venue for visitors. White wrought-iron benches provide spots for resting and people watching, though the backs of the benches slope away so sharply they offer little comfort. In the exact center of the Plaza is an obelisk erected in 1868 to commemorate fallen Civil War soldiers. The obelisk's north facade—which faces the Native Americans selling jewelry across the street—used to honor "the heroes who have fallen in the various battles with savage Indians" until several years ago when an unknown Anglo man in a hard-hat chiseled out the word "savage." In the southeast corner a smaller monument marks the end of the **Santa Fe Trail.**

In late July the Plaza is the scene of a Spanish crafts market, and, on the third weekend in August, an Indian Market, the city's busiest attraction, is held here. Arts and crafts fairs fill the Plaza on sporadic weekends. During the three-day-long September Fiesta, the Plaza is filled with food booths and dancing in the streets (not to mention some public drunkenness). For more information on these activities, see "The Main Events" on pages 13-15.
♦ Bounded by E Palace Ave and E San Francisco St, and Washington and Lincoln Aves

2 Palace of the Governors One of the oldest public buildings in the country, this block-long pueblo-style adobe structure occupies the entire north side of the Plaza. Spanish settlement of New Mexico began in 1598, when Juan de Oñate led a group of 130 families from northern Mexico into the Rio Grande Valley. In 1610 Spanish officials established the capital of the province of New Mexico at Santa Fe, laid out the Plaza, and built this structure, facing south toward Mexico City, which was the capital of New Spain. When the Pueblo Indians revolted in 1680 and attacked Santa Fe, several thousand villagers, along with their cows and goats, occupied the palace until they were forced south to El Paso. The palace and the town were occupied by the Indians until being retaken by the Spanish in 1692 in a peaceful conquest led by Don Diego de Vargas. The Spanish departmental governors ruled from the palace, and the territorial governors presided here after New Mexico was ceded to the US in 1846 following the war with Mexico.

The best known of the palace's occupants was Governor Lew Wallace, who served from 1878 to 1881 and wrote parts of his novel *Ben Hur* here. Working to suppress the violent desperadoes who roamed the region in those days, Wallace numbered among his enemies Billy the Kid, who once boasted, "I mean to ride into the plaza at Santa Fe, hitch my horse in front of the palace, and put a bullet through Lew Wallace."

Since 1909 the palace has been a museum, now housing more than 17,000 historical objects belonging to the **Museum of New Mexico.** Numerous permanent exhibits illustrate the state's multicultural heritage, ranging from ancient Indian pottery to its role in the Civil War. The **Museum Shop,** entered from Washington Avenue, offers a large selection of Southwestern literature and silver and turquoise jewelry. ◆ Admission; children under 7 free. Daily. Palace Ave (north side of the Plaza, between Lincoln and Washington Aves). 827.6483

Under the portal of the Palace of the Governors:

Indian Craft Vendors Facing the Plaza, dozens of Indians from nearby pueblos sit in front of blankets covered with hand-crafted jewelry for sale. To many visitors, this sight offers the first sharp impression of what is called "The City Different." Only Indians can sell here, and they have to certify that the wares were made by themselves or their families. (Not too long ago, an Anglo vendor challenged this practice in court, contending that it discriminated against non-Indians. The court held that the Indians under the portal were a "living historical exhibit," and therefore the policy was legal.) The jewelry—much of it silver and turquoise—is of high quality. Some of the artists will even let you bargain the prices down a bit. ◆ Daily

3 Roque's Carnitas ★★★$ In the warm months you'll be lured by the appetizing aroma of meat sizzling on the grill of Roque Garcia, a regional local, and Mona Cavalli, who emigrated from New York years ago. This is literally a moveable feast—a pushcart parked on the northeast corner of the Plaza. There's no menu, just homemade lemonade and

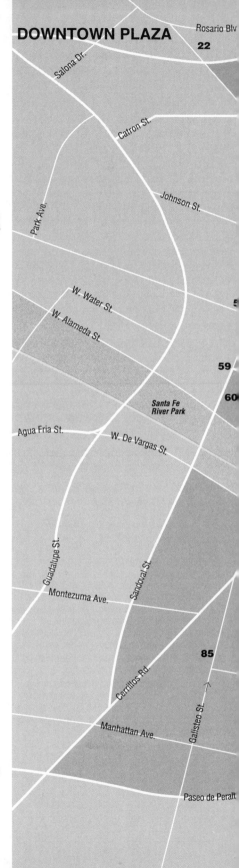

DOWNTOWN PLAZA

Paseo de Peralta

Old Taos Hwy.

Bishop's Lodge Rd.

S. Federal Pl.

25

City Hall Park

32

33

23 **24**

Griffin St.

W. Marcy St.

26

Paseo de Peralta

21

27 **29** **31**

19 **20**

30

E. Marcy St.

Grant Ave.

Sheridan Ave.

28

34

Sunset St.

17 **15**

W. Palace Ave.

Washington Ave.

Nusbaum St.

18 **14**

16

13

Lincoln Ave.

45

35

57

Burro Alley

W. San Francisco St.

55

2

3

E. Palace Ave.

44 **43** **42**

Otero St.

56

54

1 Plaza

41

53 **52**

12

4

46 **47**

Cathedral Pl.

40

Cienega St.

36

11

10

5

48

62

9 **8**

6

39

W. Water St.

61

7

E. San Francisco St.

63

70

51 **50**

37

68 **69**

71 **73**

49 St. Francis Cathedral

64 **67**

72

E. Water St.

38

Galisteo St.

75

65

Ortiz St.

Don Gaspar Ave.

74

66

82

76

83

Old Santa Fe Trail

84

Shelby St.

77

E. Alameda St.

92

Santa Fe River

Santa Fe River Park

86 E. De Vargas St. **87**

78

Boyle Pl.

88

81

89 San Miguel Mission

91

S. Capitol St.

79

93

Don Gaspar Ave.

Old Santa Fe Trail

Roundhouse

80

90

94

Acequia Madre

N

km

mi

1/8

1/4

1/4

1/2

delicious *carnitas* (Spanish for "little meat")—which are strips of prime beef or chicken, marinated in a "secret" sauce, grilled with onions and green chile, and served in a tortilla topped with homemade salsa. Doctors, lawyers, and Indian vendors have been popping over here for a quick, tangy lunch to take away since 1984. In the winter Roque and Mona head south to Mexico. ◆ New Mexican ◆ Daily lunch Apr–early Nov, weather permitting. E Palace and Washington Aves

4 **Catron Building** A lawyer and political power, Thomas B. Catron was a member of the infamous "Santa Fe Ring," which controlled the New Mexico Territory in the second half of the 19th century. He was appointed district attorney in 1866 and elected as one of the state's first two senators in 1912, amid much wheeling and dealing in the Hall of Representatives. In 1891 he contracted for a half-million bricks to construct this office building on the Plaza, where the post office once stood. The building now houses shops and galleries. ◆ Daily. 53 Old Santa Fe Trail (east side of the Plaza, between E Palace Ave and E San Francisco St)

Within the Catron Building:

Taylor A. Dale Gallery Museum-quality Native American artifacts are featured here. Also sold are tribal art pieces from Africa, Oceania, and Indonesia, including masks and textiles. ◆ M-Sa. Second floor. 988.1487

Channing Gallery A wide range of art, including American Indian crafts (textiles, bead work, baskets, and pottery), American folk art (furniture and old forged tools mounted as sculptures), and outsider art (works by unschooled artists from such institutions as correctional and psychiatric facilities), is offered in this gallery. ◆ M-Sa. Second floor. 988.1078

5 **Eagle Dancer** The pieces sold here range from the sublime to the ridiculous, as they do in many Indian art shops—from pueblo Storyteller dolls and Hopi kachinas to the biggest Santa Fe cliché of all, the seated wooden coyote howling at the moon (it's a fact of nature that coyotes howl standing up). The balcony contains the best Hopi kachinas, pottery, and jewelry. On the main floor is a room featuring high-quality, finely woven Navajo rugs, and a vault containing old and new Indian Pawn (Indian-owned jewelry sold to raise money). The cheap stuff, including "Navajo kachinas"—which are tourist schlock—is in the basement. The owners also operate **Wind River Trading Co.** (113 E San

Francisco St, between Old Santa Fe Trail and Cathedral Pl, 989.7067), **Wind River West** (Plaza Market, on the Plaza, 982.6232), and **Turquoise Trail** (84 E San Francisco St, at Old Santa Fe Trail, 983.5230). ◆ Daily. 57 Old Santa Fe Trail (east side of the Plaza, between E Palace Ave and E San Francisco St). 986.2055

6 **Packard's Indian Trading Co.** Known for its top-quality Indian crafts since 1925, highlights of this store include exquisite contemporary Indian bracelets by Don Lucas, contemporary inlaid *concho* belts by Benny and Valerie Aldrich, and the finest Zuni needlepoint turquoise (carved into fine slivers and set in silver) around. Helpful employees will fit the entire family, including infants-in-arms with Indian moccasins; kachinas are sold here, too. Owned by the Packard family for more than 50 years, the place continues to be reliable and first-rate under the aegis of the Cannon family who bought it in 1978. ◆ Daily. 61 Old Santa Fe Trail (at E San Francisco St). 983.9241

7 **La Fonda** $$$$ The oldest hotel in Santa Fe dominates the southeast corner of the Plaza. Records indicate that somewhere in the city there was a *fonda* (Spanish for "inn") to accommodate travelers early in the 1600s. The old hotel this was modeled after, also called **La Fonda**, existed on this site when it became the end of the Santa Fe Trail in 1821. Among the hotel's guests in the early days were Kit Carson, General William Tecumseh Sherman, and General and Mrs. Ulysses S. Grant. Billy the Kid is rumored to have washed dishes in the hotel kitchen. Sheriff Pat Garrett, the man who shot him, checked in just two days after Billy's death.

Visitors in recent decades have included such diverse spirits as Errol Flynn, Senator John F. Kennedy, Shirley Maclaine, and Ross Perot. During the Second World War, when the atomic bomb was being built in nearby Los Alamos, scientists on their day off would often visit the hotel's bar to drink and relax. Some of the bartenders at the time reportedly were army intelligence men who kept their ears open in case the physicists, their tongues loosened by booze, began to discuss their work.

The lobby, with its high ceilings and dark vigas (wooden beams), tile floors, oversized armchairs, and paintings by Gerald Cassidy, which date to 1922, remains a popular meeting place because of its convenient location. The 170 rooms and suites are furnished in traditional Spanish style; some have adobe fireplaces. Guests can relax in the indoor pool. In the summer the **Bell-Tower Bar,** the rooftop open-air lounge that overlooks downtown Santa Fe, is one of the city's most frequented rendezvous spots. ♦ 100 E San Francisco St (between Old Santa Fe Trail and Cathedral Pl). 982.5511, 800/523.5002; fax 988.2052

Within La Fonda:

La Plazuela ★$$$ Situated in the hotel's enclosed courtyard, this restaurant features traditional but high-priced New Mexican tacos and enchiladas, as well as steaks, chops, and seafood. You can get the local treats a lot cheaper elsewhere. Potted trees provide an outdoorsy touch, but the skylit roof creates a soft light that, while pleasant, gives one the feeling of being underwater. ♦ New Mexican ♦ Daily breakfast, lunch, and dinner. Reservations recommended for dinner. Main floor. 982.5511

Photogenesis Stunning black-and-white photographs—including many exquisite Southwestern landscapes—are available in this basement gallery. The works here feature images by such outstanding regional photographers as Eileen Benjamin, Peter Sahula, Mark Nohl, Ann Mason, and Nicholas Trofimuk. Browse among these prints for their sheer beauty, even if you can't afford to buy them. ♦ M, Th-Su. Basement level. 989.9540

Things Finer Robert M. Pettus's shop offers fine antique and contemporary jewelry, crystal, silver, and objets d'art. The romance of bygone eras—18th century, Victorian, Art Deco, Retro—pervades every inch of this store. Russian icons and enamels are a specialty. ♦ M-Sa. Ground floor. 983.5552

Señor Murphy Candy Maker This long-established Santa Fe candy store offers an irresistible selection of temptations visitors won't find back home. The emphasis is on New Mexican ingredients. One of the most popular items is red chile piñon nut brittle—a unique and surprisingly delicious snack. The factory (1904 Chamisa St, at Llano St, 988.4311), which offers guided tours to groups (generally kids on school trips, no individuals), also has a retail store. ♦ Daily. Main floor. 982.0461. Also at: 1904 Chamisa St (at Llano St), 988.4311; Villa Linda Mall (4250 Cerrillos Rd, at Rodeo Rd). 471.8899

8 Rio Grande Gallery The work of popular Taos artist R.C. Gorman, whose stylistic line drawings of Indian women are regarded by some as high art and by others as motel-room art, is sold here. Also showcased are the mystical abstractions of Tom Perkinson and the Plains Indians portraits of C.J. Wells. ♦ Daily. 80 E San Francisco St (south side of the Plaza, between Don Gaspar Ave and Old Santa Fe Trail). 983.2458

8 Andrew Smith Gallery Santa Fe native Andrew Smith's photography gallery is one of the best in Santa Fe. Classic early American photography of Edward S. Curtis, who recorded Indian life throughout the West; Ansel Adams, who traveled widely in New Mexico; Eliot Porter, who captured nature in color close-ups while based in nearby Tesuque; and Laura Gilpin, who called Santa Fe home while recording the lifestyle of the Navajos, are among the works showcased here. A large selection of contemporary photography includes pictures by W. Eugene Smith and other international stars. ♦ M-Sa; Su noon-4PM. 76 E San Francisco St (south side of the Plaza, between Don Gaspar Ave and Old Santa Fe Trail). 984.1234

9 Dewey Galleries Housed in the historic Spiegelberg building (a 19th-century mercantile store listed on the National Register of Historic Places), this gallery carries a fine selection of Navajo textiles, Native American jewelry and pottery, and contemporary fine art by American artists. ♦ M-Sa. 74 E San Francisco St (south side of the Plaza, between Don Gaspar Ave and Old Santa Fe Trail). 982.8632, 800/327.7721

9 Simply Santa Fe In 1881 this building was erected atop an older foundation to house one of the largest mercantile establishments in the region. It is now home to a three-level shop filled with some of the best work by local craftspeople. Visible in the basement is the bricked-off entrance to an underground tunnel that led to the **Palace of the Governors** (see page 19), which was the city's most fortified building. The merchandise, all unique and handmade, runs the gamut from jewelry to clothing to home furnishings. A particular joy is a steel bed frame made by Lloyd Kreitz, in which you'd wake up under a canopy of metal stars. ♦ Daily June-Christmas; M-Sa 26 Dec-May. 72 E San Francisco St (south side of the Plaza, between Don Gaspar Ave and Old Santa Fe Trail). 988.3100

10 F.W. Woolworth This may be the most revered five-and-dime in America because of its nostalgic symbolism. It's a reminder to Santa Feans of the days when the Plaza was filled with pharmacies, shoe stores, and inexpensive clothing shops, all patronized by locals. Most of these businesses are long gone to the malls, forced out of downtown by rising rents and lack of parking; **Woolworth's** is the last holdout. In addition to the normal sundries and a routine but convenient lunch counter, it features a local culinary favorite: Frito pies in a bag. They'll open a bag of Fritos, pour the chips into a plastic bowl, add beans and chili, top it off with chopped onions, and hand you a plastic spoon. Get a soda and head across the street to the Plaza (don't forget a napkin) for a lunch that's cheap and fun. ♦ Daily. 58 E San Francisco St (south side of the Plaza, between Don Gaspar Ave and Old Santa Fe Trail). 982.1062

10 Plaza Bakery/Häagen-Dazs The former **Zook's Pharmacy** became a Häagen-Dazs outlet in the late 1970s, an event that marked the point of no return in remote Santa Fe's headlong dive into the modern yuppie world. Most people pop in for take-out ice-cream cones, but there are several tables inside at which to gorge on calories and cholesterol. The rich ice cream, cakes, and cookies are tops, if you can brave the jostling mob at the counter. The **Häagen-Dazs** people claim that more of their ice cream is sold in this shop in a year than at any other location in the US. ♦ Daily. 56 E San Francisco St (south side of the Plaza, between Don Gaspar Ave and Old Santa Fe Trail). 988.3858

11 Glenn Green Galleries Though it displays the works of about 25 contemporary artists, including the sculptures of Paul Moore and the mixed-media paintings of Navajo artist Tony Abeyta, this gallery is primarily an outlet for renowned Indian sculptor Allan Houser. Recipient of the National Medal of the Arts in 1992 and the Prix de West in 1993, Houser's work is shown throughout the country. His *Offering of the Sacred Pipe* is in the courtyard of the US Mission to the United Nations in New York City, and his 12-foot-high *May We Have Peace* is temporarily sitting on Al and Tipper Gore's lawn awaiting the opening of the Smithsonian Museum for the American Indian in Washington, DC at the end of the century; the maquette for the sculpture was presented to President Clinton in 1994. ♦ Daily. 50 E San Francisco St (south side of the Plaza, between Don Gaspar Ave and Old Santa Fe Trail). 988.4168

12 Ore House ★$$$ Sit on the balcony overlooking the Plaza, sip one of 80 kinds of margaritas, and feel immune to the bustle below. By the time you've sampled a few, you may not care that the food, which includes steak, a salad bar, and a daily seafood special, is ordinary. ♦ Steaks/Seafood ♦ Daily lunch and dinner. Reservations recommended for dinner. 50 Lincoln Ave (at W San Francisco St). 983.8687

On his first visit to Santa Fe, humorist Will Rogers said of the city's disjointed maze of narrow streets: "Whoever designed this town did so while riding on a jackass, backwards and drunk."

12 Plaza Cafe ★★$ A downtown fixture as old and humble as the men who sit across the street, the simple **Plaza Restaurant** opened in 1918 and has been owned by the Razatos family since 1947. It is now operated by a new generation—brothers Len and Dan and sister Belinda—who modernized the interior and changed the name to **Plaza Cafe.** The grill has remained simple, unpretentious, and family-oriented and is definitely not a bar—no alcohol is served without a meal. The food includes huge hamburgers, New Mexican specialties, and Greek dishes. Boxed lunches can be made up to take on your day trips. ♦ New Mexican/American/Greek ♦ Daily breakfast, lunch, and dinner. 54 Lincoln Ave (west side of the Plaza, between W San Francisco St and W Palace Ave). 982.1664

13 Palace Avenue In the 19th century the stretch of this road that fronts the north side of the Plaza was the rowdiest street in town. West Palace was home to gambling halls and to many of the "fancy women" who entertained trail-weary traders and love-starved soldiers. Most prominent among the painted ladies was Doña Tules Barcelo, owner of the fanciest gambling hall, a brothel, and—cause and effect?—a bank. She was eagerly accepted in prominent society, to the despair of a few local bluenoses. Her story was fictionalized by Ruth Laughlin in the novel *The Wind Leaves No Shadows.* Today it is home to a variety of galleries and shops. ♦ From W San Francisco St to Canyon Rd

14 Museum of Fine Arts At the end of the 19th century, traditional adobe architecture was giving way to brick construction in Santa Fe; more than six million bricks were ordered by local builders in that year alone. In 1916 a local artist, Carlos Vierra, spearheaded a movement to return to the traditional adobe style. This museum was built in 1917 on the site of a former army barracks to ease overcrowding in the **Palace of the Governors.** Designed by architects **I.H. Rapp** and **William M. Rapp,** the structure has beautiful soaring curves that are breathtaking against the bright blue sky. The building helped inspire the Pueblo Revival–style (now known as Santa Fe style) architecture that has held sway in the city ever since. A 1982 renovation by **Edward Larrabee Barnes** and **Antoine Predock** increased the exhibition space. The influence of Spanish mission churches, most notably the one at **Acoma Pueblo,** is visible in the **St. Francis Auditorium** at the west end of the building (chamber music concerts are held here).

This is one of the few museums in the world that was created specifically for local artists to display their own work; no attempt was made to gather a collection of European old masters. In time, however, the open-door policy ended, and curated exhibits of contemporary art were balanced with shows featuring New Mexico's own old masters—early painters of the Santa Fe and Taos art colonies, including Joseph Sharp, Ernest Blumenschein, Irving Couse, Victor Higgins, John Sloan, and Andrew Dasburg, and photographers such as Eliot Porter, Laura Gilpin, and Edward Weston. The permanent collection includes 13 works by Georgia O'Keeffe. ♦ Admission; under 17 free. Daily. 107 W Palace Ave (between Sheridan and Lincoln Aves). 827.4455

15 Contemporary Southwest Galleries
Owners Cliff Phelps and Frank Howell display works in a variety of mediums, all in contemporary Southwestern style. They're the local representatives of Miguel Martinez of Taos, painter of a thousand faces, all of them haunting Hispanic women. Also striking are the imaginative ceramic sculptures of Gene and Rebecca Tobey, derived from Indian fetish motifs. ♦ Daily. 123 W Palace Ave (at Sheridan Ave). 986.0440

15 Horwitch LewAllen Gallery The hottest news in years on the Santa Fe art scene was the April 1994 merger between two of the city's most prestigious galleries. After the 1991 death of longtime Santa Fe gallery owner Elaine Horwitch, one of the best-known art dealers in the Southwest, the **Elaine Horwitch Gallery** languished under the absentee ownership of her son, Scottsdale art dealer Mark Horwitch, until many art watchers declared that the gallery had lost its focus and relevance. By combining the **Horwitch Gallery**'s prime location and impressive collection with Arlene LewAllen's (formerly of the **LewAllen Gallery**) local art market experience and sharp eye for contemporary painting and sculpture, it is expected that the gallery will set a new standard for modern art in Santa Fe. Under Horwitch family ownership and LewAllen management, this space exhibits the top artists from both former galleries. Among the works featured are massive, sometimes musical, stone-slab sculptures by Jesús Bautista Morelos; mixed-media painting/construction by Roy De-Forest; paintings by Australian Aborigine folk artist Clifford Possum; and the unique dalmatian paintings of the late Dick Mason. ♦ M-Sa. 129 W Palace Ave (between Grant and Sheridan Aves). 988.8997

*Susie's
Patio Cafe*

16 Susie's Patio Cafe ★★$ Located in a passageway linking Palace Avenue and San Francisco Street, this is a convenient spot to enjoy a cup of coffee or espresso, or perhaps a frittata or stuffed croissant. Susie Pond, who

left the entertainment business in Los Angeles for the quiet life, will be happy to shoot the breeze with you. Unfortunately, the once-lovely patio has been destroyed by the intrusion of the city's zillionth boutique, so eating indoors might be a better choice. ♦ Cafe ♦ Daily breakfast, lunch, and dinner. 130 W Palace Ave (in a passageway between W Palace Ave and W San Francisco St). 983.3245

17 Montez Gold Personable owner Rey Montez—whose roots here date back to the Spanish conquistadores—carries contemporary jewelry by about 50 local artists, as well as hand-painted leather and silk clothing. Catch Rey when he isn't busy and he'll be happy to discuss the family tree. A charming specialty of the shop—75 percent of the business, in fact—is custom-made wedding rings. ♦ M-Sa. 135 W Palace Ave (at Grant Ave). 983.9449

EDGE

17 Edge ★★$$$ This disco on the third floor of the **Palace Court**, a three-story shop-filled building, is a big draw with a cross-section of locals, including Santa Fe's significant lesbian and gay population. The spiffy modern decor has been labeled Pueblo Deco—a marriage of Art Deco and Southwest Indian. The small but appetizing menu features burgers, salads, such gourmet sandwiches as turkey and guacamole on sourdough bread, and other light fare. The cuisine is New Southwestern—it emphasizes the use of such uniquely Southwestern ingredients as green chile, blue corn, and piñon nuts. Diners can eat in any of the club's rooms or in the new first-floor courtyard. ♦ American/New Southwestern ♦ Daily lunch, dinner, and late-night dinner. Reservations recommended. 135 W Palace Ave (at Grant Ave), Third floor. 986.1700, 986.1714

18 Parker Books of the West Interested in reading about *Dodge City—The Cowboy Capital, Cattle Trade of the West,* or *Six-Guns and Saddle Leather?* These and hundreds of other rare, used, and new volumes about the Southwest are available in this unpretentious shop run by Betty and Riley Parker. Would you believe old Louis L'Amour works in hardback? ♦ M-Sa. 142 W Palace Ave (at Burro Alley). 988.1076

An average of three burglaries a day are committed in Santa Fe.

The median age of a Santa Fe resident is 36.1, while the median age of a Santa Fe visitor is 50.

Restaurants/Clubs: Red   **Hotels:** Blue
Shops/ 🌳 Outdoors: Green   **Sights/Culture:** Black

THE PALACE

18 The Palace Restaurant and Saloon

★★$$$ Doña Tules ran her saloon, gambling hall, and bawdy house on this site until she died in 1853. In 1959 excavation began for the present restaurant, whose rich red interiors and saloon-type doors retain the Old West flavor of the original. Popular with local politicians and realtors, this after-work drinking spot serves continental and Northern Italian cuisine. The menu, which changes seasonally, includes homemade pasta, seafood, and free-range poultry and meats such as *tagliarine di mare* (pasta with scallops, shrimp, and sun-dried tomatoes in a light pesto sauce), sautéed sweetbreads, and *petto di pollo al formaggio* (grilled chicken breast with goat cheese, herbs, and red lentils). ♦ Continental/Northern Italian ♦ M-Sa lunch and dinner. Reservations recommended for dinner. 142 W Palace Ave (at Burro Alley). 982.9891

19 Grant Corner Inn

$$$ Tucked behind a pretty weeping willow that's downright sobbing, this Colonial-style manor was built in the early 1900s as a home for a wealthy ranching family. Today it's a first-rate bed-and-breakfast inn, renovated and owned by Pat Walter, wife Louise Stewart, and daughter "Bumpy." The atmosphere here is Old World, with an assortment of four-poster beds, quilts, gooseneck lamps, and other antiques that make each of the 11 rooms a gentle time trip into another century. An extraordinary breakfast is served before a large fire in winter, outdoors in summer. Guests can also stay at a nearby Southwestern-style hacienda. ♦ 122 Grant Ave (at Johnson St). 983.6678

20 Riva Yares Gallery

For more than 25 years Riva Yares ran a gallery in Scottsdale before she moved to Santa Fe. The roster of artists whose work she has exhibited includes Milton Avery, Hans Hoffman, Alex Katz, Alexander Liberman, Larry Poons, Elias Rivera, and George Segal. ♦ Tu-Sa. 123 Grant Ave (between W Palace Ave and W Marcy St). 984.0330

David Carradine has appeared in more movies set in New Mexico than any other actor.

---

21 Pickney R. Tully House

This adobe house is an architectural curiosity: Built in 1851, it is painted to look like brick. Tully eventually deeded the place to his son-in-law, Oliver P. Hovey, who had a printing press shipped from Missouri in 1848 and began publication of New Mexico's first English-language newspaper, *The Santa Fe Republican.* The house is now home to an expensive clothing boutique. ♦ 136 Grant Ave (at Griffin St)

22 Homewood Suites

$$$$ Newly built in 1994, this all-suite hotel offers the most spacious accommodations in the downtown area. The 105 units, which are decorated in soft Southwestern rose and turquoise hues, have separate bedrooms and full kitchens with stoves, refrigerators, and microwaves. Living rooms have sofa beds, TVs with VCRs, gas fireplaces, and balconies. Amenities include an exercise room, an outdoor swimming pool, two hot tubs, a 24-hour convenience store, and an executive center wtih a copy machine, fax machine, typewriter, and computer for guests' use. The hotel provides free shuttle service to the Plaza (five blocks away) and any other desired destinations in the downtown area. Rates include a continental breakfast and evening social hour (fruit and cheese or light dinner, no cocktails). ♦ 400 Griffin St (between Paseo de Peralta and Rosario Blvd). 988.3000, 800/225.5466; fax 988.4700

23 First Presbyterian Church

In a region that is predominantly Catholic, this church has held strong since opening its doors in 1867; it's the oldest Protestant church in New Mexico. ♦ 208 Grant Ave (at W Marcy St). 982.8544

24 Sweeney Convention Center

When this was Santa Fe's mid–high school, Dolly Parton and other touring singers would perform here in the **Sweeney Gym.** In the early 1970s the city converted the school into a convention center that now hosts gatherings of up to several hundred people. Business interests are pressing for the construction of a larger, more modern facility, which won't be completed for years, if it happens at all. The **Santa Fe Convention and Visitors Bureau** is located inside. ♦ W Marcy St (at Grant Ave)

25 Federal Courthouse

A beautiful piece of Greek Revival stonework, this building stands out in adobe Santa Fe like a goddess in a sandbox. In 1850 the US Congress authorized the construction of a "capitol building" here, but appropriated a mere $20,000. Four years later, $50,000 more was added, but funds nonetheless ran out after only one-and-a-half stories had been built above the basement. The building stood without a roof for the next 25 years, falling, understandably, into increasing dilapidation. In 1883, when the site was selected for a large territorial fair, a temporary roof was added so that Indians participating in the six-week celebration could stay inside. A racetrack about one-third of a mile long was laid out in an oval around the grounds, and horse and burro races were held. A year later a stone monument to frontiersman Kit Carson was erected at the main entrance by his comrades in the Grand Army of the Republic. The building was finally completed in 1889—36 years after construction began. Rough stone for the walls was quarried in the Hyde Park region of the hills above the city. Dressed stone came from the village of Cerrillos, to the south. The building, however, never did become the capitol. On the east side of the courthouse is **Grant Park,** a tree-shaded oasis that looks like a bit of New England, and to the west is the nondescript **Main Post Office.** ♦ M-F. S Federal Pl (off Washington Ave). 988.6610

26 City Hall A bronze statue of St. Francis, the city's patron saint, stands in front of this modern building—his back to the goings-on inside—where the mayor's office and a host of other city agencies are located. The eight-member city council normally meets every other Wednesday at 4PM and 7PM. When a new development project is listed on the agenda—as it often is—the room gets crowded and the tempers grow hot. ♦ M-F. 200 Lincoln Ave (off W Marcy St). 984.6500

27 Piccolo Cafe ★★$ When you simply have to rest in your wanderings, this tiny corner hideaway is a refreshing place. Assorted pastries and bagels are available in the morning, and at lunch and dinner there's a large assortment of sandwiches, as well as Greek and garden salads. Coffees, cakes, soft drinks, nonfat frozen yogurt, sundaes, and floats are on tap well into the evening. Bag lunches can be provided. ♦ Cafe ♦ Daily breakfast, lunch, and dinner. 142 Lincoln Ave (at W Marcy St). 984.1709

28 Old Sears Building For many years locals shopped here at **Sears** until the huge department store moved out to **Villa Linda Mall.** Now renovated, this old building houses shops on the ground floor—with maroon awnings that look like they belong in Beverly Hills—and three restaurants upstairs. To get to the restaurants you can ride on the only escalator in the entire city. But it only goes up; you'll have to take the stairs or the elevator down. ♦ 130 Lincoln Ave (between W Palace Ave and W Marcy St). No phone

Within the Old Sears Building:

Garduño's of Santa Fe $$ The Garduño family has been serving food to New Mexicans for over a quarter of a century. Unfortunately, the line out the door is a testament only to their reputation. The food is much too salty, much too spicy (even for those who love chile), and made from too many ingredients

that taste defrosted. The enticing five-page menu may be more of a problem than a recommendation. But the margaritas are the size of swimming pools, which might explain the line. The family also owns four restaurants in Albuquerque. ♦ New Mexican ♦ Daily lunch and dinner. Reservations recommended. 983.9797

Cafe Escalera ★$$$ The menu changes daily in this clean, well-lighted place, though most of the choices are from the Mediterranean, particularly Morocco. While aspirations are high, the quality also seems to change daily. In keeping with the growing trend, smoking is allowed in the bar but not in the restaurant. ♦ Mediterranean ♦ M-Sa breakfast, lunch, and dinner; Su dinner. Reservations recommended for lunch and dinner. 989.8188

Babbo Ganzo

Babbo Ganzo Trattoria ★★★$$$ Classic Tuscan food as well as New Mexican specialties are prepared by chef Giovanni Scorzo, who claims his pizza—baked in a wood-burning oven—is the best in the world. Many people agree: His ultrathin crust is exactly what you would eat in Florence. The pastas are uniformly good, and the antipasto and daily seafood specials, such as halibut with mushrooms, are excellent. ♦ Italian/New Mexican ♦ M-Sa lunch and dinner. Reservations recommended Friday and Saturday. 986.3835

Kent Galleries/The Contemporary Craftsman In 1991 **Kent Galleries** absorbed **The Contemporary Craftsman,** which has remained one of the finest craft galleries in town since 1974. Droll pottery covered with rabbits made by Rabbit Art Works is a longtime favorite. Beautifully wrought ceramics range from the functional to the purely artistic. The outstanding jewelry collection includes contemporary gold and silver works, many with semiprecious stones, by regional and local artists. Jane Kent's gallery walls, which zigzag for an entire block, feature popular local landscapes in oil pastel by Maggie Muchmore. ♦ M-Sa; Su noon-5PM. 988.1001

29 Davis Mather Folk Art Gallery Coiled, brightly colored wooden snakes glare out from the walls and shelves of this tiny, jam-packed shop, along with assorted sheep, roosters, families of cats, and folk-art buses filled with animal passengers. The town's first folk-art shop opened in the mid-1970s, caught the Santa Fe wave, and is still going strong. Hang around and you might meet the owner's wife, Christine Mather, a former museum curator who coauthored the hugely successful book *Santa Fe Style*. ♦ M-Sa. 141 Lincoln Ave (at W Marcy St). 983.1660

Paul's

30 Paul's ★★★$$ Santa Feans consider this elegant little hole-in-the-wall restaurant a local secret. Among its variety of interesting menu items, chef Paul Hunsicker features a baked salmon with a pecan-herb crust in sorrel sauce. Another mouthwatering dish is roast duck with a chipotle-tomato-orange sauce. Save room for the pièce de résistance—chocolate ganache. Hunsicker won the Taste of Santa Fe award in 1994 for best dessert for this delicious confection of white and dark chocolate mixed together like a marble cake, and served on a pecan crust. If you come at breakfast you can get *migas* (eggs scrambled with tortilla strips). ♦ Continental/Southwestern ♦ M-Sa breakfast, lunch, and dinner. Reservations required. 72 W Marcy St (between Lincoln and Washington Aves). 982.8738

31 Ristorante La Traviata ★★★$$$ Two neat, white-clothed rooms offer tasteful surroundings in which to savor memorable Sicilian dishes at this charming trattoria. Opera tapes provide background music, and photographs and portraits depicting operas and opera stars adorn the walls. Owner Alberto "Ken" Calascione makes annual trips to Italy, where he stays with his cousins and pries recipes out of his family. For appetizers, both the cured salmon and the tuna carpaccio are excellent. Stand-out entrées include the chicken or veal marsala—marsala dishes don't get any better than this—or the fettuccine *all'arrabbiata* (with porcini mushrooms, basil, tomatoes, and hot peppers). For dessert, try the tiramisù; it's heavenly. And best of all, the portions are huge. One drawback: The small tables are crowded close together, which can make things a bit noisy, especially at lunch. ♦ Sicilian ♦ M-F breakfast, lunch, and dinner; Sa-Su dinner. Reservations required for lunch and dinner. 95 W Marcy St (between Lincoln and Washington Aves). 984.1091

The paint used to create designs on New Mexican pottery is usually made from natural materials such as boiled wild spinach (also known as beeweed) and the residue of boiled yucca fruit.

Restaurants/Clubs: Red   Hotels: Blue
Shops/ 🎋 Outdoors: Green   Sights/Culture: Black

32 Padre Gallegos House This Territorial-style adobe home was built in the 1850s by Padre José Manuel Gallegos a few years after he was defrocked as a priest by Archbishop Lamy, who had taken a dim view of the padre's gambling, dancing, and political activities. According to some historians, Padre Gallegos was a ringleader of the 1847 Taos revolt against the American occupation of the New Mexico Territory, in which Governor Charles Bent was assassinated. During the Civil War the building was used as a rooming house. Beginning in 1868, part of the north tier of rooms where **Santacafe** (see below) is located, served for a time as an Episcopalian chapel; it is believed that the former padre wed the widow Candelaria Montoya there. Gallegos died in 1875 and was buried in Rosario Cemetery a few blocks away. ♦ Free. Daily. 231 Washington Ave (between E Marcy St and Paseo de Peralta). No phone

Within the Padre Gallegos House:

Santacafe ★★★$$$ One of Santa Fe's finest, this restaurant offers beauty at every turn: in the soft white adobe interiors of the small rooms, in the boulder-studded courtyard where lunch and dinner are served in the warm months, and, under the watchful gaze of co-owners Bobby Morean and Judith Ebbinghaus, in the way every appetizer and entrée is presented. The menu changes with the seasons, and the combinations of ingredients are novel and usually delicious. Crab egg rolls are a traditional favorite appetizer, and the flash-fried calamari is crisp yet tender, as is an entrée of Oriental duck breast in Velarde sweet-and-sour cherry sauce. One variety of pizza is made with fresh peppers, chiles, tomatoes, basil, and Sonoma jack cheese. The pleasant staff always offers impeccable service. On occasion a subtle dish, such as scallops, may taste too subtle for complete satisfaction, or crab cakes a bit too spicy. But overall, dining here is a lovely experience. ♦ New Southwestern ♦ M-Sa lunch and dinner; Su dinner. Reservations required. 984.1788

33 Territorial Inn $$$ Just a short jaunt from the Plaza, this 10-bedroom bed-and-breakfast inn is set back from the street behind a well-kept lawn and large cottonwood trees, giving it a nice secluded feeling. The building itself, constructed in the 1890s by **George Shoch,** a Philadelphian, is a blend of stone and adobe architecture with an unusual pitched roof. Levi Hughes, a prominent local merchant, lived here in the 1920s with his wife and threw lavish society parties. In the public living room a large fire blazes on cool evenings. Two of the rooms have their own fireplaces, and eight have private baths. In the back garden, a hot tub is enclosed in a gazebo. Eat breakfast in the garden in summer or in your room. ♦ 215 Washington Ave (between E Marcy St and Paseo de Peralta). 989.7737; fax 986.1411

34 Santa Fe Public Library Once the main fire station, then converted into **City Hall,** this two-story Territorial-style building is now the main branch of the local library. Visitors cannot check out books without a local address, but they are welcome to use the **Southwest Reading Room,** which houses a distinguished collection of works on the region, both fiction and nonfiction. There is also a periodicals reading room with a modest offering of current newspapers and magazines. ♦ M-Sa; Su 1-5PM. 145 Washington Ave (at E Marcy St). 984.6780

35 Peyton-Wright Gallery Artists who dip their brushes in dreams and myths dominate John Wright Schaefer's boldly evocative contemporary gallery. Kathleen Morris, one of the gutsiest painters in the region, is not afraid to float babies in a yellow Vietnamese dreamscape or create her own revisionist tarot deck. Orlando Leyba's mixed-media works and Miguel Zapata's bronze sculptures represent the cutting edge of contemporary Hispanic art. And the Indian visions of Darren Vigil Gray churn with an inner fury. ♦ M-Sa; Su by appointment. 131 Nusbaum St (between Washington Ave and Otero St). 989.9888

36 Dancing Ground of the Sun $$$ David and Donna McClure gave up careers in Honolulu, Hawaii, to run this bed-and-breakfast inn whose name comes from an old Indian name for Santa Fe. All four of the units are casitas (bungalows), each with its own kitchen. Three have fireplaces for those cool Santa Fe evenings. A continental breakfast and afternoon refreshments are provided. ♦ 711 Paseo de Peralta (between E Palace Ave and E Marcy St). 986.9797

37 Wyeth Hurd Gallery This gallery is dedicated to paintings and prints by what may be America's foremost family of artists: patriarch N.C. Wyeth, who died in 1945; his son Andrew Wyeth, the most famous; his daughter, Henriette Wyeth, whose strong still lifes may make her the most enduring painter of the lot; Henriette's late husband, Peter Hurd, who is best known for watercolors of the New Mexico landscape; Jamie Wyeth, Andrew's son, whose portraits of celebrities are well known nationally. And on and on into the new generation. ♦ Daily. 301 E Palace Ave (at Paseo de Peralta). 989.8380

38 La Posada $$$ One of the most pleasant hotels in town, this six-acre spread of grass, fruit trees, and casitas offers 119 rooms and 40 suites—all just an easy three-block walk from the Plaza. The Victorian-style main building was constructed in the 1880s by Abraham Staab, a German immigrant who made a fortune in the mercantile business. The ghost of Staab's wife, Julia Shuster Staab, is said to be a permanent nonpaying guest in room 256. Surrounding the main house are wings of casitas, both old and new, many of which contain Native American fireplaces, flagstone floors, vigas, and skylights. There's also an outdoor pool, a rose garden, and a lovely patio with wrought-iron tables shaded by umbrellas, as well as a restaurant and bar. Joan Mondale used to stay here on frequent visits to Santa Fe when she was the Second Lady. ♦ 330 E Palace Ave (between Paseo de Peralta and Delgado St). 986.0000, 800/727.5276; fax 982.6850

Within La Posada:

Staab House ★$$$ This restaurant has a nice rustic feel to it, including a large fireplace. The breakfasts are excellent; in the summer the superb, though expensive, all-you-can-eat Sunday brunch buffet features about 40 items. Lunch and dinner, however, rarely excite. ♦ American ♦ Daily breakfast, lunch, and dinner. Reservations recommended for dinner. 986.0000

39 Palace Design Copper lamps and shades that look like tall pyramids are a leading attraction in this designer variety store, along with exotic mirrors, wrought-iron tables, candlesticks, and wall sconces. Owner James Aumell has been a trader here since 1970. ♦ Daily. 217 E Palace Ave (at Cienega St). 988.5204

Horticulturists agree: The chile pepper, one of New Mexico's official vegetables (the other is the pinto bean), is not easily defined. The produce industry calls them vegetables, but to botanists they're berries. And horticulturally, they're fruits. Worse yet, when red chiles are dried, they're considered a spice.

40 Nicholas Potter, Bookseller The oldest used-bookstore in town was started in 1969 by Chicago emigrant Jack Potter, whose son Nick took over in 1975. It is a bibliophile's heaven. If Nick doesn't have a certain volume, he'll try to track it down for you. The shop stocks about 8,500 volumes, all hardbacks, of predominantly literary and scholarly works. ♦ M-Sa. 203 E Palace Ave (between Otero and Cienega Sts). 983.5434

40 Palace Avenue Books If nothing old strikes your fancy at **Nick Potter's,** try something new next door at Judy Dwyer's bookshop, which is strong in current works on history and philosophy. The space is small, but the selection of Southwestern scholarly works may be the largest in town. ♦ M-Sa. 209 E Palace Ave (between Otero and Cienega Sts). 986.0536

41 Frank Patania Masks from Bali, tribal art from New Guinea, and carvings from Indonesia offer a welcome break from the Southwestern bazaar. Frank Patania also sells silver and gold jewelry he designs himself, as well as Navajo jewelry. ♦ M-Sa. 119 E Palace Ave (between Otero St and Washington Ave). 983.2155

42 Sena Plaza Stop in this courtyard, one of the prettiest and most serene spots in Santa Fe, and relax on benches amid the profusion of day lilies, hollyhocks, roses, and large shade trees; let the gurgling fountain blot out the traffic noise. This was once the courtyard of a single residence, that of Doña Isabel and Don Jose Sena. Starting with a small house, Sena little by little built a hacienda of 33 rooms to house his 11 children, the servants, the horses, and the chickens. Part of the second story was added when the building was restored in 1920. Now owned by prominent local art dealer and real estate mogul Gerald Peters, it houses shops, galleries, and a restaurant. But the lovely courtyard still conveys the feeling that time itself has paused to rest. ♦ 125 E Palace Ave (between Otero St and Washington Ave)

Within Sena Plaza:

Montez Gallery All his life, Santa Fe native Rey Montez watched his father, Ramon, carve traditional Hispanic *retablos* (renderings of the saints on wooden plaques), as well as animals and flowers, out of sugar pine. An electrician by trade, Ramon gave away his artwork to friends, but never tried to sell it. In 1989 Rey opened a gallery to display the art of his father and other traditional Hispanic folk artists of the area, whose work had been largely overlooked amid the myriad of Indian art stores. This tiny, friendly shop filled with *bultos* (religious wood carvings of saints), *retablos,* appliquéd straw crosses, and assorted objects of tin is the most authentic Hispanic gallery in town. ♦ M-Sa. 982.1828

La Casa Sena ★★★$$$$ This elegant and formal dining room occupies a 19th-century Territorial-style adobe house and serves wonderful local and continental fare. In warm weather you can eat under the stars. Highlights on the full New Mexican menu include *pollo en mole* (chicken in a red chile–mole–sesame sauce) and *truchas en terracotta* (trout cooked in clay). Delicious whole-wheat sopaipillas are served at lunch, and the wine list is outstanding. ♦ New Mexican/Continental ♦ Daily lunch and dinner. Reservations required. 988.9232

Cantina ★★★$$$ Adjacent to **La Casa Sena** (and under the same ownership), this laid-back eatery provides one of the most enjoyable dining experiences in town. The talented staff sing excerpts from Broadway musicals past and present while serving, and in a nightly show. Sounds corny, but it's fun. The best local ingredients are always used in the gourmet fare here. A red-chile pasta with scallops, shrimp, and salmon is wonderful, as is the avocado cheesecake (yes, avocado—try it!) with a piñon nut crust. Reservations are not taken, and since the room is L-shaped, it's best to show up half an hour before show time for a good view and an enchanted evening. ♦ New Mexican ♦ Daily dinner; shows daily 6PM, 8PM. 988.9232

Barbara Zusman Art & Antiques A large collection of antique Mexican jewelry is just one of the special finds at this treasure trove. Pamela Adger's messenger sculptures are droll clothed cylinders containing a secret hidden communiqué: When you buy your favorite doll, you get to read the message that's just for you. Zusman made her name with her individual treasure necklaces, from which hang everything but the kitchen sink. ♦ Daily. 984.1303

SOAP OPERA

Soap Opera For more than two decades, Santa Fe's bathers have been stopping by this aromatic shop to pick up exotic soaps scented with cedar and sage, piñon pine, avocado, lavender, sandalwood, and patchouli. ♦ Daily. 982.8066

43 The Shed ★★$ A few steps through a passageway off Palace Avenue, Prince Plaza—a small courtyard—houses one of downtown's busiest lunch spots. The line forms early as patrons queue up for typical New Mexican fare, including tacos and enchiladas. ◆ New Mexican ◆ M-Sa lunch. 113¹/₂ E Palace Ave (between Otero St and Washington Ave). 982.9030

44 Trujillo Plaza In 1942 nuclear physicist J. Robert Oppenheimer chose a boys' ranch (an outdoor-oriented private school) in Los Alamos, New Mexico, to be the home of the Manhattan Project—an effort to design and build an atomic bomb to bring about the end of World War II. Scientists were recruited from across America, but the project was so secret that the only address and destination they were given was 109 East Palace Avenue in Santa Fe. When their trains were met in Lamy, the nearest rail stop, they were brought here to check in, then were driven in military jeeps or buses the 40 miles to Los Alamos. Here, too, their mail arrived, so their location would remain unknown to the outside world. Today the historic address houses shops. ◆ 109 E Palace Ave (between Otero St and Washington Ave)

44 The Rainbow Man In business since 1945, this eclectic shop is housed in the rebuilt remains of a building that was wrecked during the Indian uprising of 1680. Owners Bob and Marian Kapoun display everything from historic photographs to railroad memorabilia and old dining-car china, vintage Indian blankets, and Old Pawn jewelry. There's also a collection of miniature kachina dolls, including one-inch-high wonders by Bess Yanez. ◆ Daily. 107 E Palace Ave (between Otero St and Washington Ave). 982.8706

45 The Burrito Company $ Low prices, a convenient location, and sidewalk tables are what entice all those people sitting here. If food is your top priority, keep walking. ◆ New Mexican ◆ M-Sa breakfast, lunch, and dinner; Su breakfast and lunch. 111 Washington Ave (between E Palace Ave and Nusbaum St). 982.4453

45 Inn of the Anasazi $$$$ Of all the hotels in town, this hostelry is a true work of art. Built in 1991 by the **Robert D. Zimmer Group,** it tucks 59 rooms into a small space only a half-block from the Plaza and looks like it has been here forever—which is exactly the intended effect. The outside is dark adobe with protruding vigas that cast the afternoon shadows like a sundial. Heavy wood and leather furniture fill the interior, which has the allure of a cozy cave dwelling hideaway. All of the rooms have ceilings constructed of vigas and *latillas* (cross beams), along with four-poster beds, gaslit fireplaces, Indian rugs, and hand-carved cabinets that hide the modern TVs and VCRs. Service is prompt and first-rate, except for the valet parking in the underground garage, which may take some

time because of the narrow property site. ◆ 113 Washington Ave (between E Palace Ave and Nusbaum St). 988.3030, 800/688.8100; fax 988.3277

Within the Inn of the Anasazi:

Anasazi Restaurant ★★$$$ The same dramatic Southwestern ambience that characterizes the hotel imbues this 96-seat restaurant. The tables are made of rough-hewn wood, and the *bancos* (adobe banquettes) are upholstered with handwoven textiles from Chimayó. Up to 12 guests can dine together in the private wine cellar. The menu, created primarily from food grown in the region, features such exotic combinations of New Mexican and Native American dishes as organic tenderloin of beef with white cheddar, mashed potatoes, and mango–red-chile jelly, and wood-grilled natural chicken with country-style corn pudding, garlic, sage, and organic vegetables. Although the taste is usually quite good, its richness sometimes taxes the digestive system. ◆ New Mexican/Native American ◆ Daily breakfast, lunch, and dinner. Reservations recommended. 988.3030

45 Hotel Plaza Real $$$ Right next door to the **Inn of the Anasazi,** and built about the same time, this hotel strives for a brighter atmosphere. The Territorial-style architecture features brick trimwork and white-painted columned porticoes extending out from the pale beige walls. Many of the 100 rooms and suites contain wood-burning fireplaces, and some have balconies. Continental breakfast is complimentary, and underground parking is available. At times, however, the service—such as "prompt" wake-up calls—can leave a lot to be desired. ◆ 125 Washington Ave (between E Palace Ave and Nusbaum St). 988.4900, 800/279.7325

46 James Reid Ltd. Since 1980 James Reid has been showcasing his own silver work—especially buckles and belt-tip sets—as well as that of other local artists. In an unusual concept, his stable of artisans works together and collaborates on the design and creation of all sorts of excellent silver jewelry. ◆ Daily. 114 E Palace Ave (between Washington Ave and Cathedral Pl). 988.1147

47 Gusterman's Silversmiths Unusual for downtown Santa Fe, the jewelry found here has the simple clean lines of Scandinavia. Co-owners and sisters Britt and Kerstein Gusterman learned the trade from their father, a master silversmith from Sweden. The family emigrated to Colorado where the elder Gusterman owned several successful silver shops. Kerstein manages the business, while Britt continues the family smithing tradition. Two local smiths help her craft the exquisite earrings, necklaces, bracelets, and pins of gold and silver that are all created on site. Custom-made pieces are also available. ♦ Daily. 126 E Palace Ave (at Cathedral Pl). 982.8972

48 Institute of American Indian Arts Museum In a classic juxtaposition of church and state, the block-long structure across from the **St. Francis Cathedral** (see below) used to be the **Federal Building.** Local residents would come here to pick up their tax forms from the Internal Revenue Service, among other things. When the feds vacated the place a few years ago, the **Institute of American Indian Arts (IAIA),** an art school for Indian students, took over and converted the building into a museum, which opened in 1992. Today the *National Collection of Contemporary Indian Art*—more than 8,000 pieces of sculpture, pottery, basketry, beadwork, and paintings—is housed here.

The museum's goal is to entice people to view Indian art the way Indians do, in a meditative,

quiet mood. Toward that end, the main entrance opens into the **Lloyd Kiva New Welcoming Circle,** a space for quiet contemplation with a fire pit in the center. Visitors are urged to meditate here before continuing on. Inside, one permanent exhibit features the works of graduates of the institute since its founding in 1962, including Earl Biss, Kevin Red Star, Dan Namingha, and others. Another exhibit, *Early Innovators,* traces the development of Indian art in this century through the sculpture of Allan Houser, the paintings of Pablita Velarde, the jewelry of Charles Loloma, and much more. The **Allan Houser Art Park** is a lovely outdoor sculpture garden with changing exhibits.

The **IAIA** is currently operating out of temporary quarters while planning and raising money for a new campus on privately donated land south of the city. ♦ Admission. M-Sa; Su noon-5PM. 108 Cathedral Pl (between E Palace Ave and E San Francisco St). 988.6281

49 St. Francis Cathedral Built in the 1800s, this was the seat of the Archdiocese of Santa Fe until 1974 when the current archbishop, Roberto Sanchez (the first Hispanic to hold that position), moved the headquarters to Albuquerque after his elevation to the post. One of the most historically interesting buildings in town, the cathedral (pictured below) is still used for regular church services, weddings, and funerals.

In 1851, when New Mexico was one of the wildest outposts of the Wild West, French

St. Francis Cathedral

bishop Jean Baptiste Lamy was sent to Santa Fe by the pope to try to tame it with culture and religion. Lamy believed a dominant religious symbol was needed, so he laid plans for a huge cathedral; the cornerstone was set in 1869. Huge blocks of yellow stone were mined at quarries about 20 miles south of town, loaded onto wagons, and brought to the site. (Lamy, a village not far from the stone quarries, was named after the bishop.) His French Romanesque–style cathedral was built around an older parish church dating from 1714. Stained-glass windows imported from France were installed in 1884, and the cathedral was dedicated to St. Francis, the patron saint of Santa Fe, two years later. Its twin towers were supposed to be topped with steeples 160 feet high, but these were never added.

The old Spanish-style parish church was incorporated into one corner of the cathedral, where it remains as a chapel dedicated to the oldest wooden Madonna known to exist in North America. This statue was carved in Mexico and brought to Santa Fe around 1625; it was taken with the populace driven into exile by the Pueblo Revolt from 1680 to 1692, when it was carried by the legions of Don Diego de Vargas, who retook the city from the Indians. Originally called **Our Lady of the Assumption,** it was renamed **La Conquista-dora** (Our Lady of the Conquest) after the city was reconquered. The most venerated religious object in Santa Fe went by that name until the summer of 1992, when Archbishop Sanchez agreed with Indian protestors that the moniker was offensive and formally dubbed it **Our Lady of Peace.** A local woman dresses the statue in different clothing every day. Each June the statue is carried through the streets in a solemn procession that symbolizes the retaking of the city.

Archbishop Lamy, a scholar with European tastes, had a profound influence in the taming of Santa Fe and is commemorated by a bronze statue, which stands in front of the cathedral. When Willa Cather began to spend time in Santa Fe in the 1920s, seeking inspiration for a novel to be set here, she found it in the story of Lamy, told in her classic anecdotal book *Death Comes for the Archbishop.* A wonderfully readable tale, it is a staple in all the local bookstores. **Cathedral Park,** alongside the church, provides a fine, shady resting place. If you're in town in summer, don't miss the free afternoon concerts performed in the cathedral by artists from the **Santa Fe Opera.** ♦ 213 Cathedral Pl (between E Palace Ave and E San Francisco St). 982.5619

50 Tom Taylor With 45 years of experience, Tom Taylor creates hand-crafted boots that are stunning (except perhaps to animal activists), as well as custom-made belts. He uses 15 types of leather, including ostrich, Italian calf, snakeskin, and alligator. His wife, Jean Taylor, crafts the buckles and other silverwork. Boots made to order take four to six months. ♦ M-Sa May–early Sept; M-W, F-Sa mid-Sept–Apr. 108-110 E San Francisco St (between Washington Ave and Cathedral Pl). 984.2231

51 French Pastry Shop ★$ Pastries, crepes, croissants, and cappuccino are available in this crowded coffeehouse. ♦ Coffeehouse ♦ Daily. 100 E San Francisco St (between Washington Ave and Cathedral Pl). 983.6697

52 Fourth World Cottage Industries Owned by Lydia and Marines Perez, these two second-floor shops keep whole families in Guatemala employed turning out handicrafts. The colorful work extends from clothing to jewelry. Crafts from Indonesia, Thailand, China, Japan, India, Peru, Ecuador, and Morocco are also available. ♦ M-Sa; Su noon-5PM. 102 W San Francisco St (between Don Gaspar Ave and Galisteo St), Second floor. 982.4388

52 Alla In 1980 James J. Dunlap and Barbara A. Sommer opened a business that seemed most unlikely to succeed—a second-floor book-store limited almost exclusively to books in Spanish. They're still going strong, having added more space across the hall, and now carrying works in French and Portuguese, as well as some books in English dealing with Latin America. ♦ M-Sa. 102 W San Francisco St (between Don Gaspar Ave and Galisteo St), Second floor. 988.5416

53 Plaza Mercado Spanning half a block, this three-story collection of shops and restaurants was created in the mid-1980s and expanded in 1991 by Gerald Peters on the site of older, humbler businesses. Enter from either San Francisco, Water, or Galisteo Streets. ♦ 112-122 W San Francisco St (between Don Gaspar Ave and Galisteo St)

Within Plaza Mercado:

San Francisco Street Bar & Grill ★★★$ The best hamburger in town (try it with green chile) is served at Robert C. Day's convenient, casual restaurant, one of the few downtown where you can eat during off-hours. The Santa Fe sausage plate with black beans is a special treat at dinnertime. Despite its basement location, this place, more of a grill than a bar, has a spacious feel. A **Patio Grill** pushcart in the rear courtyard is open summer afternoons. ♦ American/New Mexican ♦ Daily lunch and dinner. 114 W San Francisco St, Downstairs. 982.2044

Body Beautiful Dip your body in mud right in the heart of town. Or how about trying a cellulite herbal wrap, seaweed body facial, aromatherapy, or a paraffin manicure? Half-hour foot massages are also available, in case you've been doing too much sight-seeing. ♦ M-Sa. 112 W San Francisco St, Third level. 986.1200

Santa Fe School of Cooking If you fell in love with New Mexican food and want to learn how to prepare it yourself, take a two-hour cooking class here. In the end you get to eat the meal that you made. An adjacent market sells all the foodstuffs you'll need to do it at home. ♦ Group rates are available. Call for schedules. 116 W San Francisco St, Third level. 983.4511

Nambé Mills Showroom Cast at a foundry in the southern part of Santa Fe, Nambéware consists of dishes, bowls, plates, and platters made of a secret metal alloy that contains no silver, lead, or pewter, though its silver color suggests all three. It can be used for cooking, yet the metal still glows. Some of the designs have been displayed by New York City's Museum of Modern Art. Seconds are also sold here at reduced prices. ♦ Daily. 112 W San Francisco St, First level. 988.3574. Also at: 924 Paseo de Peralta (at Alameda St). 988.5528

Blue Corn Cafe ★★$ Since its 1992 opening, this New Mexican restaurant has proved to be a welcome addition to the downtown scene. The Southwestern-style space is attractive; the mood is youthful and lively; and the food is consistently good, with homemade tortilla chips, fresh, light tortillas kept warm at your table, and excellent burritos and *chile rellenos*. Best of all, the moderate lunch prices don't go up a penny at dinner: most entrées are under $6, which is amazing for the Plaza area. ♦ New Mexican ♦ Daily lunch and dinner. 133 W Water St, Second level. 984.1800

Eclectica Wonderful Mexican works—tin bird cages, hand-carved and hand-painted full-size altarpieces, Talavera pottery from Mexico, Zapotec rugs—as well as replicas of Mexican antiques pack this tiny shop. Owner Efrain Aguirre-Prieto is an artist from Mexico who designs a lot of the tin and wrought iron.

If you want a dozen matching tin candelabras, he'll design them, have them crafted in Mexico, and ship them off to you. ♦ Daily. 112 W San Francisco St, First level. 988.3326

Jane Smith If you're looking for exquisite handmade Western wear for men and women—including doeskin leather cowboy gloves complete with beadwork, Plains Indian–style leather tunics with shells and beads, handmade boots, and broomstick skirts—you'll find them here. ♦ Daily. 122 W San Francisco St, First level. 988.4775

54 Evangelo's This used to be a macho local bar where outsiders feared to tread. But since Nick Klonis took over from his father in 1984, it hums with the "in" crowd. No food is served, but nearly 300 imported beers are offered. The South Seas decor is off-the-wall here in the high desert. There are pool tables downstairs. ♦ Daily. 200 W San Francisco St (at Galisteo St). 982.9014

55 The Santa Fe Bookseller Art and the Southwest are the only two subjects handled by Jan Nelson in this specialty bookstore featuring both new and out-of-print works. ♦ M-Sa. 203 W San Francisco St (at Galisteo St). 983.5278

56 Collected Works Book Shop Selling mostly paperbacks, this independent bookstore is owned by Lynne Moor, who does a good job of stocking literary backlists, such as the complete works of Hemingway. ♦ Daily. 208B W San Francisco St (between Galisteo and Sandoval Sts). 988.4226

56 Tia Sophia's ★★$ Three siblings in the Maryol family, who grew up in Albuquerque, now run New Mexican restaurants in Santa Fe. This one is Jim Maryol's, and it's strong on *huevos rancheros* (fried eggs served on corn tortillas, smothered in red- or green-chile salsa) and bacon-and-egg rolls. Breakfast burritos, a house specialty that has become popular in many parts of the country, were invented here. ♦ New Mexican ♦ M-Sa breakfast and lunch. 210 W San Francisco St (between Galisteo and Sandoval Sts). 983.9880

57 Lensic Theatre Built in 1930 and dedicated to the people of Santa Fe, this is one of the few old-fashioned movie palaces in the country that have not been carved up into a hundred-plex. It's worth catching almost any film on the huge screen under the soaring roof just to recapture the special feeling that movie-going once provided. ◆ 211 W San Francisco St (between Galisteo and Sandoval Sts). 982.0301

58 Eldorado Hotel $$$$ Santa Fe's largest hotel (218 rooms) is located in the building most hated by locals. Built in 1986 on the site of a former lumberyard, its massive, square-block, five-story bulk is beyond the human scale that the city has tried to preserve. The structure is bathed in the requisite fake adobe color, the lounges and rooms are decorated in trendy Southwestern style, and the rates are designed to keep out the riffraff. You'll feel as if you never left the big city. There's an indoor swimming pool as well as a number of shops on the premises. ◆ 309 W San Francisco St (at Sandoval St). 988.4455. 800/955.4455; fax 982.0713

Within the Eldorado Hotel:

Eldorado Court ★★$$ The hotel lobby doubles as a restaurant with a small menu. Sandwiches and salads are featured at lunch and dinner, but there are also several hot entrées. An expensive, but sumptuous, all-you-can-eat brunch featuring eggs Benedict, pheasant medaillons, and kiwi fruit salad is served on Sunday. ◆ New Southwestern ◆ Daily breakfast, lunch, and dinner. Reservations required for Sunday brunch. 988.4455

The Old House ★★$$$$ The **Eldorado Hotel** was built around an old adobe house the developers did not dare demolish in the face of local opposition. Instead, they covered it over and turned it into an upscale restaurant. No beans and *posole* are served here. Instead, there's usually a rattlesnake appetizer, roasted rack of lamb with a mustard-and-cracked-pepper crust, grilled veal with shiitake mushrooms and hazelnut sauce, a pasta, and a seafood special. ◆ Continental ◆ Tu-Su dinner. Reservations required. 986.1864

59 Hilton of Santa Fe $$$ Unlike the developers of the **Eldorado Hotel**, this worldwide chain was satisfied with designing what is probably the world's shortest **Hilton**—a two-story, Territorial-style building with 159 guest rooms. In the early 1700s this was the site of the home of a prominent and notorious local family named Ortiz. The house later became a large mercantile establishment, then, rumor

has it, a brothel. The hotel was built around the old home, whose courtyard was preserved as the **Chamisa** restaurant. Southwestern style predominates, of course. One reason for the fealty to local customs may be that Conrad Hilton was born in the tiny New Mexico village of San Antonio, about 150 miles to the south. ◆ 100 Sandoval St (at W Water St). 988.2811

Within the Hilton of Santa Fe:

Chamisa ★★$ An atmospheric breakfast and lunch spot in the courtyard of the old *casa*, this establishment adds a touch of originality to some standard fare, such as including a steak salad in its salad list. A lunch buffet offers samples of American Indian, New Mexican, and traditional American foods. ◆ American/New Mexican/American Indian ◆ Daily breakfast and lunch. 988.2811

Piñon Grill ★$$$ More formal than **Chamisa** (see above), this dining room is set with white cloths and flower bouquets. Assorted beef, chicken, and seafood dishes are available, including lamb chops marinated in chile, smoked quail on a bed of roasted peppers, and king salmon with citrus salsa. Game is a hot item here; try the mixed game grill of antelope, venison, and wild boar in a wild-mushroom sauce. The menu sounds tempting but the food and service can sometimes disappoint. ◆ New Southwestern ◆ Daily dinner. Reservations recommended. 988.2811

60 Alpine Sports On winter mornings the parking lot of Harvey Chalker's establishment is jammed with skiers renting skis before heading out to the slopes. In the afternoons they return with their brightly colored lift tickets hanging from their clothes as if they're for sale. Skis are also sold here, as are all the requisite ski equipment and clothing. A full line of hiking and mountain-climbing gear takes care of the summer months. ◆ Daily Dec–mid-Mar; M-Sa mid-Mar–Nov. 121 Sandoval St (between W Water and W Alameda Sts). 983.5155

61 Santa Fe Weaving Gallery Want to put on the dog, literally? Nancy Paap creates lush coats and jackets from the hand-spun hair of pedigreed chow and Samoyed show dogs. (The prices are pedigreed, too.) Paap and 19 other fiber artists, most from New Mexico, are represented. Victoria Rabinowe shows fine hand-painted silk garments, and Kate Boyan, a designer from Alaska, creates exquisite beaded bags in jewel and earth tones using elk and deer skins. ◆ Daily Apr-Oct; M-Sa Nov-Mar. 124½ Galisteo St (at W Water St). 982.1737

62 Montecristi Custom Hat Works Row after row of hats line the walls of this offbeat shop. Each chapeau is custom designed and tailored to fit your head perfectly. Step inside and you can see hats being steamed into the proper size and shape. Since 1978 Milton Johnson and his workers have been crafting exquisite Panamas and fine fur felts, as well as rare and unusual hat bands. ◆ M-Sa. 118 Galisteo St (between W Water and W San Francisco Sts). 983.9598

63 Foreign Traders Established in 1927 as **The Old Mexico Shop** by Tony Taylor, the brother of Lady Bird Johnson, this business is now owned by Taylor's grandson, Alex Tschursin. A direct import store, it is filled with heavy wooden tables, chairs, and cabinets, as well as ceramic dishes and tiles. Most items hail from Mexico. ◆ Daily Memorial Day-Labor Day; M-Sa the rest of the year. 202 Galisteo St (between W Water and W Alameda Sts). 983.6441

64 Artesanos Mexican designs entice browsers and collectors in this huge family-run import shop owned by Polo Gomez. There are 170 styles of Talavera tile alone, as well as lead-free dishware, UL-approved Mexican lights, pigskin furniture, hand-blown glass, traditional Mexican folkloric art, and the largest selection of Mexican artifacts in Santa Fe. Most of the tiled kitchens in town probably were born here. A private shipping department will mail chilegrams—*chile ristras* (strings) or wreaths—to your friends back home. ◆ M-Sa. 222 Galisteo St (between W Water and W Alameda Sts). 983.5563

TAOS FURNITURE

65 Taos Furniture Despite the name, Santa Fe is home base for Andy Peterson's worldwide business that perpetuates and updates the plain furniture designs of the region's early settlers. The heavy wooden furniture is rugged and simple, yet includes more than 80 styles of beds, chairs, tables, and cabinets. The craftspeople start with local ponderosa pine and kiln-dry it to increase stability. The wood is planed by hand, then burnished with river rocks. Joints are handfitted using mortise, tenon, and dowels, and the drawers are dovetailed. Short people may find the long surfaces of this furniture uncomfortable. Nevertheless the business has outlets in New York, Paris, Milan, Geneva, Tokyo, and Aspen. ◆ M-Sa. 232 Galisteo St (at W Alameda St). 988.1229

66 Jackalope Station This is the downtown outlet of **Jackalope Pottery**, a huge, sprawling Mexican market several miles from downtown (see "Additional Highlights of Santa Fe" chapter). Mexican crafts are particularly highlighted, but folk art from other Latin American countries are on hand as well. There is a wide selection of animal pottery and weavings at both locations. In fact, every craft item at the main site is available here, but in smaller amounts. The **Soon-to-be-Famous Jackalope Café** (★$, 989.7494) serves mesquite-grilled hamburgers while live musicians from all over the world play their native music. ◆ Daily. 231 Galisteo St (at W Alameda St). 989.7494. Also at: 2820 Cerrillos Rd (between Camino Carlos Rey and Clark St). 471.8539

67 Overland Sheepskin Sheepskin coats hanging high grab your eyes, and the pungent smell of leather infuses your nose in Jerry and Marge Leahy's sprawling shop. Also sold here are leather and canvas coats, luggage, and accessories. ◆ Daily. 225 Galisteo St (between W Alameda and W Water Sts). 988.5387

68 Galisteo News ★$ Locals and visitors alike enjoy coffee, cakes, and sandwiches indoors or out at this combined newsstand and coffee bar. It was the first of its kind in town when it opened in the early 1980s. A large selection of magazines is for sale. ◆ Sandwiches/Pastries ◆ Daily. 201 Galisteo St (at W Water St). 984.1316

69 Coyote Cafe ★★★$$$$ You might think that the decor of Mark Miller's trendsetting place-to-be-seen—the staircase is painted in a surreal mix of colors and a menagerie of carved wooden animals peers down from a desert scene on the balcony overlooking the dining room—is a tough act to follow in the kitchen. Just wait for the food—the restaurant's forte is the elevation of New Mexican regional food into an upscale cuisine by making, for instance, duck tamales instead of beef, and by serving rib chops with red-chile onion rings and blackened tomato salsa. When it works, it's great, and it works fairly often. Dinner is restricted to a fixed-price, three-course meal, which can be a lot to stomach. For a better bargain and less food, come for lunch or head upstairs to the **Rooftop Cantina** (★★★$$). Here, similarly exotic combinations—such as a very spicy barbecued duck and jack-cheese quesadilla, or mild soft tacos stuffed with sea bass—are available under an outdoor canopy at much lower prices. ♦ New Mexican ♦ Coyote Cafe: M-F dinner; Sa-Su lunch and dinner. Rooftop Cantina: daily lunch and dinner Apr-Oct. Reservations required. 132 W Water St (between Galisteo and Ortiz Sts). 983.1615

On the street level of the Coyote Cafe:

Coyote Cafe General Store In addition to the souvenir T-shirts, aprons, and mugs, this shop offers a mélange of Southwestern food products, including dried chiles, fresh organic produce, and wild game—enough items to pretend you're Mark Miller in the privacy of your own kitchen (and the cookbooks to show you how). For those who want a little spice in their life, there's a wide array of *hot* sauces. ♦ Daily. 982.2454

70 American Country Collection As jam-packed as a country attic, this shop features reproductions of antique furniture (and some actual antiques), as well as lamps, rugs, and collectibles with a down-home motif. The company's larger store, where much of the furniture is made, is located at 620 Cerrillos Road, at Paseo de Peralta (984.0955). ♦ Daily. 129 W Water St (between Don Gaspar Ave and Galisteo St). 982.1296

71 Arius Santa Fe Art Tile Just about every design you could possibly think of painting on a tile is on display here, from traditional Southwestern and Indian scenes to Jewish themes surrounding the word Shalom. In 1972 Roberta Goodman began experimenting with hand-painted tile art in a small studio. Soon after, she opened this shop downtown and built it into a worldwide business. All the tiles are still hand-painted locally. A popular specialty is custom-painted tile murals to set into the outer wall of your home, surrounding your house number. But all sorts of custom murals and individual tiles are possible. These tiles make tasteful, inexpensive souvenir gifts. ♦ Daily. 114 Don Gaspar Ave (between W San Francisco and W Water Sts). 988.1196

71 Lindee's Original Santa Fe Fiesta Fashions For three days every September, Santa Fe indulges in an orgy of food, drink, and dancing known as Fiesta. Traditional fiesta costumes led Lindee Shaw in 1969 to spin off an entire line of locally produced fashions for both sexes and all ages, which have since been featured in some of the nation's leading department stores. Broom-stick skirts in cotton or taffeta form the basic line; up to 10 yards of fabric are used per skirt. But fiesta fashion also includes handmade Navajo velvet shirts, ribbon shirts, and peasant blouses. ♦ M-Sa. 118 Don Gaspar Ave (between W San Francisco and W Water Sts). 986.5078

72 Hotel St. Francis $$$ A hotel built on this spot in 1880 was destroyed by fire. The current structure, which opened in 1924 as the **De Vargas Hotel,** often was alive with the wheeling and dealing of local politicians. Falling into disrepair, it became Santa Fe's cheapest hotel in the 1970s, offering run-down, $12-a-night rooms two blocks from the Plaza and just around the corner from the old bus station (now a parking lot). It was reno-vated in the mid-1980s and given its present name. High ceilings and casement windows lend the 83 rooms old world charm and are reminders of the hotel's long history. After-noon high tea is served in the now high-class (though overstuffed) lobby that suggests a British boarding house. The bar, with outdoor wrought-iron tables, is a convenient spot to watch the passing parade. The building is a National Historic Landmark. ♦ 210 Don Gaspar Ave (at W Water St). 983.5700

Within the Hotel St. Francis:

On Water ★★$$$ The menu changes weekly in this restaurant opened in 1992 by Don Fortel and Robert Packard. A mix of "New World" cuisine borrows from Asian, French, Mexican, and traditional American cooking. Typical dishes include grilled organic chicken breast with garlic butter and braised Atlantic salmon. ♦ Continental ♦ M, W-Sa breakfast, lunch, and dinner; Su brunch. Reservations recommended. 982.8787

73 Pasqual's ★★★$$ Some people swear by this place, one of the few downtown restaurants that is open for breakfast. They like the large center table where loners can find company. Others swear *at* the place because of the uncomfortable cane-backed chairs. The homemade muffins and scones are great ways to start the day. Lunch and dinner selections include gourmet sand-wiches, soups, and salads. ♦ Sandwiches/Salads ♦ M-Tu, Th-Su breakfast, lunch, and dinner; W breakfast and lunch. 121 Don Gaspar Ave (at E Water St). 983.9340

Restaurants/Clubs: Red		**Hotels:** Blue
Shops/ ♠ **Outdoors:** Green		**Sights/Culture:** Black

Tales from the Land of Enchantment

Northern New Mexico is a region where the human spirit has sometimes battled the ruggedness of the land and sometimes lived with it in fragile harmony, and where different cultures have responded to the trials of life in different ways. These conditions have attracted many writers, some who come to live, others merely to visit and record what they have discovered. The following books are noteworthy for the way they evoke and illuminate the people and the land.

Alburquerque by Rudolfo Anaya (1992; University of New Mexico Press) In this historical novel, Anaya—one of New Mexico's most celebrated literary figures—traces the growth of Albuquerque and the role of Hispanic culture there from the 17th century to the present.

Betty Crocker's Southwest Cooking (1989; Prentice Hall) While the presumably mythical Betty might be a creation of Madison Avenue, she knows her New Mexican food. Amid the dozens of ritzier regional cookbooks available, this is one of the best, not only because of the appetizing pictures and the fairly simple recipes, but because the resulting dishes are usually excellent.

Bless Me, Ultima by Rudolfo Anaya (1972; Tonatiuh International) Anaya, who lives in Albuquerque, has won a growing national reputation based largely on this early Chicano novel.

Ceremonial Costumes of the Pueblo Indians by Virginia More Roediger (1941, reissued 1991; University of California Press) Explanations of the significance of the costumes worn in ceremonial dances are accompanied by drawings.

Dance Hall of the Dead by Tony Hillerman (1973; Harper & Row) This Albuquerque author won the Edgar Award for his mystery set at **Zuni Pueblo,** and he has since written about 10 more mysteries steeped in the lore of the Navajo and Pueblo Indians. Many of Hillerman's latest books—including *Talking Gods* and *Coyote Waits*—have become huge best-sellers. Every detail is authentic.

Death Comes for the Archbishop by Willa Cather (1990; Vintage) First published in 1927, this is a classic anecdotal novel of the life and deeds of Archbishop Lamy, whom Cather has named Father Latour.

The Delight Makers by Adolf F. Bandelier (1971; Harcourt Brace Jovanovich) A novel about the prehistoric Pueblo Indians, in which the foremost archaeologist of the region blends fact and fiction.

Georgia O'Keeffe, A Life by Roxana Robinson (1989; Harper & Row) The most authoritative of a spate of recent biographies about the region's best-known painter.

Georgia O'Keeffe—In the West edited by Doris Bry and Nicholas Callway (1980; Alfred A. Knopf) An oversized book of plates containing many of the artist's most distinctive paintings of the region.

Great River by Paul Horgan (1984; Farrar, Straus, & Giroux) A monumental biography of the Rio Grande that won the Pulitzer Prize for history.

Lamy of Santa Fe by Paul Horgan (1975; Noonday Press) A detailed biography of the archbishop who helped shape the city, this book won Horgan the first of his two Pulitzers.

Laughing Boy by Oliver La Farge (1971; Signet edition) This 1929 novel about a Navajo boy won the Pulitzer Prize for fiction.

Mayordomo by Stanley Crawford (1988; University of New Mexico Press) The author, who lives on a garlic farm between Santa Fe and Taos, elegantly conjures up nature and the land along one of Northern New Mexico's *acequias* (irrigation ditches).

The Milagro Beanfield War by John Nichols (1974; Holt, Rhinehart and Winston) This novel, set in a village near Taos where the author lives, is long, wonderful, and folksy. (Robert Redford's movie version, while pleasant, is not an adequate substitute.) Nichols wrote two subsequent books in a New Mexico trilogy, *The Magic Journey,* and *Nirvana Blues.*

Red Sky at Morning by Richard Bradford (1968; Harper & Row) This coming-of-age story is set in Northern New Mexico during World War II and was later made into a movie.

River of Traps by William deBuys and Alex Harris (1990; University of New Mexico Press) Words and photographs are used to depict life in a small Hispanic village in Northern New Mexico in this widely acclaimed book.

The Santa Fe and Taos Colonies: Age of the Muses, 1900-1942 by Arrell Morgan Gibson (1983; University of Oklahoma Press) This book provides a detailed look at the early art colonies in both cities.

Stories Behind the Street Names of Albuquerque, Santa Fe & Taos by Donald A. Gill (1994; Bonus Books) Insights into the origins of street names in New Mexico are given.

Taos by Irwin R. Blacker (1959; Brooke House) This huge historical novel is set in the early days of the Indian and Spanish settlements.

73 The Chile Shop Everything you ever wanted to know about Southwestern food, the ingredients to prepare it, and the requisite wares for setting a Southwestern table is available in one fascinating shop owned by SuAnne Armstrong. This is headquarters for china and pottery, cookbooks, more than a dozen varieties of chile and chile powder, red- and green-chile salsas, blue cornmeal, blue corn chips, and the wonderful corn-based stew *posole*—in short, the stuff that makes life in Santa Fe worth living. The chile ranges from mild to hot to call-the-fire-department— the clerks will be happy to tell you which is which and how to tame the hot ones. Gift boxes can be made to order and shipped; send one back home to yourself and savor your visit for months to come. ♦ M-Sa; Su noon-6PM. 109 E Water St (between Don Gaspar Ave and Old Santa Fe Trail). 983.6080

74 El Centro This two-story adobe-colored building was one of the first downtown structures to be subdivided in order to house a cluster of stores. There are half a dozen small artsy-craftsy shops within, but the only ones worth noting are **Joe Wade Fine Art**s and **Prairie Edge.** ♦ Daily. 102 E Water St (at Shelby St)

Within El Centro:

Joe Wade Fine Arts There are three Western art galleries here run by Joe Wade. By far the most interesting is **Wade Contemporary,** which features a kind of Western impressionist art—adobe churches and other subjects presented in bright colors and dancing brush strokes. Among the most pleasing works are the pastel landscapes by Victoria Taylor-Gore. This gallery is sure to brighten your day. ♦ M-Sa. 988.2727

Prairie Edge In a city where Pueblo and Navajo arts and crafts dominate the shopping scene, this bright, spacious American Indian gallery offers an intriguing counterpoint: an array of contemporary Lakota and Oglala Sioux works using traditional materials of the Plains tribes—bone, leather, fur, feathers, and beads. From traditional and contemporary Plains Indian jewelry to ceremonial pipes and elaborately beaded buckskin fashion wear, Indian crafts enthusiasts will find out-of-the-ordinary gift items and collectibles here. The owners also run the **Sioux Trading Post** (1428 Cerrillos Rd, across from the Santa Fe Indian School, 820.0605), which specializes in such supplies as beads, hides, and animal horns. ♦ Daily. 984.1336

India Palace ★★★$$ An appendage to the rear of **El Centro** used to house the down-home New Mexican restaurant **Little Chief Grill.** That place is history now; the building was renovated and painted deep pink, and the local food was supplanted by superb East Indian cuisine prepared by chef Bal Dev Singh.

The current kitchen is hailed as first-rate even by world-traveled gourmands. A variety of excellent curries tops the menu. The breads, including spinach *paratha,* are memorable. ♦ Indian ♦ Daily lunch and dinner. Reservations recommended for dinner. 227 Don Gaspar Ave (in El Centro, enter through the Water St parking lot). 986.5859

75 Old Santa Fe Trail From 1821 to 1880—when the Midwest was linked to the Pacific Coast by rail—a steady stream of goods flowed over this trail, which circled to the south of the Sangre de Cristo Mountains. The city was a welcome sight to traders as they raced down the hill after weeks or months of driving goods in covered wagons over rugged terrain occupied by sometimes hostile Indians. Ahead lay good profits, warm meals, and women that money could buy. ♦ From E Palace Ave to E Cordova Rd, where it becomes the Old Pecos Trail

75 Char Char Vasquez has been designing suede (made mostly from lamb) and leather clothing since 1977. Locally produced, her creations have even graced the cover of a national fashion magazine. The shop also includes a nice selection of hats, jewelry, and other one-of-a-kind specialty items. ♦ Daily. 104 Old Santa Fe Trail (between E San Francisco and E Water Sts). 988.5969

ANTONIO COCILOVO

76 Loretto Chapel The first Gothic structure built west of the Mississippi, this chapel (pictured above) was constructed from 1873 to 1878 near **St. Francis Cathedral** for the Sisters of Loretto, the first nuns to come to New Mexico. In 1853 they had established **Loretto Academy,** a school for young women, in Santa Fe. The chapel was designed after Ste-Chapelle, Paris's Gothic jewel. Most attention today focuses on what is called the **Miraculous Staircase.** Legend has it that the chapel's French architect was killed by John

Lamy, the archbishop's nephew, because he was suspected of adultery with Lamy's wife. He left no plans for the stairway that would have to be built to reach the choir loft; indeed, there was not even enough room left for a conventional staircase. The sisters prayed for help to St. Joseph, the patron saint of carpenters, and an unknown carpenter soon appeared. He built an amazing spiral staircase with two 360-degree turns, using no nails, and giving it no central or visible support. His only tools were a T-square, a saw, and a tub of water for softening the wood. He left without taking money and without even leaving his name. Whether or not it's a miracle, the staircase is very real (and marvelous) and can be viewed within. The chapel is now a private museum owned by the **Inn at Loretto.** ◆ Admission. Daily. 219 Old Santa Fe Trail (at E Water St). No phone

77 Inn at Loretto $$$ Santa Fe's most picturesque architectural addition in years is this Best Western motel whose tiered design was inspired by the **Taos Pueblo.** It stands on the site of the **Loretto Academy.** The inn, decorated in Southwestern style throughout, has 140 rooms and suites, an outdoor swimming pool, and a routine restaurant/coffee shop. Assorted shops can be found in the lobby. ◆ 211 Old Santa Fe Trail (between E Water and E Alameda Sts). 988.5531, 800/727.5531; fax 984.7988

78 Garrett's Desert Inn $$ While this may just be an ordinary motel, it boasts a convenient location just two blocks away from the Plaza. Rates for the 88 guest rooms are lower than at most of the downtown hotels, but higher than similar routine accommodations on Cerrillos Road's motel strip. **Le Café on the Trail,** located in the motel's lobby, serves breakfast, lunch, and dinner. ◆ 311 Old Santa Fe Trail (just south of the Santa Fe River). 982.1851, 800/838.2145; fax 989.1647

79 Pink Adobe ★★$$$ Called "the Pink" by many locals, this is the closest thing to an institution among Santa Fe restaurants. An old adobe building with many small rooms, all with fireplaces, it has been serving hearty fare since the end of World War II. The steaks, smothered in fresh mushrooms or green chile, are as good as you can find anywhere in the land, and unless you're seven feet tall, you'll probably want to take home half for breakfast. The rest of the menu, including a small selection of shrimp, lamb, pork, and New Mexican dishes, is undistinguished. The adjacent bar, in which a tree grows through the roof and free popcorn is served, is one of the most popular in town, both among local residents and visiting movie stars. ◆ Steaks ◆ Daily lunch and dinner. Reservations recommended. 406 Old Santa Fe Trail (between E De Vargas St and Paseo de Peralta). 983.7712

Child's Play

When talk of visiting yet another gallery elicits groans from the little ones, what's a parent to do? Here are ten tips for keeping the kids entertained in Northern New Mexico:

1 Visit the more than 10,000 different handmade toys and dolls from around the world at the **New Mexico Museum of International Folk Art** in Santa Fe.

2 Ride a burro and see a living prairie dog village at **Jackalope Pottery** in Santa Fe.

3 Learn to make pottery or weave on a Navajo loom in the activities area of the **Museum of Indian Arts and Culture** in Santa Fe.

4 Walk (or run) around the park filled with huge sculptures at **Shidoni Foundry** in Tesuque, then watch molten bronze being poured to make a statue.

5 Listen to Indian storytellers such as Joe Hayes and Pablita Velarde who frequently appear at various Santa Fe locations including the **Wheelwright Museum of the American Indian,** the **Santa Fe Children's Museum,** and the **Old Santa Fe Trail Bookstore & Coffeehouse.**

6 Climb wooden ladders up to the cliff dwellings at **Bandelier National Monument** where Indians lived 800 years ago.

7 Make a stop in the Wild West at the **Kit Carson Home** in Taos and see the leather outfits mountain men wore and the guns and knives they carried.

8 Tour the home of a Native American at **Taos Pueblo** or at any of a dozen other Indian pueblos between Albuquerque and Taos.

9 Stand inside the glowing, rumbling volcano simulation at the **New Mexico Museum of Natural History** in Albuquerque.

10 Look at (but don't touch) the live baby rattlesnakes in the **American International Rattlesnake Museum** in Albuquerque's **Old Town.**

79 The Bull Ring ★$$ Although not named after all the bull that's thrown here by local politicians, it could be. When the state legislature is in session in January and February at the nearby **Roundhouse,** the air is thick with the smell of wheels being greased and backs being scratched (or stabbed) over margaritas or Coors. Waitresses have been known to quit after one night when the legislators are here, their behinds sore from being pinched. The food, mostly New Mexican, is fit for a politician; it's good but won't distract congresspeople and lobbyists from the business at hand. ◆ New Mexican ◆ M-F lunch and dinner; Sa-Su dinner. Reservations recommended. 414 Old Santa Fe Trail (between E De Vargas St and Paseo de Peralta). 983.3328

80 Roundhouse The seat of government of the State of New Mexico, this round building supposedly was designed after a Pueblo kiva, a ceremonial structure where the Indians meditate with their gods. Whether the same sort of wisdom passes inside, in the offices of the governor and the legislators, is debatable. Territorial-style motifs—brick trim and white columns—were added to give the building a more official look. From the air, the walkways emanating from four sides help create the shape of the Zia sun sign, which is the state symbol. Works by New Mexican painters adorn the interior walls, and large bronze sculptures by several local artists grace the grounds. The interior is a modern and functional cylinder of offices and meeting rooms. No one ever uses the official name: **Capitol Building.** Tours are available, if you insist (call for information). ♦ Old Santa Fe Trail (at Paseo de Peralta). 986.4589

81 New Mexico State Library There is a larger collection of books on the Southwest and a more complete reference room here than at the city library. Old magazines in the upstairs stacks date back to the early part of the century. Visitors can make arrangements at the circulation desk to check out books. ♦ M-F. 325 Don Gaspar Ave (between E De Vargas St and Paseo de Peralta). 827.3800

82 Real Burger ★★$ Very good hamburgers and sandwiches are ordered at a wooden counter in this little barn filled with booths and wonderful cooking smells. The crinkle-cut fries, which come with a bit of chile in the flavoring, are far superior to the plain fries; in fact, they shouldn't be missed. ♦ American ♦ M-Sa breakfast, lunch, and early dinner. 227 Don Gaspar Ave (between E Water and E Alameda Sts). 988.3717

82 Santa Fe Village An adobe-style shopping mall built in the 1970s, this sprawling structure is a dark catacomb filled with shops and one excellent restaurant. ♦ 227 Don Gaspar Ave (between E Water and E Alameda Sts). No phone

Within Santa Fe Village:

Fabio's ★★★$$$ Authenticity in Tuscan cooking is the mantra of Pilar and Fabio Macchioni, and it serves the palate well. Try spaghetti *alla puttanesca* (with Greek olives, capers, and freshly diced tomatoes) or the ricotta-and-spinach ravioli, another traditional recipe that is served with a choice of two sauces—cream, basil, and diced tomatoes, or baked tomato. The *pollo alla diavola* (cornish hen marinated with sage and black pepper, grilled under hot bricks, and served with spinach and potatoes) is a delicious traditional Florentine dish. Lobster, flown in daily from Maine, is sautéed in garlic, olive oil, and clam juice. ♦ Tuscan ♦ Daily dinner. Reservations required. 984.3080

83 Inn of the Governors $$$ Long taken for granted as a downtown motel, this sprawing and unpretentious hostelry has taken pains to upgrade itself in recent years with a renewed emphasis on Southwestern decor. The 106 guest rooms are bright and airy, and the location is convenient. ♦ 234 Don Gaspar Ave (at W Alameda St). 982.4333, 800/234.4534; fax 989.9149

Within the Inn of the Governors:

Mañana Restaurant and Bar ★$$ The food here is an undemanding mix of local and standard American fare—roast beef, spaghetti, and rainbow trout—none of it out of the ordinary. The bar is a popular local meeting place. ♦ New Mexican/American ♦ Daily breakfast, lunch, and dinner. 982.4333

84 Alameda Street One of the prettiest streets in town, this east-west passage runs along the north side of the Santa Fe River, which is a river only in the spring when the snow on the Sangre de Cristo Mountains is melting and running off. The rest of the time it is a dry ditch. But **Santa Fe River Park,** a narrow strip of grass running along both sides of the river, is a peaceful venue of tall shade trees—a nice place to sprawl out and rest. Picnic tables are spotted along the park, which totals 19 acres but is shaped like a long ribbon. ♦ From Calle Nopal to Rim Rd

85 Bataan Memorial Building Across the **Santa Fe River Park,** this sprawling government office building was the state capitol before its dome was removed when the **Roundhouse** opened in 1951. Today it houses, among other things, the attorney general's office and its consumer fraud division. The building was named in honor of those who survived the infamous Bataan Death March in the Philippines during World War II, and those who did not. ♦ M-F. 460 Galisteo St (between Manhattan Ave and W De Vargas St). No phone

86 East De Vargas Street Though the Santa Fe River is dry about 10 months of the year, this area, just south of the river, is believed to have been the first part of Santa Fe to be settled. The Indians named it *analco* (the other side of the water). In the early Spanish colonial period of the 1600s, it became the other side of the tracks. Spanish soldiers and priests resided on the Plaza side of the Plaza, which is close to the safe haven of the **Palace of the Governors;** their Mexican and Indian servants lived here in what was then called the Barrio de Analco. During the Pueblo Revolt of 1680, the barrio was the most vulnerable area and was totally destroyed. The barrio, however, was rebuilt early in the 18th century. At first, the social divisions still prevailed, and primarily laborers lived here; later, more prominent residents moved into some of the same houses, often adding rooms. A walk along this narrow street is a peaceful retreat away from the bustle of shopping and into history. Most of the buildings are still private residences and can be viewed—except for **The Oldest House** (see below)—only from the outside. Those listed below have been designated by the Historic Santa Fe Foundation as worthy of preservation. ♦ From Don Gaspar Ave to Delgado St

87 Roque Tudesqui House The exact age of this building is not known, but at least one wall was built partially of puddled adobe, indicating Indian construction from the pre-Spanish period. Puddled adobe is made with poured mud, rather than adobe bricks. Many of the walls are three feet thick. By 1841 it was the residence of an Italian trader, Roque Tudesqui (the only thing recorded about him is that he was 38 and single). In late spring, beautiful and ageless wisteria vines bloom on the patio. This is a private house. ♦ 129-135 E De Vargas St (between Don Gaspar Ave and Old Santa Fe Trail)

88 The Oldest House Maps dating to 1882 label this the "oldest building in Santa Fe," and it may appear on an earlier map from 1768 that shows a structure at this approximate location. The house is made of puddled adobe, and tree-ring cuts taken from some of the vigas indicate a cutting date of from 1740 to 1767. If the promotion of this building as the "oldest house in the US" is mainly for the tourist trade, however, it nevertheless is a good example of early adobe construction. Visible inside are dirt floors, very low log ceilings, a corner fireplace, and puddled mud walls. You must first pass through a gift shop. ♦ Donation requested. Daily. 215 E De Vargas St (between Old Santa Fe Trail and Boyle Pl). 983.8206

89 San Miguel Mission Across from **The Oldest House** and believed to be the oldest church in the US, this chapel (illustrated below) dates to the earliest years of the Spanish settlement, around 1625. It was originally used as a mission church for the Tlaxcalan Indian servants in the Barrio de Analco, who had been brought from Mexico by the Spaniards. Much of the church was destroyed during the 1680 Pueblo Revolt, but some walls were left standing. When the Spanish rebuilt the chapel in 1710, they put up new walls outside the old ones. The restoration turned the church into a kind of fortress, with the windows high up and adobe battlements on the roof. The current square tower was added around 1887. Inside the chapel is an altar screen dating to 1798, which displays a statue of St. Michael, the patron saint of the chapel. The paintings on the screen were created in Mexico in the 18th century. Colonial paintings on buffalo hide are also on display. The interior was restored in 1955. The chapel and a gift shop are owned and run by the Christian Brothers. ♦ 401 Old Santa Fe Trail (at E De Vargas St). 983.3974

90 Old Santa Fe Trail Bookstore & Coffeehouse A high-ceilinged, two-story Victorian building houses this popular bookstore that is a hangout for Santa Fe's lively literary subculture. Appropriately, cookbooks are found in a foyer adjoining the kitchen, and gay and lesbian literature is shelved in a conspicuously marked closet. With quality titles in all categories, the store has especially good selections of Judaica and women's topics. Poetry and prose readings, book signings, and kids' storytelling hours are presented several times a week. The indoor-outdoor coffeehouse in the back serves exceptional green salads, great margaritas, plus soups, daily specials, and gourmet coffees. Live folk music is performed Thursday through Saturday evenings. ♦ Daily. 613 Old Santa Fe Trail (between Buena Vista and Paseo de Peralta). 988.8878

San Miguel Mission

M. BLUM

91 Boyle House Another of Santa Fe's oldest houses, this adobe was built of walls more than four feet thick in some places. Ceilings of *rajas* (split wood overlaid with straw and earth) are further evidence that it dates to the early period of Spanish settlement. At various times it belonged to US soldiers, the Catholic church, and Spanish landowners. In the 1800s it was acquired by the Boyle family. It is still a private residence. ♦ 327 E De Vargas St (between Boyle Pl and Paseo de Peralta)

92 Inn on the Alameda $$$$ Across from **Santa Fe River Park,** this lovely small hotel built in Pueblo style blends in nicely with its surroundings. The 56 tasteful rooms and suites are individually decorated with local crafts; some have private balconies. The old feel blends nicely with the new, as in a year-round outdoor Jacuzzi. Although it's just a short walk from both the Plaza and Canyon Road, the inn is removed from the downtown bustle. A complimentary breakfast buffet includes bagels, pastries, fruit, and cheese. ♦ 303 E Alameda St (at Paseo de Peralta). 984.2121, 800/289.2122

93 Adolph Bandelier House Adolph Bandelier, the archaeologist who conducted many of the original studies of pueblo sites in New Mexico, Arizona, and Mexico, lived in this house with his first wife, Josephine Huegy, from 1882 to 1892 and used it as his headquarters. Despite its designation, he never owned the house but rented it. In 1919 Santa Fe merchant Henry S. Kaune, whose wife, Elizabeth Carol Bandelier, was Bandelier's second cousin, purchased the house. A private residence, it is still owned by the Kaune family. ♦ 352 E De Vargas St (between Paseo de Peralta and Delgado St)

94 Nedra Matteucci's Fenn Galleries This gallery feels almost like a museum: partly because it occupies its own building on the Paseo, partly because of the dim adobe interior, and partly because most—though not all—of the artists represented are dead. Established in the early 1970s by Forrest Fenn and purchased in 1988 by Nedra Matteucci, the gallery is a great place to roam among the buffalo—and other paintings and bronzes reminiscent of the Old West—created by Charles Russell and Frederic Remington. All of the Taos founders are exhibited, as are more modern painters such as John Marin and Marsden Hartley of the old Alfred Stieglitz school. There is also a fine collection of paintings by the late artist/architect **Nikolai Fechin**. Out beyond the gallery building is a lovely pond and a sculpture garden of spirited works in bronze and stone by Glenna Goodacre and Doug Hyde, among others. The owner runs another gallery, Nedra Matteucci Fine Art (555 Canyon Rd, between Delgato Rd and Camino Escondido, 983.2731). ♦ Daily May–mid-Sept; M-Sa mid-Sept–Apr. 1075 Paseo de Peralta (at Acequia Madre). 982.4631

Bests

Mary Sweitzer
Graphic Designer, Mary Sweitzer Design, Santa Fe

My Santa Fe favorites include:

Baja Tacos—Best and cheapest take-out Mexican food anywhere. Say hello to Bob, the owner.

Diego's Cafe in **De Vargas Center Mall**—Best margaritas this side of Juárez and good *carne adovada*.

Canyon Road—Go gallery hopping anytime and take home some art. You love it and we love it.

American Country Collection—For home furnishings, from ashtrays to love seats.

Southwest Adventure Group—Best adventure/tour operator in New Mexico, with all sorts of excitement to choose from in Santa Fe and Albuquerque.

Bell Tower Bar at **La Fonda Hotel**—View a sunset from here, but be sure to bring a jacket.

Woolworth's on the **Plaza**—Best Frito pie in the world.

Lensic Theatre—Watch any movie or event in this grand old place.

Mañana Restaurant and Bar at the **Inn of the Governors**—Small, intimate piano bar that's perfect for after-hours celebrations.

Joseph Hoffman
Owner/Real Estate Broker, Santa Fe Futures Real Estate

Cafe Escalera—The best place in Santa Fe for lunch and/or dinner. Fresh taste, seasonal food, light, casual atmosphere.

Farmers' Market at **Sanbusco Market Center**—Tuesday and Saturday mornings—Fabulous fresh produce, flowers, baked products, etc. Everybody goes.

The **Santa Fe Opera**—July and August. World renown. Under the stars, absolute magic.

Cookworks—Three stores on **Guadalupe Street:** cooking equipment, and tabletop and food products. Makes Williams-Sonoma look like amateurs.

Laura Carpenter Fine Art—Gallery openings through the year. Our best contemporary gallery with world-renown artists.

Best of all—the people and the community: nonjudgmental, accepting, supportive, interesting, exciting.

Second best—the weather: cool, dry, clean air—fabulous.

Hiking and picnics in the **Jemez Mountains** northwest of Santa Fe above Los Alamos.

The **Coyote Cafe Rooftop Cantina**—for Saturday or Sunday lunches in the summer.

Canyon Road

If you like the earthy cachet of adobe architecture, then you may find **Canyon Road** the most sensually pleasing street in America. Once an Indian trail leading to the distant **Pecos Pueblo**, the ruins of which are now a National Historical Site, the road begins at **Paseo de Peralta** and winds for more than a mile on a slight incline toward the **Sangre de Cristo Mountains**. In late afternoon, the clarity of light makes the mountains appear closer than they are. The narrow, curving street is lined on both sides with old adobes, many with their doors and window frames painted bright turquoise. Some were built in past centuries by local families, others around the turn of this century by such early members of the Santa Fe art colony as Fremont Ellis. For many years Canyon Road was the focal point of the local art colony. A trailblazing group of artists, "Los Cinco Pintores" (the five painters), all lived along the road or on the intersecting **Camino del Monte Sol**. As recently as the early 1970s, painters, potters, sculptors, and glassblowers could be seen working in their studios here, their doors open to the public.

Today much of that scene has changed. Some of the homes are still private residences, but nearly all of today's painters have been driven farther afield in search of cheaper rent. The old adobes are now filled with close to a hundred art galleries. Stroll the street leisurely and enjoy the sensual experience. The eye is pleased by the brightly colored contemporary and primitive paintings at the **Cline Fine Art Gallery**, housed in one of the most exquisitely wrought of all the adobes, and the sense of touch delights in the bronze sculpture at the **Meyer Gallery**. The sixth and perhaps most important sense, the sense of humor, is served by the droll paintings and satiric sculptures in the **Lightside Gallery**. Canyon Road satisfies all the other senses as well. With only a single lane of one-way, slow-moving traffic, the relative silence is an old-fashioned

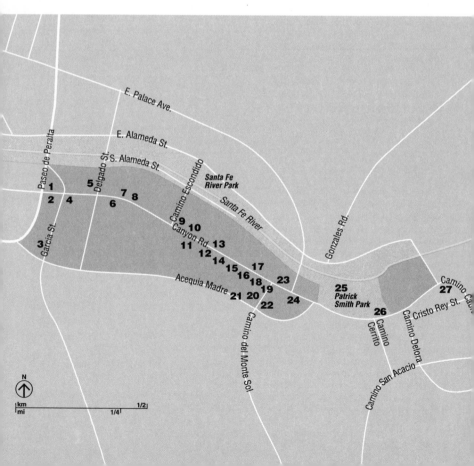

pleasure. The biting smell of cut piñon and pine logs piled high at the **Ríos Wood Yard,** which is a wonderful anomaly still tucked in among the galleries, is guaranteed to delight. And for fine taste sensations, have a light lunch at **Celebrations** and dinner at **Geronimo.**

Art and commerce end where Palace Avenue enters Canyon Road. But do yourself a favor and keep walking. The street narrows even more, the sidewalks disappear, and all sense of hucksterism fades. What's left as you amble here amid the brown mud walls and homes is a bit of silent time travel into the Santa Fe of centuries past.

1 The Munson Gallery This establishment traces its ancestry to a gallery on the East Coast that opened in 1860, making it one of the oldest in the country. It has been operating in Santa Fe since 1979, but one of the most interesting painters here is originally from New York. A realist, Richard Segalman tends to isolate women on beaches and in open fields or at the window of uncertain rooms, lending them the evocative sadness of a lonely life. After the glut of Western clichés in many local galleries, Segalman offers a welcome taste of genuinely emotional art that transcends the commercial horde. Melissa Zink's abstract collages, a blend of painting and sculpture, also leave the buck-chasing herd in the dust. Another interesting artist is Elmer Schooley, who paints large-scale close-ups of New Mexican landscapes in a pointillisticlike style. Local landscape painters Forest Moses and Douglas Atwill are also shown here. ♦ Daily. 225 Canyon Rd (between Paseo de Peralta and Garcia St). 983.1657

LIGHTSIDE

1 Lightside Gallery The name of this gallery says it all. Only artists with a sense of humor and a wry and sprightly view of the world need apply. Carlos Ferreyra paints gently humorous portraits of people in oil on formica. Roberta Laidman creates wonderful ceramic and bronze dogs. The walls are usually hung with the paintings of Joanne Battiste, whose fleshy pink female figures cavort on the canvas and seem to enjoy every minute of it. ♦ Daily. 225 Canyon Rd (between Paseo de Peralta and Garcia St). 982.5501

1 Meyer Gallery Men and women perch on the edge of chairs and talk to each other, or do not talk to each other, depending on how you position them. A peaceful boy sprawls alone in a garden, reading. A bird takes flight from the hand of a fascinated girl. These are the lifelike, romantic bronze figures of Dennis Smith, an internationally known sculptor whose work evokes every human emotion in pieces ranging from a few inches to life-size. The accuracy with which he captures in bronze the motion of people in mid-flight—as with a

mother swinging her young daughter at arm's length—is uncanny. Kent R. Wallis uses rich colors to paint impressionistic landscapes of the forests and valleys of Utah and northern California. William C. Hook's acrylic land- scapes, done in broad, confident strokes, come alive with the vividness and vitality of oils. ♦ Daily. 225 Canyon Rd (between Paseo de Peralta and Garcia St). 983.1434

2 Moondance Gallery The focus at this all- women gallery is on works with mythological, ecological, and ceremonial themes. Especially noteworthy are the colorfully Jungian ink- on-scratchboard illustrations by Meinrad Craighead, who enjoys a growing inter- national following. On the lighter side are the whimsical ceramic animal totems, guardians, and allies created by Kathy Lostetter. ♦ Daily. 233 Canyon Rd (between Paseo de Peralta and Garcia St). 982.3421

2 Gary Mauro Gallery The molded female form is the primary subject matter of artist Gary Mauro, whose works are featured here. He's best known for his bas-reliefs, in which he draws forms on muslin, then sculpts the contours into them with a quiltlike textile, over which he applies strokes of color. Sometimes he makes molds from the bas-reliefs and casts them in bronze or aluminum. His drawings and paintings are also on display. ♦ Daily. 233 Canyon Rd (between Paseo de Peralta and Garcia St). 988.3048

La Bajada, the spot between Albuquerque and Santa Fe where the Santa Fe plateau drops 1,500 feet to the Rio Grande rift, marks the boundary between the Rio Arriba (upper river) and the Rio Abajo (lower river) regions of New Mexico and has posed a challenge to travelers between the two cities since colonial times. Literally meaning "The Descent," the stretch is dotted with the graves of those killed while attempting to climb or descend the hairpin-curved trail in horse-drawn wagons. In the early 1900s motorists found the grade to be a strain on radiators and trans- missions. Even today the highway can be tricky during high winds or after a heavy snow.

Restaurants/Clubs: Red **Hotels:** Blue
Shops/ 🌳 Outdoors: Green **Sights/Culture:** Black

3 Garcia Street Books As you browse in the Canyon Road area's only general-interest bookstore, you get the feeling that each title has been carefully handpicked. The travel and arts sections here are especially good. The shop shares the building with **Downtown Subscriptions** (★★$, 983.3085), a magazine store and cafe with a spacious outdoor patio where many Santa Fe authors hang out when they're not writing—and sometimes when they are. ♦ Daily. 376 Garcia St (between Canyon Rd and Acequia Madre). 986.0151

4 Linda Durham Gallery If this building looks like an old brick schoolhouse, that's because it used to be one. In 1906 the Board of Education built the **First Ward School** at a cost to taxpayers of $5,311, replacing an earlier, smaller school that had been built in 1876. The school board sold the building in 1928, and it has been used at various times since as a zoo, a theater, an apartment house, and an antiques store. Since 1980 it has been the home of Linda Durham's gallery. A devotee of nonobjective art, Durham for many years provided the only showcase in town for New Mexico's abstract artists. Although there is now some competition, Durham still represents the most challenging forms of minimalist and installation art. ♦ M-Sa. 400 Canyon Rd (at Garcia St). 988.1313

5 Kachina House and Gallery A few steps away from Canyon Road, this gallery started by Ruth Holmwood in 1951 is a halfway house for kachina dolls—halfway from the Hopi and Zuni reservations to your house. Kachinas are elaborate wooden carvings representing the Hopi and Zuni gods. They've been used in religious ceremonies for centuries; now they are carved for sale as well. The very best—the collectors' items—are intricately carved from a single piece of cottonwood root. Only authentic wooden kachinas are sold here—no Navajo rip-offs in leathers and trinkets. Owner Holmwood's personal collection of about 300 older kachinas, which are not for sale, hangs from the ceiling. ♦ M-Sa. 236 Delgado St (between E Alameda St and Canyon Rd). 982.8415

Blue cornmeal can be used to make corn bread instead of the more widely known yellow kind. For a brighter blue hue, substitute buttermilk for half the milk in the recipe. *Atole,* a soup made by boiling finely powdered blue cornmeal, is used by both Spanish *curanderas* and Indian healers to cure illness.

6 Cline Fine Art Gallery Formerly the **Wiggins Gallery,** this rambling structure of classic adobe brown with turquoise trim was at one time a ranch house that belonged to the Sena family. Now owned by Geoff and Helen Cline, former residents of Tulsa, Oklahoma, the gallery features the work of fellow Tulsan Alexandre Hogue, known for his Dust Bowl paintings, and who at almost a hundred is still painting. The wonderful flowing landscapes of K. Douglas Wiggins are also shown here; they're the canvas equivalents of *The Milagro Beanfield War.* One room in the gallery, set up as a small apartment, is the **Eli Levin Gallery.** Levin, who came here as a young man in the 1960s, is a dedicated recorder and satirist of the local scene. The better-known Taos and Santa Fe founders are also on display. ♦ Daily. 526 Canyon Rd (between Delgado St and Camino del Monte Sol). 982.5328

7 El Zaguán Two towering chestnut trees, a lovely garden, and a sprawling hacienda make up one of Santa Fe's cherished locations. A prominent local merchant, James Johnson, purchased the property in 1849 when it was just a small, old mud house. Johnson added many rooms, converted the house to Territorial style, planted an orchard and a cornfield out back, and built corrals for the oxen and horses that hauled goods to be sold in his general store on the Plaza over the Santa Fe Trail. One of the new additions was the "chocolate room," where chocolate was ground and served in the afternoons. He also built a private chapel and a large library. The name comes from the Spanish word, *zaguán,* a covered passageway that runs the length of the house in the rear.

The Victorian garden west of the house was designed in the 1880s by Adolph Bandelier, the renowned anthropologist. Bandelier imported the peony bushes from China; the two chestnut trees were already here. The building was threatened with destruction in 1927 but was saved by Mrs. Charles H. Dietrich when she bought it. A private school for girls was housed in the building in the 1930s. Today it is owned by the Historic Santa Fe Foundation (983.2567), an organization dedicated to preserving the historic architecture of Santa Fe; its offices are in apartment No. 3. The rest of the place is made up of rental apartments, but the garden is open to the public. On any given day you might find a "live artist" painting there. To enter the garden use the courtyard entrance and bear left under the portal. ♦ 545 Canyon Rd (between Delgado St and Camino Escondido)

Miles of Mountains

The richly colored granite and red-gold volcanic rock formations of Northern New Mexico's mountains—all part of the **Rocky Mountains**—are set off by tall, silent forests of ponderosa pine, and shimmering stands of aspen (at elevations above 9,000 feet). Atop the majestic crags of the highest peaks, steep slopes covered with Douglas fir give way to alpine meadows. Hundreds of unpaved roads (some suitable for passenger cars and others only for high-clearance and four-wheel-drive vehicles) wind into these vast stretches of wilderness; where these rugged roads end, narrow trails continue, taking hikers, horseback riders, mountain bikers, fishers, and skiers (downhill and cross-country) into this region's remote interior, home to eagles, bears, and elk.

The greatest and highest of New Mexico's mountain ranges is the **Sangre de Cristo Mountains.** These tremendous peaks (the highest is **Wheeler Peak** northwest of Taos at 13,161 feet) rise abruptly from the eastern city limits of both Santa Fe and Taos and extend northward in a solid wall of forbidding rock for more than 200 miles to central Colorado. The New Mexico segment of the mountain range spans two national parks, the **Carson National Forest** (headquarters 758.6200) and **Santa Fe National Forest** (headquarters 988.6940). Together, they contain more than 400 miles of trails, numerous trout streams, high-country fishing lakes, dozens of campgrounds with a total of 899 tent and RV sites, and seven downhill ski areas.

A half-dozen crests in the Sangre de Cristos are high enough to be covered with snow for almost nine months of the year. Temperatures average 25 to 30 degrees cooler than in Santa Fe and Taos year-round, causing clouds to condense around the summits and drop about 40 inches of precipitation a year—almost four times as much as in Santa Fe. Snow and rain in these mountains provide almost all of the drinking and irrigation water for Santa Fe, Taos, and Albuquerque.

At the heart of the Sangre de Cristos, the 223,667-acre **Pecos Wilderness** encompasses some of the most spectacularly varied high-mountain scenery in the state. Hugging its summits are enormous thickets of spruce and fir, flower-filled meadows, high-altitude lakes, and two spectacular peaks, **Santa Fe Baldy** (elevation 12,622 feet) and **Truchas Peak** (13,102 feet), with its ancient forest and remote fishing lakes. Motorized and wheeled vehicles are prohibited in the wilderness area; it is only open to hikers, cross-country skiers, horseback riders, and llama trekkers (the llamas carry your gear as you walk with them).

Beyond Santa Fe, smaller mountain ranges rise from the desert. Between Santa Fe and Albuquerque, **Sandia Crest,** a single massive mountain with a ridgeline that runs 30 miles north and south, offers panoramic views of Albuquerque (and approximately half the state of New Mexico) from a wilderness vantage point a mile above the city. North of Albuquerque, on the western horizon from Santa Fe, the **Jemez Mountains** around **Bandelier National Monument** and **Los Alamos** were formed by a huge prehistoric volcano; here, visitors will find surreal forest landscapes with hot springs, strange lava and ash formations, ancient Indian pueblos and cliff dwellings, and colorful cliffs that plunge straight down for as much as a thousand feet.

8 Fremont F. Ellis Studio/Gallery One of the early members of Santa Fe's art colony, William Penhallow Henderson, designed this lovely roadside adobe in the 1920s. Long known as the **Edwin Brooks House,** it served from 1956 to 1985 as the home and studio of another of the city's best-known painters, Fremont Ellis, a member of Los Cinco Pintores. The building is owned by the late artist's family. ♦ By appointment only. 553 Canyon Rd (between Delgado St and Camino Escondido). 982.5008

9 Ernesto Mayans Gallery Established in 1977 by writer Ernesto Mayans, this has consistently been one of the most interesting galleries in town for contemporary representational art. A special highlight is the stunning black-and-white photography of André Kertész. Local painters represented include David Barbero, Ralph Leon, Joel Greene, and Cathy Folk-Williams. ♦ Tu-Sa. 601 Canyon Rd (at Camino Escondido). 983.8068

10 Celebrations Restaurant & Caterers ★★$ A stroll up Canyon Road can be tiring and thirst-making, especially in the heat of a New Mexico summer. This is the best place to break for a light lunch, where you can eat on one of two pleasant patios as well as indoors. The menu features imaginative seafood presentations, including crawfish étouffée and seafood fettuccine, as well as traditional New Mexican dishes. You can get breakfast all day, including cholesterol-free omelettes. ♦ Continental/New Southwestern ♦ M-Tu, Su breakfast and lunch; W-Sa breakfast, lunch, and dinner. Reservations recommended. 613 Canyon Rd (between Camino Escondido and E Palace Ave). 989.8904

The Jemez Mountains above Bandelier National Monument and Los Alamos form a circle around a central volcanic caldera called Valle Grande. Many geologists believe that when the volcano was active—about 1,700,000 years ago—it reached a height greater than Mount Everest.

Restaurants/Clubs: Red Hotels: Blue
Shops/ ♣ Outdoors: Green Sights/Culture: Black

11 David Ross Studio/Gallery Step into this shop and you will enter a magical mystery zoo populated by sly and seductive wooden dalmatians, zebras, tigers, and rabbits. This sweet folk art is carved and painted by David Ross, a former scenic designer, who'll be glad to talk with you while he's working. Ross had a studio in Florence until he was driven out by the 1966 flood. Soon after arriving in Santa Fe in 1972, he started his brightly colored menagerie, whose most prominent denizens are hand-carved dalmatians (pictured above), painted with tempera, that adorn the sides of portable library stairs. Bring him a picture, and Ross will carve your favorite animal to order. More practical items include animalistic chests and headboards. ♦ Daily. 610 Canyon Rd (between Camino Escondido and Camino del Monte Sol). 988.4017

12 Running Ridge Gallery Abstract, non-functional pieces in sculptured glass and ceramics, as well as modern paintings, fabric art, and jewelry, are featured in this airy space. Run by Barbara G. Grabowski and Ruth Farnham, the gallery has been here since 1979. ♦ M-Sa. 640 Canyon Rd (between Delgado St and Camino del Monte Sol). 988.2515, 800/584.6830

12 Keats Gallery When Swiss-born Iren Schio came to Santa Fe in the 1970s, her art centered on three-dimensional boxes constructed from found objects, in the manner of Joseph Cornell. A doll's hand, a broken watch, a rusty spoon were combined to make powerful statements. In more recent years she has turned to abstract works on paper and manages to fashion simple geometric shapes into equally moving statements about the forces in balance—or out of balance—in the universe. Her art predominates in this small gallery run by Martha Keats, who handles only works on paper. The acclaimed collages of Dana Newmann are also on display. ♦ M-Sa. 644 Canyon Rd (between Delgado St and Camino del Monte Sol). 982.6686

13 The Compound ★★$$$$ One of the priciest restaurants—and certainly the most formal restaurant—in town is situated down a sloping driveway off Canyon Road. Whether this formality is justified by the continental food (pâté de foie gras, caviar, and rack of lamb are among the menu selections) is a matter of opinion, and opinion varies. However, the surroundings, mostly in white, are a visual delight as designed by **Alexander Girard,** who converted a 19th-century hacienda into several dining areas. ♦ Continental ♦ Tu-Sa dinner. Reservations required. No infants or small children allowed. 653 Canyon Rd (between Camino Escondido and E Palace Ave). 982.4353

14 Helen Hardin Estate/Silver Sun The renowned Indian painter Pablita Velarde is from Santa Clara Pueblo and now lives in Albuquerque. Her granddaughter, Margarete Tindel, is a young artist who also lives there. Sadly missing is the middle generation: Pablita's daughter and Margarete's mother—Helen Hardin. As a child Helen would hear her mother get up in the middle of the night to paint under naked bulbs while the family slept. After becoming an artist, Helen did the same thing. Her work was less traditional than Velarde's; Hardin combined sacred Indian mythology with a more modern sensibility and a subtle sense of humor. Her fame rivaled her mother's when she died of cancer in 1984 at the age of 41. The true cause of her death, her mother has been quoted as saying, was that she made public the Indian spirit world that is supposed to remain private. For seven years after her death, her work remained in storage, until her heirs, including husband Cradoc Bagshaw, a photographer, decided her legacy of etchings and acrylics should be available to the public, and this gallery was opened in 1991. Cheryl Ingram, who had owned Silver Sun at this spot since 1976, became the estate representative and gave Hardin's work a place of honor and a room of its own in her store. Ingram also shows small Navajo sculptures and delicate miniature pottery from Acoma Pueblo, and Native American handmade jewelry. There's a wide range of turquoise and silver earrings ranging in price from affordable to high-end traditional. ♦ Daily. 656 Canyon Rd (between Delgado St and Camino del Monte Sol). 983.8743

14 Tresa Vorenberg Goldsmiths Unique gold and silver jewelry by local and national jewelry designers adorn the showcases of this store. The contemporary designs range from inlay to diamonds. Also offered are abstract, landscape, and figurative paintings by local artists. ♦ M-Sa; occasionally Su. 656 Canyon Rd (between Delgado St and Camino del Monte Sol). 988.7215

Restaurants/Clubs: Red   **Hotels:** Blue
Shops/ 🌸 Outdoors: Green   **Sights/Culture:** Black

15 Fletcher Gallery According to artist Susan Bennerstrom, most people think pastels are "mushy." Hers are anything but. They are powerful evocations of ominous and lonely moods, created out of buildings set in landscapes that are usually about to erupt into some kind of storm. "There aren't any stories in a blue sky," she says. Bennerstrom, who lives in the state of Washington, is the preeminent force in this gallery, but finely detailed landscapes by Jane Shea achieve similarly powerful effects with an exquisite watercolor technique. Among the other work shown are lots of still lifes by such painters as R.B. Sprague, Guy Diehl, and John Nava. ♦ M-Sa. 668 Canyon Rd (between Delgado St and Camino del Monte Sol). 983.9441

16 The Graphics House Gallery Two artists share this studio space: Anne Sawyer, who has an etching press on one side of the building, and David E. Brighton, who keeps an art-engraving workshop on the other. Both are fine craftspersons. Sawyer's miniature etchings are among the most affordable art in town. ♦ Daily. 702 Canyon Rd (between Delgado St and Camino del Monte Sol). 983.2654

16 Gypsy Alley More than a half-dozen shops and galleries await down this quaint, narrow alleyway. Paintings, folk art, jewelry, photography, and Mexican rugs are all available. Shop owners here are friendly and helpful. ♦ 708 Canyon Rd (between Delgado St and Camino del Monte Sol)

Within Gypsy Alley:

Leaping Lizard Gallery Several local artists, with tongues in their cheeks, show brightly colored yet sophisticated drawings and sculptures of anthropomorphic animals and mystical creatures of their own divining in this, the most fun of the **Gypsy Alley** galleries. Zookeeper Lily Waters calls it a new mythology. Max Lehman's hilarious ceramics are "neo-Maya," who include Maya Minnie and Queenie Quark. Whimsical animal silkscreens are offered by children's book illustrator Tom Ross, the gallery owner, whose earth-loving

LEAPING LIZARD

dinosaur, It Zwibble, has starred in children's books and an **HBO** special. ♦ Daily. 1 Gypsy Alley. 984.8434

'Oot'i Gallery Stroll farther down the alley for a look at the cowboy and Pueblo photographs of Janis Schwartz-Stegall. While based in New York, Schwartz-Stegall roamed the world shooting in color. Then she moved to New Mexico and switched to black and white. It was an inspired choice; her pictures are simply luminous. The name of the gallery, by the way, is the Navajo word for vision. ♦ Daily. 7 Gypsy Alley. 984.1676

17 Artisans "Through This Door Pass the Finest Artists in the World." So proclaims a sign at the entrance to Santa Fe's largest art supply store. Flattery may get you anywhere, but that's not the only reason local artists have been flocking here for their cadmium reds and cobalt blues since Bill Banta and Jack Young opened shop in 1975. This is one of the most complete art supply stores in the Southwest, stocking every major brand (plus some minor brands) of oil paints, watercolors, acrylics, and pastels, as well as brushes, canvas, paper, inks, pens, pads, erasers, and how-to books—supplies for everyone from the beginner to the accomplished master. ♦ M-Sa. 717 Canyon Rd (between Camino Escondido and E Palace Ave). 988.2179

18 Geronimo ★★★$$$ This is the third restaurant in recent years to occupy the **Borrego House,** an adobe whose history can be traced to a smaller structure that stood here in 1753 on a farm that extended back about a hundred yards to the *Acequia Madre,* the "mother ditch," which supplied the farm's water. In the 19th century it was owned for 75 years by the Borrego family, who added the large front room and the front portal for entertaining. From then until 1939 the house was willed to various children and heirs room by room, a fairly common local practice in those days; at times even parts of a room were bequeathed. Between 1928 and 1939, all the rooms were purchased individually from the heirs by Mrs. Charles Dietrich, who then restored the house. But the inside, with its uneven floors and walls, retains the essence of true Santa Fe style. The building has changed hands and restaurant incarnations several times since.

49

The present restaurant owners, Cliff Skogland and Brent Jones, serve first-rate food and deserve to last longer than some of their culinary predecessors. The grilled tournedos of beef with acorn squash are excellent, as are the steamed manilla clams and fettuccine in curry sauce and the blackened sea bass with yellow-tomato–sage vinaigrette. This is the only restaurant in town that serves full dinners until 1AM. ♦ Continental ♦ M dinner; Tu-Su lunch and dinner. Reservations recommended. 724 Canyon Rd (at Camino del Monte Sol). 982.1500

19 Camino del Monte Sol Beginning in the 1920s, this street, which intersects Canyon Road just past the **Borrego House** (see page 49), was the home of Los Cinco Pintores, five painters who banded together by that name and came to symbolize the vitality of the Santa Fe art colony. They were Fremont Ellis, Walter Ufer, Joseph Bakos, Willard Nash, and Will Shuster. The group bought a tract of land together and built their homes and studios here. Other painters, and writers such as Mary Austin, also built in the area. The street was previously called Telephone Road because it followed the main telephone line into town, but artist and resident William Penhallow Henderson and his wife, Alice Corbin, a poet, preferred something more literary and renamed it after a nearby mountain. For the most part the homes remain private residences. About a half-mile up the road is **St. John's College,** where the curriculum is designed around the "great books" program advocated by educator R.M. Hutchins. ♦ From Canyon Rd to Old Santa Fe Trail

20 Ríos Wood Yard Mountains of freshly cut logs reach toward the sky in this unfenced rural roadside enclave. Inhale the deep wood smells and gaze at the tree rings that speak of nature's endurance. For generations the Ríos family has been supplying much of Santa Fe with the piñon and pine that make those Indian fireplaces crackle on snowy winter evenings. You won't be tempted to buy something and ship it home. On the other hand, these logs may induce you to move here. ♦ Daily. 324 Camino del Monte Sol (between Canyon Rd and Acequia Madre). 982.0358

21 Acequia Madre In the days before piped-in water and deep wells, *acequias* (ditches) were the vessels of life; after rainfall and during the spring runoff, they carried the water that made farming, and survival itself, possible in this region. Ditch irrigation in the Indian regions began as much as a thousand years ago. Water rights belong to all those who own property along the ditch, according to the size of their property. The landowners all had to help with the maintenance of the *acequias,* clearing the winter's debris in spring so water could flow through. Each ditch had a

mayordomo (steward) who supervised the cleanings. The practice still exists today, though the water here is used more for maintaining gardens than for growing food. Running alongside the ditch is a quiet residential street bearing the same name. If you've had your fill of shops and galleries, you can walk down Acequia Madre to Garcia Street, then turn right; one block will bring you back near the base of Canyon Road. You'll also pass **Acequia Madre Elementary School,** whose walls feature a mural painted by a prominent local artist, Frederico Vigil. ♦ From the Santa Fe River at the upper end of Upper Canyon Rd, along Upper Canyon Rd to Acequia Madre St, to the Santa Fe River just south of downtown

Staged in Santa Fe

Santa Fe has a number of theaters used by both local and touring companies and musical groups. They offer drama and dance, as well as orchestras, chamber music, and pop concerts. Check the local newspapers to see what entertainment is available while you're in town. The following is a roster of theaters in Santa Fe:

Center for Contemporary Arts (art films) 291 Barcelona Ave (between Old Pecos Trail and Don Gaspar Ave). 982.1338

Greer Garson Theater College of Santa Fe, 1600 St. Michael's Dr (between Llano St and Cerrillos Rd). 473.6511

James A. Little Theater New Mexico School for the Deaf, 1060 Cerrillos Rd (between St. Francis Dr and Baca St). 827.6760

Paolo Soleri Amphitheater Santa Fe Indian School, 1501 Cerrillos Rd (between Baca St and San Jose Ave). 989.6300

Railyard Performance Center 430 West Manhattan Ave (between Guadalupe St and St. Francis Dr). 982.8309

St. Francis Auditorium Museum of Fine Arts, 107 W Palace Ave (between Lincoln and Sheridan Sts). 827.4455

St. John's College (art or classic films are shown on Saturday nights) Camino de Cruz Blanca (between Camino del Monte Sol and Camino Cabra). 982.3691

Santa Fe Community Theater 142 E De Vargas St (between Don Gaspar Ave and Old Santa Fe Trail). 988.4262

New Mexico produces more chile than the rest of the US combined, and exports more than 70 million pounds of it each year, mostly in the form of ground red-chile powder.

22 Mary Austin House This refurbished old adobe has long been a focal point of the local art scene. Austin, an early Santa Fe writer and feminist, built the house in the 1920s with the help of architect **John Gaw Meem** and artist William Penhallow Henderson. Painter John Sloan created the decorative windows in the rear of the building, and photographer Ansel Adams lived here when he and Austin were working on books together. Willa Cather wrote much of her novel *Death Comes for the Archbishop* in the house library. And photographer Laura Gilpin lived just to the north. ♦ 439 Camino del Monte Sol (between Canyon Rd and Acequia Madre)

Within the Mary Austin House:

Gerald Peters Gallery A former student at **St. John's College,** Gerald Peters went from "great books" to creating Santa Fe's most successful art gallery while buying up much of the prime real estate downtown. More of Georgia O'Keeffe's paintings pass through this gallery than any other gallery in the world. Not coincidentally, Peters also handles the sculptures of Juan Hamilton, O'Keeffe's longtime companion and one of her principal heirs. The floral still lifes of Carol Mothner are exquisite, while her evocative studies of puppets and toy soldiers capture the darker side of the human condition. The usual assortment of early Santa Fe and Taos painters is also on display. ♦ Daily May-Sept, M-Sa Oct-Apr. 988.8961

23 Imperial Wok ★★★$$ This dining establishment—perhaps the best of Santa Fe's half-dozen Chinese restaurants—is owned by Benny and Marta Hung, who also have restaurants in New York state, Colorado Springs, and Albuquerque. The specials are priced a bit high for Chinese food, but they are extremely good, especially the seafood dishes. Don't miss the Club Seafood—king crabmeat, shrimp, and scallops sautéed with Chinese vegetables in a white wine sauce. Lunch is less expensive, but the chef's specials are not available. In the evening the covered courtyard has a dark, romantic air that's found in few Santa Fe restaurants. There's also a parking lot. ♦ Chinese ♦ M-Sa lunch and dinner; Su dinner. Reservations recommended. 731 Canyon Rd (at Camino del Monte Sol). 988.7100

24 El Farol ★★★$$$ One of the city's longest-running restaurants, housed in an atmospheric, centuries-old adobe with many small rooms, this dining spot features tapas, those wonderful small dishes that originated in Spain. The problem here is choosing among the wide array of dishes, such as baby squid fried in beer butter; scallop seviche; chorizo (sausage) with green peppercorn and mustard sauce; sautéed wild mushrooms with spaghetti squash; or hickory-smoked chicken breast with cucumber. The hosts suggest three or four dishes per person, but two might fill you up unless you're really hungry; you can always order another later. The extremely popular bar, which is decorated with murals painted by Alfred Morang, features live blues, jazz, and folk entertainment. ♦ Tapas ♦ Daily dinner. Reservations recommended. 808 Canyon Rd (at E Palace Ave). 983.9912

25 Patrick Smith Park A few steps past 943 Canyon Road is a small entryway into this park, more commonly known as "Canyon Road Park." The lovely 5.4-acre patch of greenery has a softball field, soccer field, and basketball hoops but is also used for tossing a football or Frisbee, picnicking, or reading a book in the shade of a tall tree. The park's far side, bordering the Alameda, offers more parking space.

Beyond this point on Canyon Road there are no more shops, just old adobe buildings—many have not been restored in a long time—that are private residences, and a few artists' studios. The sidewalks disappear here, and the slope toward the mountains becomes steeper. But this narrow, curving stretch of road retains much more of the European feel that once permeated all of Santa Fe than the lower part. Since most visitors don't make it this far, a walk here offers a feeling of peace and serenity. Watch out for the cars that come from both directions. ♦ Between the Santa Fe River and Canyon Rd (near Camino Cerrito)

26 Frederico Vigil Studio Probably the best-known Hispanic artist in Santa Fe, Frederico Vigil is a master of the ancient art of *buon fresco*—painting murals in wet plaster, much the way Michelangelo painted the Sistine Chapel during the Renaissance. His murals are colorful mélanges of Hispanic and regional imagery that often summarize hundreds of years of history in a single work. They can be found on the inside and outside walls of schools and churches throughout the area. Several years ago a mural he had painted at nearby **St. John's College** was verbally attacked by the college's new president as being in bad taste, and then was physically attacked by a disgruntled former student, touching off a local furor. Vigil collects and grinds his own pigments, slakes his own lime months in advance, and draws his designs in the studio before transferring them to wet plaster, where there is little margin for error. When he is not out working on a wall, Vigil draws and paints in this studio, which is open to visitors if he is around. ♦ Hours vary. 1107 Canyon Rd (at Camino Cerrito). 983.9511

Cristo Rey Church

ANTONIO COCILOVO

27 Cristo Rey Church In 1540 Spanish explorer Francisco Vásquez de Coronado and his expedition blazed the first European trail through the Southwest. Four hundred years later, to commemorate that event, Santa Feans built one of the largest adobe structures in existence (illustrated above). **John Gaw Meem** designed the beautiful church in the Spanish-mission Classical style. Nearly 200,000 adobe bricks made from the soil at the site were used in the construction. Local residents performed the work under the guidance of professional builders. The church was specifically designed to contain a superb stone reredos (altar screen) that had been carved in Mexico in 1760. The reredos had been installed in a military chapel on the Plaza called **La Castrense.** Later it was placed in a parish church. Archbishop Lamy, who with his French pretensions did not like local art, had the reredos concealed behind a wall of **St. Francis Cathedral** when the cathedral was being built on the site of the parish church in 1869. Today the reredos is on prominent display in this church, which is open to visitors. ♦ 1120 Canyon Rd (at Camino Cabra). 983.8528

Bests

Ellen Kleiner
Managing Editor, *Mothering* magazine

Family Magic:

Sunset Storytelling by Joe Hayes outside the summer tipi at the **Wheelwright Museum of the American Indian** on Camino Lejo.

The touch-all-you-want outdoor sculpture garden at **Shidoni Foundry** on Bishop's Lodge Road, just yards from perfect skipping stones along the banks of the Little Tesuque River.

Afternoons at the **Santa Fe Children's Museum** on Old Pecos Trail, with hands-on-discovery and guided rope climbing.

Descending into the kiva after exploring the ruins of the long-abandoned 13th-century pueblo at **Pecos National Monument** east of Santa Fe.

The prairie dog village set between folk art, pottery, and furniture at the indoor-outdoor mercados of **Jackalope** on Cerrillos Road.

Scooping up *just a little* "magic clay" from the ever-deepening well of curative earth in the anteroom beside the altar at the **Santuario de Chimayó**—a 180-year-old adobe church in the Chimayó Valley north of Santa Fe.

Romance galore:

The **Canyon Road Walk** on summer Fridays at 5PM, when the galleries serve up refreshments as well as art.

Sena Plaza, off East Palace Avenue, for courtyard dining, cobblestone strolling, and fragrant dreaming amid the wishing wells and lush foliage of a mid–19th-century colonial hacienda.

The spectacular outdoor amphitheater at the **Santa Fe Opera**—high drama set against rising stars and hilltop silhouettes.

Morning hikes at the **Randall Davey Audubon Center,** a 135-acre nature-and-wildlife sanctuary at the very top of Upper Canyon Road, teeming with coyotes and mule deer (bashful) as well as butterflies and hummingbirds (far more social).

Hot-tubbing year round at **Ten Thousand Waves** on Ski Basin Road, beneath piñon trees and a moon you can almost touch. Bring a guava for dessert.

And always mystery:

Perched in a niche at **St. Francis Cathedral** is *La Conquistadora,* the oldest Madonna in the United States. Generations of Santafesiños say that this 370-year-old, 31-inch hand-carved wooden statue of the Blessed Mother inspires love in the land and in the heart. It's got to be true.

Christine Mather
Author

Santa Fe's pleasures come in simple, small, sweet, and discreet ways. Early mornings downtown or at night after a heavy snowfall, Santa Fe returns to its pre-auto life, quiet and simple with the small scale of a little colonial frontier town. This is a great time for an early-morning caffè latte at **La Traviata.** For a tiny town it's scary how many great places there are to eat. My regulars include lunch at **Paul's** and **Escalera,** and dinner at the bar of the **Coyote Cafe.** The kids love **Zia Diner, The Burrito Company,** the tatami rooms at **Sakura,** and anything from **Señor Murphy's** candy store. Meanwhile, the hunter-gatherer of the family, my husband, Davis, likes to stalk his food fresh and spends hours at the **Farmers' Market** at **Sanbusco Market Center,** weather permitting.

Acequia Madre lit up with *farolitos* at Christmas; **Ghost Ranch** near Abiquiu in the summer; at home with a piñon fire or up the high road and down the low road to Taos in the autumn to see the aspens and cottonwoods; lilacs on **Camino del Monte Sol** in spring—New Mexico has a very seasonal landscape. While on the high road to Taos, stop at **Las Trampas Church** after visiting the **Santuario de Chimayó.** The best of Taos includes **Ranchos de Taos Church;** the **Pueblo**—go early or late in the day and just sit quietly for a spell and try to block out the 20th century; **Millicent Rogers Museum; Brett House** for dinner; and **Michael's Kitchen** for breakfast or lunch.

In Albuquerque we often head to **Albuquerque International Airport**—the best in the West. We like to have lunch at the **New Mexico Museum of Natural History** while staring at the pterodactyls after taking in the volcanoes or the time machine.

Shopping in Santa Fe is perhaps how the city got its moniker—the City Different—since it is far easier to buy great Navajo jewelry or other art than it is to find plain white socks or anything prosaic. The **Davis Mather Folk Art Gallery** is perfect if you've run out of wooden snakes or need a killer wooden pig. It is getting hard to keep up with all the galleries and shops, so your best bet is to walk around the **Plaza,** down **San Francisco Street,** and up **Canyon Road.** My favorites include the **Chile Shop** and the **Museum Shop** at the **Palace of the Governors.**

My favorite free (or pretty darn close to it) activities include: the **Santa Fe Children's Museum**—hold the hissing cockroaches, I dare you; walking around the **Randall Davey Audubon Center; Las Golondrinas** festivals; **Pecos** and **Bandelier National Monuments;** and Indian dances, especially at **San Ildefonso Pueblo.**

Linda Durham
Owner/President, Linda Durham Gallery, Santa Fe

Hiking the **Windsor Trail** in **Santa Fe National Forest/Hyde Memorial State Park,** climbing **Santa Fe Baldy** (elevation 12,622 feet), and feeding the marmots while the ravens and hawks circle. Do it all early in the day before the lightning storms.

Breakfast burritos at **Tia Sophia's.**

Flying kites at the **Cross of the Martyrs.**

Summer fund-raisers for the environment on the grounds of the **Randall Davey Audubon Center.**

The Pet Parade, held during September Fiesta de Santa Fe.

Friday night gallery hopping and people-watching; collectors in denim and diamonds; dealers with and without attitudes; artists in various states of array or disarray.

Formal tailgate dinners in the parking lot of the **Santa Fe Opera** on the season's opening night.

Caffe latte at the **Aztec Street Cafe.**

The bar at **La Posada de Santa Fe.**

Chamber music concerts at **St. Francis Auditorium** on Sunday evenings.

Randy L. Burge
Part-time cowboy and folk artist, Santa Fe

In Santa Fe:

KOLT-106 on the FM dial—Best country station west of Texas.

St. John's College soccer field—A great place to watch sunsets above the **Jemez Mountains.** Take along a bottle of wine.

Downtown Subscriptions—Best newsstand and coffee shop in Santa Fe.

Tecolote Cafe—For a delicious breakfast in the morning. The place is closed Monday.

Santa Fe Children's Museum—Fun and frolic for young and old people.

Artisans—Supplies for all artists.

Big Rocks ski run, **Santa Fe Ski Basin**—A little bit of tree skiing to test one's sanity. Watch out for the boulders and cliffs past the trees.

Shidoni Foundry in **Tesuque**—A bronze foundry and outdoor gallery with the world's best collection of yard art for sale. This is serious sculpture with both large and small works. Visitors on Saturday can watch bronze pourings. Take along a picnic lunch.

Tales of spirits are part of the Hispanic heritage of Santa Fe, and ghosts thrive here. The late Sister Miriam George, who was the librarian at the now defunct Loretto Academy, a former Catholic school for girls, reportedly still hangs around the gift shop at the Inn of Loretto, singing and moving merchandise. The Nuclear Dancers, on the other hand, only "half manifest themselves" for about 10 seconds on the sidewalk in front of the Palace Avenue building that was the office for the Manhattan Project, which built the atomic bomb. Ghost Tours will take you on a walking tour of the city's haunted sites. You'll get lots of history, but no guarantees that a ghost will make an appearance. Tours leave at 8PM from Wednesday through Saturday at the southeast corner of the Plaza, next to the Old Santa Fe Trail marker. For more information and reservations, call Southwest Adventure Group (983.0876).

Restaurants/Clubs: Red **Hotels:** Blue
Shops/ Outdoors: Green **Sights/Culture:** Black

Guadalupe Street

Many Americans first heard of Santa Fe through the big-band tune "The Atchison, Topeka, and Santa Fe." The irony is that the railroad that carries the same name never stopped in Santa Fe. The main rail line in 1879 reached the village of Lamy, 20 miles to the south, beyond the rugged Sangre de Cristo Mountains, and only a narrow spur line used mostly for freight cars connected the railroad with the capital city. The spur line ended on Guadalupe Street, where the old, vacant station is still visible. This was a logical spot for the line's terminus because a few hundred yards away was the end of **El Camino Real** (the Royal Road), a 1,500-mile overland trade route from Mexico City, and debarking passengers had only a short walk to the hotels near the Plaza.

In the late 1800s, warehouses were built in this area to serve the railroad, and Guadalupe Street became a commercial hub. After the trucking business got into gear, however, the rail-shipping industry slowed down and some of the warehouses were abandoned while others became the homes of automobile dealerships, auto repair shops, and other utilitarian businesses patronized by local residents. When tourism became a big business in Santa Fe in the late 1970s, Guadalupe Street was refurbished and put into play. The auto dealers moved to the far south end of town, and the abandoned spaces, just a few blocks from the Plaza, were renovated into shops and restaurants that today line the busy thoroughfare as well as the narrow side streets. The district has joined the Plaza and Canyon Road as one of the city's major areas in which to browse and shop.

A few good art and photo galleries dot the district, notably the **Laura Carpenter Gallery** for world-class sculpture and installation art and **Scheinbaum & Russek Ltd.** for photography. Several New Age bookstores cater to the large number of Santa Fe residents fascinated by astrology and the occult, yet most of the shops tend to be utilitarian, selling fine cookware, luggage, and stationery—a welcome change from the glut of Indian jewelry stores near the Plaza. You can indulge in excellent New Mexican and American dishes at **Guadalupe Cafe**, fine American food at **Zia Diner**, choice Italian fare at **Pranzo Italian Grill**, gourmet French seafood at **Encore Provence**, and sushi and other Japanese dishes at **Sakura** and **Shohko Cafe**. You can even find New York–style bagels, bialys, and Reuben sandwiches at **Bagelmania**, and the homespun **Aztec Street Cafe** is a pleasant hideaway for a coffee break.

The street takes its name from the **Santuario de Guadalupe**, an 18th-century adobe church dedicated to the Virgin of Guadalupe, the most venerated religious figure in Mexico. It is divided into South Guadalupe and North Guadalupe by the **Santa Fe River.** Between the grassy banks of this "river" there is, for 10 months of the year, nothing but a dry ditch. Only in April and May, when the snows on the mountains are melting, does a small river flow. But the **Santa Fe River Park** along the banks, sprinkled with benches and picnic tables, is a convenient place for resting or a picnic lunch.

1 Santuario de Guadalupe One of the city's most visually dramatic landmarks, this adobe church was built between 1776 and 1795 by Franciscans. The site was chosen to mark the end of El Camino Real, a 1,500-mile trade route that ran from Mexico City all the way to Santa Fe. In the beginning, the church was a simple adobe structure with a flat roof and a tower on one side, typical elements of New Mexican churches at that time. Mass was celebrated only occasionally, by itinerant priests, until Archbishop Lamy converted the run-down building into a regular parish church in 1880. The French archbishop, ever

eager to improve on local taste, had it renovated into a Romanesque, New England–style church with a pitched roof, a steeple, and a white picket fence. In 1961 a much larger, more modern church, **Our Lady of Guadalupe Parish,** was built behind the chapel, which soon fell into disrepair. There was talk of tearing down the old building—whose walls are three to five feet thick—and replacing it with a parking lot. But a nonprofit group was formed to rescue it. The archdiocese deeded the chapel to the Guadalupe Historic Foundation, which in 1976 undertook another renovation

and removed most of the external ornamentation and restored the chapel closer to the original style. Weakness in the structure of the bell tower led to further renovation in 1991. The former church is now used for occasional concerts by the **Desert Chorale** and art exhibitions.

The chapel is dedicated to Our Lady of Guadalupe, the most revered religious figure in Mexico. Featured prominently is an oil-on-canvas reredos of the Virgin of Guadalupe painted in 1783 in Mexico by José de Alzibar, a prominent artist of the time. The huge

55

canvas was brought north in several sections on the backs of mules and assembled in the church. Alzibar's signature and the lines where the canvas was joined are clearly visible. ◆ 100 S Guadalupe St (between Agua Fria St and the Santa Fe River). 988.2027

2 Agua Fria Street This narrow street (its name is Spanish for cold water) follows the path that was the end of El Camino Real 200 years ago. Today it is the principal artery through the unfashionable west side of town. A drive along this street to its southern terminus at Airport Road (about 10 minutes away) offers a clear picture of how most native Santa Feans live, far from the upscale glitz introduced to the downtown area to serve the newly arrived millionaire set. With the renovation of Guadalupe Street, however, real estate prices have climbed at the street's northern end. ◆ From Guadalupe St to Airport Rd

3 Guadalupe Cafe ★★★$ Informal and without pretensions, this is one of those rock-solid restaurants that every city should revel in. It was here years before nouvelle New Mexican cuisine came to town and, if there is any justice, it will be here long after that fad passes. Chef and co-owner Isabel Koomoa serves consistently good hearty fare, whether it be a cooked-to-order hamburger with excellent fries, any of a half-dozen enchiladas—from the standard chicken to a nontraditional (for landlocked New Mexico, anyway) seafood version—spaghetti, breast of chicken *relleno* (stuffed with cheese and rice), or a variety of overstuffed sandwiches. You can even get half a sandwich with soup or salad, as well as fine desserts. For breakfast try the *migas* (eggs scrambled with tortilla strips and bacon grease) or the fresh raspberry pancakes. The three dining rooms are pleasant and casual, and during lunch, dinner, and Sunday brunch, locals are crammed into the waiting area. Reservations are not taken, so get here early or be prepared to wait with everyone else. ◆ New Mexican ◆ Tu-Sa breakfast, lunch, and dinner; Su brunch. 313 S Guadalupe St (at W De Vargas St). 982.9762

In Santa Fe it is a sign of prestige to live on a dirt road—but only on the exclusive east side. On the less fashionable west side of town, dirt roads are found mainly in the barrio.

4 Cookworks When renowned chef and author Julia Childs comes to town, she has book signings at this outstanding kitchenware store, which occupies three storefronts along Guadalupe Street. Supplying both Santa Fe's fine restaurants and the large number of Santa Feans who enjoy cooking gourmet dishes as much as eating them, this store offers an impressive selection of pots, pans, woks, knives, espresso makers, and all manner of unusual cooking utensils—great for browsing even if you're not into baking. ◆ Daily. 316, 318, 322 S Guadalupe St (between Agua Fria St and Montezuma Ave). 988.7676

5 Herbs Etc. Unpainted wooden shelves are jam-packed with Chinese and other medicinal herbs, vitamins, and homeopathic remedies in this funky drug-free pharmacy for the New Age. Simply taking a whiff of the pungent air inside might cure what ails you. ◆ M-Sa. 323 Aztec St (between S Guadalupe and Sandoval Sts). 982.1265

5 Aztec Street Cafe ★★$ This small coffeehouse furnished with bare wooden tables is filled with writers, painters, and other creative types who pass the time reading newspapers, playing checkers, or philosophizing over good coffee and serviceable desserts. Some day the successful ones will reminisce about the good old days spent here. Meals tend to be simple; sandwiches and green-chile burgers are among the typical choices. ◆ Cafe ◆ Daily breakfast, lunch, and dinner. 317 Aztec St (between S Guadalupe and Sandoval Sts). 983.9464

6 Access Maps & Gear No relation to the ACCESS® Press guidebooks, this shop occupies a corner of **FrameCrafters** (988.2920), a framing shop that was opened by Mardes York and Ginny York almost 20 years ago. Most locals probably don't know it exists, but tourists will delight in the cornucopia of antique maps and reproductions of the same, globes in all sizes, topolopes (envelopes made from topographical maps), topographical jigsaw puzzles, and relief maps. Prints of early New Mexico are also sold. A mail-order catalog is available. ◆ Tu-Sa. 321 S Guadalupe St (between Aztec St and Montezuma Ave). 982.3330

The largest contiguous aspen forest in the world paints the Sangre de Cristo Mountains around Santa Fe Basin brilliant yellow and orange in October. Unlike other parts of the Rockies, the mountain slope here is broad and gentle in the 9,000- to 11,000-foot elevations where aspens grow.

6 Santa Fe Pottery Fourteen local potters show their work in Frank Willett's small, charming shop, which has been here since 1972, before Guadalupe Street was redis-covered. Dinnerware, cookware, stoneware lamps, and sconces line the white shelves. Potters used to work in the back room with their wheels and kilns, but the space is now used only for display. ♦ M-Sa. 323 S Guadalupe St (between Aztec St and Montezuma Ave). 988.7687

7 Zia Diner ★★$$ Meat loaf like your mother never made is the unlikely standout on the menu here. It's chock-full of piñon nuts—tasty without being greasy—and you can get it with mashed potatoes and a vegetable, or as a sandwich on French bread. Other old-fashioned diner items include an open-faced hot turkey sandwich. The homemade pies—especially the strawberry rhubarb—are wonderful. Daily specials at lunch and dinner are a bit more fashionable—quiches, angel-hair pasta with sun-dried tomatoes, that sort of thing. A large, sprawling, popular place, this restaurant has booths and tables on two levels, an outdoor patio for warm weather days, as well as a soda fountain with stools (good when you're by yourself). This is a favorite haunt of actor Gene Hackman, a regular-type guy. Wine and beer are available. ♦ American ♦ Daily lunch and dinner. Reservations recommended. 326 S Guadalupe St (between Agua Fria St and Montezuma Ave). 988.7008

7 Zia Bakery ★★$ Beth Koch and Susan Murishing, who opened the doors of **Zia Diner** (see above) in 1986, later spun off this bakery a few steps across the patio walkway. It has become a small mecca for Santa Fe's cafe culture. Coffee and pastries are served. ♦ Coffeehouse ♦ Daily. 328 S Guadalupe St (between Agua Fria St and Montezuma Ave). 988.5155

7 Scheinbaum & Russek Ltd. One of the most professional photography galleries in Santa Fe, this shop deals in rare and contemp-orary prints. The list of photographers whose works have been shown here comprises a who's who of the art. Standouts among many are Manuel Alvarez Bravo, Henri Cartier-Bresson, Judy Dater, Laura Gilpin, Beaumont Newhall, Eliot Porter, and Edward Weston. ♦ M-Sa. 328 S Guadalupe St (between Agua Fria St and Montezuma Ave), Suite M. 988.5116

8 Sanbusco Market Center The word Sanbusco is an acronym for Santa Fe Builders Supply Company, which operated here in the late 19th and early 20th centuries out of a large warehouse and 2.5 acres of sheds and shipping docks. Shelves were stocked with lumber, nails, paint, and other supplies. By 1972 the compound was virtually abandoned and, in recent years, has been renovated into a sprawling complex of shops by builder Joe Schepps, who retained the old name. ♦ Daily. 500 Montezuma Ave (one block west of S Guadalupe St). 983.9136

Within Sanbusco Market Center:

Encore Provence ★★★$$$ One of Santa Fe's finest, this elegant dining establishment in a yellow wooden house is owned by a French couple, Patrick and Claude Benrezkellah, who previously ran restaurants in Paris and Connecticut. The menu—which changes daily—is pure French (the only true French restaurant in town), mostly offering seafood flown in from both coasts, and it is exquisite. Among the superb appetizers, you might want to try the smoked salmon or the seafood terrine; entrées typically include a choice of perfectly prepared and presented fish and seafood. Rabbit, chicken, or lamb dishes are usually offered for fish-phobics. The desserts are sublime, including as good a crème brûlée as you'll find anywhere. The service is friendly and impeccable. Wine is served by the bottle only, and you can choose from a fine assortment of French and California labels. ♦ French ♦ M-Sa dinner. Reservations required. 548 Agua Fria St (at Montezuma Ave), or enter through the rear of the Sanbusco parking lot. 983.7470

Pranzo Italian Grill ★★★$$$ This lovely restaurant has soft peach walls, formal white-clothed tables, a gently curving bar, plus a patio that's open in warm weather. The food is usually excellent—some locals put it right up there with Santa Fe's best; others have found it a bit uneven. An assortment of pizzas and pasta, ranging from spaghettini with baby shrimp, olive oil, garlic, sun-dried tomatoes, peas, and provolone to linguine with sausage and roasted bell peppers in a basil-tomato sauce are included on the menu. Most dishes are priced a bit lower than the competition. Chicken, veal, and seafood are at the higher end of the range. There is a good selection of recent-vintage wines. ♦ Italian ♦ Daily lunch and dinner. Reservations recommended. 540 Montezuma Ave (one block west of S Guadalupe St). 984.2645

On Your Feet Shoes pinching your toes from all this trekking around town? Planning to hike in **Hyde Park** or **Bandelier** and forgot your hiking boots? This store is devoted to walking shoes and other casual styles for men and women. And if any of Santa Fe's sights knock your socks off, they've got those, too. ♦ M-Sa; Su noon-5PM. 530 Montezuma Ave (one block west of S Guadalupe St). 983.3900

The Winery If you're planning a picnic and want to bring a bottle of white wine to cool in a mountain stream, or if you're looking for a gift for your hosts, you're sure to find what you need here. This shop stocks somewhere between 800 and a thousand different labels. ♦ M-Sa. 500 Montezuma Ave (one block west of S Guadalupe St). 982.9463

Farmers' Market Small farmers from throughout the area bring fresh produce into town to sell at an outdoor market set up in the **Sanbusco** parking lot. Writer Stan Crawford is likely to be here selling the garlic he grows near his home in nearby Dixon, about which he's written a book, *A Garlic Testament.* Strands of garlic or chile *ristras* (decorative dried strands of red chile strung together) are easy to transport home and make good gifts. In addition to fresh melons, fruit, and corn in season, canned and baked goods, sauces, and spices are sold. ♦ Tu, Sa morning June–mid-Nov

The Jamison Galleries Opened downtown in 1964 by Margaret Jamison, this Western gallery, now owned by Zeb B. Conley Jr., is probably the longest-running gallery in town. Works by the Taos and Santa Fe old masters are usually on display, as well as early works, offered for resale, by such contemporary Indian painters as Fritz Scholder, Earl Biss, and Kevin Red Star. ♦ M-Sa. 982.3666

9 University Plaza In the 1880s Protestant evangelists who wanted to convert the Catholic locals, whom they looked on as heathens, constructed this unusual corner building as a school. With its mansard roof and nonadobe construction, this is an architectural oddity for Santa Fe. It was named the **University of New Mexico**—no kin to the current university in Albuquerque—and was supposed to be a center of "moral education." But the locals didn't much care for the idea, and the missionaries didn't care much for life in Santa Fe. They packed up and moved on, to no one's disappointment. The building later became the **Franciscan Hotel,** and its mansard roof was removed when a third story was added; in the 1970s the roof was restored in an attempt to recover some of the structure's old charm. Today it's an office building. ♦ 330 Garfield St (at S Guadalupe St)

Within University Plaza:

Worldly Possessions This eclectic store fills most of the ground floor rooms in

University Plaza with wood carvings from Africa, tribal art of Australia, collector-quality artifacts from southeast Asia, handmade textiles and feather jewelry from Indonesia, and much more. Two rooms present gallery-style exhibitions of contemporary folk art, while another contains a wide selection of trade beads and findings. ♦ Daily. 983.6090

10 Thao ★★★$$$ Set in a modest Victorian house, this cozy restaurant serves "high Thai" cuisine, a gourmet mix of French colonial and southeast Asian influences with results that are spicy and sometimes magical. Try the Thai bouillabaisse, a seafood stew in carrot-peanut broth served with cassava root, spinach, and ginger. Other specialties include lacquered duck and salmon cakes in yellow-curry sauce. The homemade three-spice ice cream may be just the perfect pick-me-up on a hot June afternoon. ♦ Thai ♦ M-F lunch and dinner; Sa-Su dinner. Reservations recommended. 322 Garfield St (between S Guadalupe and Sandoval Sts). 988.9562

11 Old Railroad Depot The **Atchison, Topeka, and Santa Fe Railroad** has been hailed in story and song, but the name was a misnomer. The main track of the railroad, which in 1880 linked the Midwest by rail to the Pacific coast and made the Santa Fe Trail obsolete, never did touch Santa Fe, thanks to the greed of some local residents. The railroad company planned to lay tracks through a narrow pass between Glorieta and Santa Fe, but several Santa Feans bought part of it, then demanded a large price from the builders. Instead of paying up, the railroad rerouted the tracks to Albuquerque which became a boomtown, while Santa Fe remained off the beaten path.

After much lobbying by Archbishop Lamy, a 20-mile spur line was built along another route linking Santa Fe to the main track. Today the village of Lamy sits at the junction. In recent decades only occasional trains of a few cars each carried freight to Lamy to be transferred to the main line, and the railroad ultimately discontinued service and spoke of tearing up the tracks. A group of investors, including actor Michael Gross of TV's "Family Ties," formed the **Santa Fe Southern Railway,** which carries passengers to and from Lamy either to meet the daily east-west trains or to go on a sight-seeing ride. These trains arrive and depart from the other end of town (see **Santa Fe Southern Railway** on page 65). The old depot still stands, however, its beige walls and sloping roof an abandoned monument to a bygone time.

The acreage around the depot is the last undeveloped area near downtown and has been the subject of years of controversy over how it should be developed. The construction of *Outside* magazine's headquarters just across the old tracks from historic warehouse buildings housing book publishers Bear & Co. and John Muir Publications, suggests that the railroad yards may emerge as Santa Fe's "publishers' row." ♦ Off S Guadalupe St (at W Manhattan Ave)

12 Tomasita's ★$ Situated in a former rail yard warehouse, this restaurant is owned by Georgia Maryol, one of the three Maryol siblings who run local New Mexican restaurants (brother Jim heads up **Tia Sophia's** and sister Toni runs **Diego's Cafe**). In one of life's injustices, this is the most popular of the trio despite being the least pleasant. At lunch and dinner people crowd in and are willing to wait from 45 minutes to an hour to eat in a large hall that is jam-packed and noisy and to endure rude service; after all that waiting, they'll shoo you out for quick turnover. The food is no better than most New Mexican restaurants, and not as good as some. ♦ New Mexican ♦ M-Sa lunch and dinner. 500 S Guadalupe St (at W Manhattan Ave, in the railroad yards). 983.5721

13 High Desert Angler Probably the least publicized art form in Santa Fe is the art of tying fishing flies. If you want to learn, this is the place. Jan Crawford not only rents and sells rods and reels, flies, and all manner of fishing gear, she gives classes in every aspect of fly-fishing. She also offers classes just for women. With a ready smile she'll teach you everything from casting to landing and releasing fish, and—according to her brochure—how to think like a trout. She'll even lead you to water in New Mexico. ♦ Daily. 435 S Guadalupe St (entrance on Read St). 98.TROUT (honest)

14 Laura Carpenter Fine Art A beautiful old house with stained-glass windows has been transformed into one of the few galleries in this section of town that specializes in contemporary art. Open since 1991, the gallery continues to present a program of lectures surrounding the exhibitions and has expanded its space to include shows in an adjacent gallery. Among the nationally known artists shown recently were James Lee Bayers, Eric Fischl, Ellsworth Kelly, Agnes Martin, Ed Ruscha, Kiki Smith, and Richard Tuttle. ♦ Tu-Sa. 309 Read St (between S Guadalupe and Sandoval Sts). 986.9090

15 Hotel Santa Fe $$$ A novel commercial enterprise, this hotel is a partnership between a group of private investors led by builder Joe Schepps, and **Picuris Pueblo,** the smallest Indian tribe in New Mexico, which is situated near Taos. By allowing the pueblo to own 51 percent of the hotel, the investors were able to get 90 percent of their loans guaranteed by the federal government under a program aimed at encouraging Native American enterprise. Opened in 1991, the hotel is big, yet nicely designed and set back from the street. The 131 spacious, bright rooms are tastefully furnished and decorated in Southwestern style. The deli serves breakfast or sandwiches later in the day. Other amenities include an outdoor pool and hot tub, and a number of the staff members are from the pueblo. Another plus is that the rates here are somewhat lower than lodgings closer to the Plaza. ♦ 1501 Paseo de Peralta (at Cerrillos Rd). 982.1200, 800/825.9876; fax 984.2211

16 Luna Built as a movie theater in the 1940s, this huge, dark, black-lighted barn is 9,000 square feet, with a capacity of 800 people. Co-owner Scott Crane, who started the club with businessman Randy Mulkey, is a partner in the Ace of Clubs nightspots in Nashville and Knoxville, Tennessee. DJ-played dance music is featured on Friday and Saturday nights, live local and national acts play during the week; charges change accordingly. Among the better-known musicians who have played here is Michelle Shocked. Crane describes his club as "a cool and soulful, hip, rockin' little dance joint." Little it's not. No food is served, but the bar is about half a block long. ♦ Cover. Daily. 519 Cerrillos Rd (between W Manhattan Ave and Paseo de Peralta). 989.4888

Although New Mexico became a state in 1912, its Native Americans were not recognized as US citizens until 1924. They also were not permitted to vote until 1948.

Restaurants/Clubs: Red **Hotels:** Blue

Shops/ 🌳 Outdoors: Green **Sights/Culture:** Black

17 Santa Fe Travelodge $$ This standard chain motel is remarkable only because its 48 guest rooms are the lowest-priced accommodations (even so, the rates are no bargain) within walking distance of Santa Fe's downtown Plaza. You'll find the usual road-side amenities—air-conditioning, cable TV, and in-room phones, as well as a small outdoor heated pool (a rarity in water-scarce Northern New Mexico). Other affordable motels can be found farther east along Cerrillos Road, the commercial strip that is Santa Fe's busiest street. ◆ 646 Cerrillos Rd (between Paseo de Peralta and S Guadalupe St). 982.3551

18 O.J. Sarah's ★$ A sign above the entrance of this eatery declares it an "American Museum of Post-Hippie Culture." It is indeed a living museum because many of the customers at the checkered-cloth tables are graduates of the counterculture. This spot is particularly well-known for breakfasts of eggs or pancakes and lunches of sandwiches or salads, and vegetarian dishes are always available. The restaurant is serviceable, but somehow the food rarely arrives at your table hot. ◆ American ◆ M, F-Su breakfast, lunch, and dinner; Tu-Th breakfast and lunch. No credit cards accepted. 106 N Guadalupe St (between W Water and W San Francisco Sts). 984.1675

18 Corn Dance Cafe ★★★$$$ Santa Fe's only American Indian restaurant is a dream come true for proprietor Loretta Barrett Oden, a member of the Potawatomi Indian Tribe of Oklahoma. Following three years of travel to collect recipe ideas as healthy as they are deli-cious from tribes throughout the Americas, she bought this low-ceilinged, atmospheric res-taurant in 1994, redecorated it with contem-porary works by Indian artists, and created one of the most unusual and tantalizing menus in town. Try the whole Tlingit salmon with a rosehip puree or the sassafras wood-smoked bobwhite quails served with jicama, grilled red banana, papaya-lime salsa, and achiote cream. A house specialty is "Little Big Pies," a fat-free gourmet version of Indian tacos (similar to a thick-crust cheeseless pizza) with a choice of such toppings as Potawatomi prairie chicken and barbecued buffalo brisket. The buffalo and most other ingredients are raised on reser-vations around the US and flown in fresh. The staff, mostly American Indians, must surely be the most cheerful bunch of restaurant workers in Santa Fe. ◆ American Indian ◆ Daily lunch and dinner Mar-Sept; M, W-Su dinner, Su brunch Oct-Feb. 409 W Water St (at N Guadalupe St). 986.1662

Chances that a resident of Santa Fe is a "healer" of some kind: 1 in 52.

19 Vanessie ★★$$$ Don't step inside these doors unless your appetite is huge. Only the basics are served—beef, chicken, rack of lamb, and fresh fish—but the portions are gigantic, and everything is à la carte. If you order a baked potato, it's likely to weigh 22 ounces. A side salad is enormous, and so is dessert. A piano bar that gets rolling around 9PM and keeps going until 1AM or 2AM is a big draw. ◆ Continental ◆ Daily dinner. Reservations recommended. 434 W San Francisco St (between N Guadalupe St and Park Ave). 982.9966

20 Sakura ★★★$$ The best sushi in town is served here, at Santa Fe's second-oldest Japanese restaurant. The interior is divided into tables on one side and private tatami rooms on the other, with an outdoor patio facing a grassy courtyard in warm weather. Singles can eat on stools at a small bar and watch their sushi being prepared. The salmon teriyaki, the raw tuna dishes, and the California rolls are divine. This is an especially good bet at lunchtime. ◆ Japanese ◆ Tu-F lunch and dinner; Sa-Su dinner. Reservations recommended for dinner. 321 W San Francisco St (at N Guadalupe St). 983.5353

21 Shohko Cafe ★★★$$ Back in the mid-1970s, Shohko Fukuda and her husband, Hiro, opened Santa Fe's first Japanese restaurant at another location when anything but an American or New Mexican menu was risky business. But good food conquered provincialism as the city grew more cosmopolitan. Within a few years Shohko moved to this larger site, added a sushi bar, and is now the proud ancestor of the city's slew of Asian restaurants. The sushi is a bit tame (the rice is not pickled), but sure pleasers are the shrimp or vegetable tempura, the chicken teriyaki, and the yakitori dinner. ◆ Japanese ◆ M-F lunch and dinner; Sa dinner. Reservations recommended Friday and Saturday. 321 Johnson St (at N Guadalupe St). 983.7288

22 Allene Lapides Gallery An old and abandoned Spanish Baptist church was converted in 1988 into this sleek, modern, bright, and cavernous gallery of contemporary paintings and sculpture. Owner Lapides gives annual shows to celebrity photographer Herb Ritts, who moved to Santa Fe in 1991 and who happens to be her nephew. Also on display are ghostly black and white hand-rubbed paintings of horses by Joe Andoe, and works by Alex Katz and Ida Kohlmeyer, among others. ◆ M-Sa. 217 Johnson St (between Grant Ave and N Guadalupe St). 984.0191

23 Bert's Burger Bowl ★★$ One Location Worldwide is the proud boast of this locally owned fast-food place, as proclaimed on the T-shirts sold inside. Also sold here is the best fast food in Santa Fe. It has been popping off the grill in this very spot since the 1950s. The charbroiled hamburger with onions and green chile and the charbroiled cheeseburger with green chile are local legends, mainly because the hot green chile tastes fresh from the field. There are no tables inside and just a few stone ones out front, so it's best to pick up your order and head for **Santa Fe River Park,** or your own favorite hideaway, to eat. ♦ Hamburgers ♦ Daily lunch and dinner. 235 N Guadalupe St (at Catron Pl). 982.0215

24 Bagelmania ★★$ This bagel emporium is a bright spot located in a converted auto-body shop. Opened in 1992, it is a very popular downtown hangout. The influx of big-city residents used to this kind of food has continued unabated, and for the most part owners Jeff, Faurest, and Gary Schwartzberg are doing things right. (They should; the family has been in the business in New York since 1932.) Bagels and bialys are baked daily on the premises. The corned beef is lean, the chopped liver is the real thing—made fresh every day from chicken livers—and the atmosphere is casual and pleasant, the walls filled with black-and-white photos of the Big Apple and old-time movie stars. If the place is a bit noisy, well, that's New York for you. ♦ Deli ♦ Daily breakfast and lunch; W-Su dinner; bakery open daily. 520 Catron Pl (between Griffin and N Guadalupe Sts). 982.8900

25 Diego's Cafe ★★★$ Open since 1989, this is the newest of the three New Mexican restaurants run by one of the Maryol siblings, in this case sister Toni Hill, who is co-owner with husband John Hill. It's also the best. The New Mexican food, while not original in concept, is consistently excellent. Toni is one of the most cheerful hostesses in town, the prep work in the kitchen is careful, and the ingredients are top quality. The nacho appetizer is a meal in itself—it can be easily shared four ways—the chicken enchiladas are stuffed with juicy meat, and the hamburgers, humanely slim, are nonetheless cooked medium rare if that's how you order them. This is a big everyday favorite with local residents. ♦ New Mexican ♦ M-Sa lunch and dinner; Su lunch. De Vargas Center Mall (Guadalupe St, at Paseo de Peralta). 983.5101

25 Furr's Cafeteria ★$ Part of a Southwest chain, this cafeteria is better than most at quality control. There is a wide selection of small salads; entrées such as chicken-fried steak, baked cod, chopped steak, and roast beef; and assorted pies and cakes. The price is right—including all-you-can-eat meals for under $6—and the food is tasty. Alcohol is not available. ♦ American ♦ Daily lunch and dinner. De Vargas Center Mall (N Guadalupe St, at Paseo de Peralta). 988.4431. Also at: Coronado Shopping Center, 522 W Cordova Rd (at St. Francis Dr). 982.3816

26 Santa Fe National Cemetery One of the most stirring sights in Santa Fe occurs every evening when the sun, setting low in the west, shines on the slopes of this veterans' cemetery and nearly 18,000 identical white tombstones glow against the green hills in brilliant ranks. In the early days of World War II, New Mexico had more casualties per capita than any other state—mostly at Bataan in the Philippines—and these hills resemble a mini-Arlington. Just to the south is **Rosario Cemetery,** where most of the city's non-military funerals have been held for more than a century. ♦ 501 N Guadalupe St (off Paseo de Peralta, across from the De Vargas Center Mall). 988.6400

Bests

Arlene LewAllen
Director, Horwitch LewAllen Gallery

Having been in New Mexico for over two dozen years, my favorite restaurant is the **Bobcat Bite,** out on the Old Pecos Highway. It is run by the same family that raises their own beef, with the best burgers in New Mexico!

Heading up to Taos, I enjoy stopping at the **Embudo Station** for a home-cooked meal along with their homemade beer. You're right on the Rio Grande River, sitting among the cottonwoods.

Of course, anywhere you drive, you see the spectacular skies with the endless horizon. Always a wonder. The best spot in Santa Fe to see sunsets is the **Cross of the Martyrs.**

Larry Munson
Owner, The Munson Gallery

Celebrations Restaurant & Caterers—old adobe charm/outdoor patio dining.

Extraordinary mountain bike trails through the **Sangre de Cristo** mountain range.

Cultural events—world class opera, symphony, and art exhibitons.

Santa Fe diversity!

K.C. Compton
aka "Samurai Mama" newspaper columnist, *The New Mexican*

Evangelo's—Santa Fe's most famous dive bar. Play pool in the basement if you're ever lucky (or charming) enough to snag a table.

Ore House—Nothing beats coming here on Friday after work, drinking tequila shots on the balcony, and watching people come and go on the **Plaza.**

Pick up *carnitas* from **Roque's** and go sit on the monument in the Plaza and wait to see if some long-lost friend shows up. There's a saying that if you want to locate anyone in America, all you have to do is sit long enough on Santa Fe's Plaza.

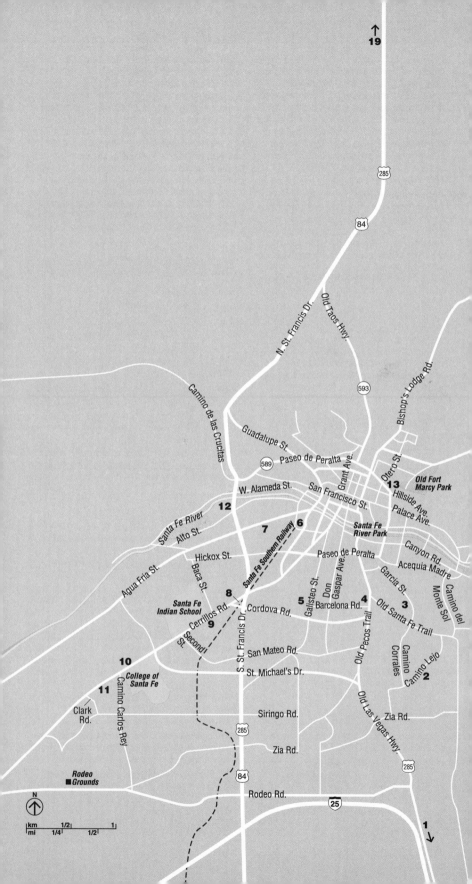

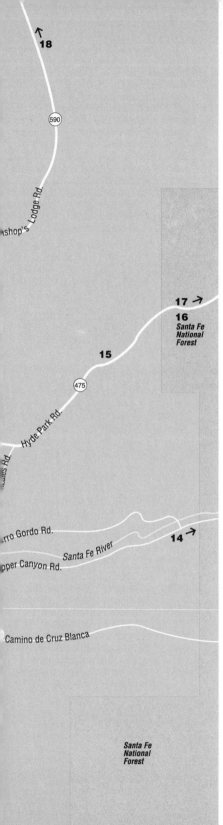

Additional Highlights of Santa Fe

Some of Santa Fe's premier attractions are situated just off the beaten path or a short drive away—including several you won't want to miss. The *Girard Collection* of toys, dolls, and masks from around the world set up in hilarious dioramas is the best permanent exhibit in town. It's housed in the **Museum of International Folk Art,** which is about two miles from the Plaza. Children will also enjoy the first-rate hands-on **Santa Fe Children's Museum.** In summer you might want to hit both ends of the economic scale in a single day by browsing through **Trader Jack's Flea Market** in the afternoon, then heading next door to the world-famous outdoor **Santa Fe Opera** at night (you'll need to get opera tickets in advance—and take along a warm sweater). In late September or early October, the most memorable experience is a drive into the **Santa Fe National Forest,** where whole mountainsides of aspen trees have turned bright gold. And in winter, outdoor types will want to head up the same road to the **Santa Fe Ski Basin,** where you won't be tempted to buy anything more than a lift ticket and a cup of hot chocolate.

1 Harry's Roadhouse ★★$$ Located on the southeastern outskirts of town, this old adobe house has been converted into the kind of restaurant where Santa Feans go to enjoy hefty portions of creative variations on familiar New Mexican dishes—without paying tourist prices. Typical menu items include meat loaf and a vegetarian burrito packed with black beans, eggplant, and tempeh (a soy product similar to tofu). Dine in one of several rooms in the cozy, old-fashioned interior or alfresco on the patio, which is set in a lovely, landscaped yard complete with an artificial stream cascading through a succession of pools in the shade of tall trees. ♦ Southwestern/American ♦ Daily breakfast, lunch, and dinner. Old Las Vegas Hwy (take Old Pecos Trail south to Old Las Vegas Hwy; continue south on Old Las Vegas Hwy about 1.5 miles). 989.4629

1 Bobcat Bite ★★$ Huge, sizzling green-chile cheeseburgers keep Santa Feans coming back for more at this long-established, rustic little eatery southeast of town on the old highway that parallels I-25. Known for its generous portions, "The Bite" also serves thick, juicy steaks for dinner. ♦ American/New Mexican ♦ Tu-Sa lunch and early dinner. Old Las Vegas Hwy (take Old Pecos Trail south to Old Las Vegas Hwy; continue south on Old Las Vegas Hwy about 2.5 miles). 983.5319

2 Wheelwright Museum of the American Indian A traditional Navajo hogan (a dwelling made of logs and mud) was the inspiration for the design of the eight-sided building housing this privately owned museum. The Navajo exhibits are especially strong, revealing much about Navajo daily life, though baskets, pottery, and jewelry from many other Southwestern tribes are also featured. The museum was created in 1937 by Mary Cabot Wheelwright, a wealthy New England heiress who traveled to the Navajo reservation in 1920 when she was 40 years old. While there she met Hosteen Klah, an influential Navajo singer and healer. Though they did not speak each other's language, they became colleagues and began to work together to preserve Navajo culture. The museum was originally called the **Museum of Navajo Ceremonial Art,** but the name was changed so that art from all American Indian tribes could be included. Recent exhibitions have included paintings by Navajo artist Frank Salcido Comes Charging, and *The Image Weavers: Contemporary Navajo Pictorial Textiles*. A research library contains manuscripts, rare photographs, and recordings of Navajo ceremonies. Hands-on demonstrations include sheep shearing, yarn spinning, natural dyeing, and traditional loom weaving. ♦ Donation requested. Daily. 704 Camino Lejo (off Old Santa Fe Trail near Camino del Monte Sol, behind the Museum of International Folk Art). 982.4636

2 Museum of International Folk Art There is little doubt that this is the best museum in Santa Fe. Founded in 1953 to show the work of craftspeople from around the world—just plain folks, as opposed to an artistic elite—it has undergone two significant expansions in recent years. The first was through the beneficence of the late **Alexander Girard,** the renowned architect and fabric designer who moved to Santa Fe shortly after World War II. **Girard** roamed the world seeking inspiration

for his work, and while doing so he became an inveterate collector of folk art, including handmade toys. By the time he quit globe-trotting, he had amassed more than 100,000 objects, which he donated to the museum. In 1982 he personally oversaw the construction of the **Girard Wing,** in which about 10,000 pieces from his collection are on permanent display—not on sterile shelves, but in intricate and colorful dioramas that he designed to show village life in the colonial US and in countries around the world (not to mention heaven and hell). Holes are cut in the dioramas at the level of children's eyes so they, too, can enjoy all the wonders and delicate humor.

In 1989 the museum opened the **Hispanic Heritage Wing,** which displays about 5,000 folk art objects dating from the 1600s to the present. Religious art, tinwork, jewelry, and textiles from Northern New Mexico and throughout the Spanish Colonial empire are emphasized. ♦ Admission. Daily May-Sept; Tu-Su Oct-Apr. 706 Camino Lejo (off Old Santa Fe Trail near Camino del Monte Sol). 827.6350

2 Museum of Indian Arts and Culture In 1931 the Laboratory of Anthropology was established in Santa Fe to preserve artifacts unearthed in New Mexico. Before land can be developed, the laboratory must certify that the site is not of historical significance. The state opened this museum in 1987 to display much of the collection of the adjacent laboratory, which numbers more than 50,000 artifacts. Rotating exhibits deal with every aspect of the Indian culture of the region from pre-Columbian days to the present. Artists in residence are often on the premises demonstrating the techniques of pottery, basketry, and other Indian arts. ♦ Admission. Daily May-Sept; Tu-Su Oct-Apr. 710 Camino Lejo (off Old Santa Fe Trail near Camino del Monte Sol). 827.6344

3 School of American Research This nonprofit institution for archaeological research has been prying into the secrets of the old Southwest since 1907. The school sponsors scholarly research and publications. A large collection of Indian art and textiles is housed inside. ♦ Fee. Tours F 2PM. Reservations required. 660 E Garcia St (between Arroyo Tenorio and Camino Corrales). 982.3584

SANTA FE
CHILDREN'S
MUSEUM

4 Santa Fe Children's Museum Big smiles and engrossed looks on the faces of happy children are the biggest attractions here. Hands-on exhibits let kids draw pictures, create their own cartoon movies, make magnetic constructions, divert water streams, and do many other things that are both fun and educational. They can even see live giant cockroaches—definitely not a hands-on display. Founded in 1987 by codirectors Ellen Biderman, Ellyn Feldman, and Londi Carbajal, this is a private, not-for-profit institution that children from roughly ages two to nine and their parents have a hard time leaving. ♦ Admission. Th-Su. 1050 Old Pecos Trail (at Barcelona Rd). 989.8359

5 Hollywood Vintage Would you like to own jewelry worn by Joan Crawford when she portrayed all those suffering rich women on screen in the 1940s? Or a suit that Marlene Dietrich donned when she knocked 'em dead with her voice and her style in the 1930s? Or baubles sported by glamour girl Jean Harlow in her sexy put-ons? The back room of a private home on Galisteo Street is set up like the boudoir of a 1930s movie star, with a large mirror, feather boas, dresses, shoes, and jewelry strewn about. Here Gayle McDonald, who was a movie costumer for the Disney studio and others for 12 years, sells pre-owned Hollywood clothing and jewelry, as well as other vintage clothing for women. The costumes on display change with the seasons, from summery crepes to winter woolens. Gayle's jewelry dates from 1910 to 1940, and one of her specialties is a huge assortment of Bakelite jewelry—which collectors obsess over—from the 1930s. Scattered about the boudoir are autographed photos of stars she's worked with (but those are not for sale). Gayle's husband, James "Scotty" McDonald, a sculptor who works with bronze and sometimes works in the backyard, has shows in regional galleries. ♦ Call for hours and directions. 986.3935

6 Santa Fe Southern Railway The re-creation of an old-time railroad trip through the Southwest is available on this small privately owned railway that opened in 1992. The line hauls freight from Santa Fe and meets with the main line at the village of Lamy, 20 miles to the south. Passengers ride in an old **Santa Fe Railroad** caboose that holds 16 people as the train winds its way through the hilly landscape for one and a half hours. Most people eat lunch at the **Legal Tender** restaurant (★★$$; 100 Main St, 466.8425) in Lamy (a one-street town), or bring a picnic. ♦ Fee. Departs M, W, F at 11AM and returns to Santa Fe at 4PM. Reservations recommended. 410 S Guadalupe St (just south of Montezuma Ave). 989.8600

7 Ark Books Santa Fe is known for its large "New Age" population, from serious astrologers and psychics to crystal healers, UFOlogists and assorted flaky characters. This bookstore is the town's New Age information clearinghouse. Besides a full range of the latest books on everything from holistic health

to shamanism, the occult and Eastern religions, there is a good selection of hard-to-find audio tapes, incense, and offbeat gift items. A bulletin board contains fliers pinned up by many local teachers, healers, and psychics, peddling their services and announcing their upcoming workshops. ♦ 133 Romero St (between W Manhattan Ave and Agua Fria St). 988.3709

8 Wild Oats Community Market One of the most popular grocery stores in town and the perfect place to pick up an extraordinary picnic lunch, this market stocks an amazing array of health and gourmet food items, locally made food products, exotic vegetables, grains in bulk, dietary supplements, natural personal care products, Chinese herbs, and gift items from cookware and incense to "Save the Rainforest" T-shirts. There is also a full deli featuring sandwiches, a salad bar, and such ready-made dishes as tabbouleh and guacamole. The indoor dining counter and outdoor tables make this a popular local gathering place. A licensed massage therapist is on duty at all times, offering refreshing, low-cost 15-minute massages right in the middle of the busy store. ♦ Daily 8AM-11PM. 1090 S St. Francis Dr (at Cordova Rd). 983.5333. Also at: St. Michael's Village (1708 Llano St, at St. Michael's Dr). 473.4943

9 Tecolote Cafe ★★$ This plain-and-simple little coffee shop is where locals go for great breakfasts. Menu choices range from the perennial New Mexican favorite, *huevos rancheros* (fried eggs served on a corn tortilla, and smothered in chile salsa), to more familiar fare including overstuffed omelettes, flapjacks with maple syrup, and biscuits and gravy. Lunch features the best chicken-fried steak in town, as well as a standard selection of New Mexican dishes; the green-chile stew is exceptionally good. ♦ American/New Mexican ♦ Tu-Su breakfast and lunch. 1203 Cerrillos Rd (at Baca St). 988.1362

10 Baja Taco ★★$ Set inconspicuously beside the city's most traffic-clogged street, this tiny take-out place hardly looks like it would be worth driving out of your way for, but locals will tell you that they serve some of the best green chile around—at some of the best prices. Stock up on the generous-sized burritos, soft tacos, and enchiladas (one will make a meal), and head for the mountains, or at least the nearest park, to enjoy a spicy picnic. ♦ New Mexican ♦ Daily lunch and dinner. 2621 Cerrillos Rd (between Maez Rd and Maclovia St). 438.7196, 471.8762 (to place an order)

There are 59 churches in Santa Fe.

Restaurants/Clubs: Red	**Hotels:** Blue
Shops/ ♠ Outdoors: Green	**Sights/Culture:** Black

Tinseltown among the Tumbleweeds

The rolling, piñon-studded hills and sandy arroyos of Northern New Mexico have long attracted filmmakers in search of a place to shoot old- and new-fashioned Westerns. Among the films that brought actors and camera crews to the Santa Fe/Taos/Albuquerque area are the following:

Billy Jack (1971) Tom Laughlin and Delores Taylor star in this quirky modern classic about a Vietnam vet who cares for wild horses and a wild teenager.

Butch and Sundance: The Early Days (1979) This "prequel" to the 1969 blockbuster (below) features Tom Berenger and William Katt.

Butch Cassidy and the Sundance Kid (1969) Paul Newman and Robert Redford dashingly rob their way through the Southwest and into Central and South America, until showdown time in Bolivia.

City Slickers (1991) Billy Crystal, among others, is an urbanite who signs on to a cattle drive for his vacation.

Easy Rider (1969) This tough and tender road movie about two lost souls on motorbikes stars Peter Fonda and Dennis Hopper.

Every Which Way But Loose (1978) Clint Eastwood plays the brawling trucker who wins a brawling orangutan in a prize fight.

Fool for Love (1985) Based on a Sam Shephard play and featuring him along with Kim Basinger, Randy Quaid, and Harry Dean Stanton, this heavy drama-in-a-hotel deals with incest between half-siblings.

The Fortune (1975) This thriller about a rich heiress, set in the 1920s, stars Jack Nicholson, Warren Beatty, and Stockard Channing.

Indian Day School (1898) This 19th-century film was directed by inventor Thomas Alva Edison and se at the **Isleta Pueblo.**

The Man Who Fell to Earth (1976) David Bowie is the tragic protagonist of this visitor-from-another-planet science fiction film.

The Milagro Beanfield War (1988) Robert Redford directed this tale of a battle over precious land in Nev Mexico starring Sonia Braga and John Heard.

The Muppet Movie (1979) Yes, even Kermit the Frog has visited New Mexico—on his way to Hollywood.

Oklahoma! (1955) As in the famous stage version, cowhands woo women with song and dance in the dusty West; this production starred Shirley Jones, Gordon Macrae, and Rod Steiger.

Outrageous Fortune (1987) Bette Midler competes with a female rival for a lover; the FBI and CIA want him, too.

Silkwood (1983) Meryl Streep plays Karen Silkwood a real-life victim of radiation and corporate conspiracy; Cher plays a morgue cosmetician.

Twins (1988) A perfect (genetically engineered) Arnold Schwarzenegger discovers he has an all-too-imperfect "twin" (Danny DeVito).

11 Jackalope Pottery This huge, sprawling Mexican market created in 1975 by Darby McQuade showcases every kind of craft known to Mexico, where McQuade has his own crew of buyers. Vast amounts of folk art arrive by the tractor-trailer load, including animal pottery, and weavings. Other Latin American countries are represented as well. More than just a place to shop, there's also a prairie dog village, an aviary, demonstrations by artisans from Mexico, strolling musicians, and a pleasant and inexpensive outdoor cafe here. ♦ Daily. 2820 Cerrillos Rd (between Camino Carlos Rey and Clark Rd). 471.8539. Also at: 221 Galisteo St (at W Alameda St). 989.7494

12 Seckler Studio/Monteverde Gallery Orange sparks fly and grinding wheels whine indoors and out as four goggled workers translate into steel the sculptural designs of Frank H. Seckler—wonderful Indian mythic figures based on petroglyphs. They are crafted into unusual tables, chairs, screens, light fixtures, wall hangings, and freestanding steel figures. Seckler spent most of his life in the cattle and meat-packing business in Colorado and sculpted as an avocation for 20 years. He moved to New Mexico and started working full time in 1990, opening a studio in Taos late in 1991 and one in Santa Fe a year later. Today galleries throughout the country show his work. His son, Frank B. Seckler (don't call him junior), runs the Taos studio. Adjacent to the working area is the **Monteverde Gallery**—which sells the pieces—run by the artist's wife, Magdalena Monteverde, who hails from the Canary Islands and Spain. She also shows paintings by local artists. Visitors are welcome. ♦ Daily. 150 S St. Francis Dr (at Alto St). 989.4371

13 Cross of the Martyrs During the 1680 Pueblo Revolt against Spanish domination, more than 20 Franciscan priests were killed. A large cross atop a hill above the city is dedicated to their memory. Plaques telling the history of Santa Fe are posted along a brick walkway that leads up the hill. At the top you get a bird's-eye view of the city and can see the broad sweep of three mountain ranges that rim the plateau: the Sangre de Cristos immediately to the northeast, the Jemez 40 miles to the west, and the Sandias, near Albuquerque, 60 miles to the south. ♦ Walkway begins at Paseo de Peralta (between Otero St and Hillside Ave)

14 Randall Davey Audubon Center In 1847, when New Mexico became a US territory, a sawmill was built on what is now Upper Canyon Road to provide planks for an army establishment at nearby Fort Marcy. Water diverted from the Santa Fe River powered the mill. When the mill was closed in 1856, the property was transformed into a residence with several outbuildings in a rolling, wooded area. A number of families lived here until it was purchased in 1920 by painter Randall Davey, who had just moved to Santa Fe from the East. Davey used the original mill building, which had 16-inch-thick stone walls, as his home, and a former mill storeroom as his painting studio. He lived here until he was killed in an automobile accident in 1964. The Davey home and studio remain intact amid the greenery, and many of his paintings are on display.

The property is now owned by the National Audubon Society and is maintained as a 135-acre wildlife refuge and environmental education center. More than one hundred bird species have been observed at the refuge in Santa Fe Canyon, including, most typically, nuthatches, goldfinches, warblers, stellar jays, brown creepers, and yellow-bellied sapsuckers. Mammals such as raccoon, coyotes, black bears, mule deer, bobcats, and mountain lions sometimes pay visits. The visitor center bookstore specializes in natural history. Call for schedules of tours of the Davey home. ◆ Donation requested. Daily May–mid Nov; M-F mid-Nov–Apr. 1800 Upper Canyon Rd (beyond the pavement's end). 983.4609

The only successful removal of European colonists in North America by indigenous people began on 10 August 1680. On that day, thousands of New Mexico Pueblo Indians joined Popé, a San Juan Pueblo Indian who was whipped publicly by Franciscan friars for practicing his native religion, in a bloody rebellion against the Spanish colonists. Now known as the Pueblo Revolt, the Native American revolutionaries succeeded in forcing the Spanish out of New Mexico. The Spaniards retreated south to El Paso and did not return to the area until 1692.

15 Ten Thousand Waves Japanese Health Spa When Duke Klauck came to this city in 1978, he brought with him a dream of building a traditional Japanese *onsen* (outdoor hot springs resort) in the high desert setting of Santa Fe. A hot springs connoisseur and avid fan of Japanese culture, Klauck had spent years traveling to more than 250 hot springs around the US as well as to the famous Japanese *onsens* of places like Kyoto and Beppu. To the Japanese, soaking in hot teakwood tubs is a daily ritual, but to Klauck's knowledge no one in America had ever simulated the *onsen* setting. Purchasing a prime parcel in the city's north hills, Klauck set out to see if the legendary three cultures of Santa Fe were ready for a fourth.

Combining the best of Japan and New Mexico, Klauck began building his business according to Japanese design, substituting native New Mexican materials such as adobe and aspen wood for hard-to-get Japanese mud-wattle and bamboo. Today East meets West here in a simple Japanese-style building that sits quietly at 8,000 feet in the piñon-shrouded hills above Santa Fe. Ten exotically designed outdoor hot tubs dot the hillsides. Steamy saunas and icy cold plunges also await adventurous bathers who flock to the bathhouse in all kinds of weather to don kimonos and follow wilderness footpaths to tubs that overlook Santa Fe's fabled mountain views.

But "The Waves," as locals know it, boasts more than bathing. With some 60 massage therapists on hand, visitors choose from everything from soothing Swedish to *watsu* (underwater) massage, as well as facials, herbal wraps, and more. A small retail area features healthy snacks, kimonos, T-shirts, and skin-care products. And after bathing or massage, clients convene to a cozy reception area or outdoor deck where they can sip Japanese tea and coo over the handsome bathhouse dog, Kojiro, a 110-pound Japanese Akita and a practicing Buddhist, according to Klauck.

Located on the road to the Santa Fe ski area, this is a favorite with the après-ski set, who like to warm up here after a hard day on the slopes. And with its relaxing ambience and moonlit vistas, "The Waves" consistently rates with voters in the local weekly's annual "Best of Santa Fe" poll as the "most romantic" getaway in the city. Nature-lovers may even spy a jackrabbit or two prancing about the mountain property. ♦ Daily; hours vary. Reservations recommended. Hyde Park Rd (off Washington Ave), 3.5 miles from Santa Fe. 982.9304

16 Santa Fe National Forest/Hyde Memorial State Park For one of the most beautiful sights in the world, visit Santa Fe in late September and early October when the aspen trees that cover the mountain slopes turn a bright burnished gold. Many visitors come just to drive the winding mountain road and walk amid this stunning natural beauty. The largest pull-over spot is known, appropriately, as Aspen Vista. You can park there and walk among the golden coinlike leaves. Twelve miles northeast of Santa Fe on Ski Basin Road, the state park offers picnic tables, camping grounds, clear mountain streams, and 350 acres of mountain slopes crisscrossed with hiking trails. It is set in the national forest, which contains thousands of acres of slopes covered with pine and aspen trees and dotted with hiking trails. **Windsor Trail** is the main path. Detailed maps of the hiking trails are available from the **Santa Fe National Forest Headquarters** (1220 St. Francis Dr, Santa Fe, 988.6940). ♦ Take Hyde Park Rd north from Santa Fe and follow the signs

17 Santa Fe Ski Basin Thousands of skiers descend on Santa Fe in the winter months, creating a second visitor season for the city. This basin, at 12,000 feet, is one of the highest ski slopes in the country. From the peak you can see 80,000 square miles of mountain ranges and high desert. Most of the runs at the ski basin are for intermediates and beginners, but several, including **Wizard, Parachute, Big Rocks,** and **Tequila Sunrise,** will challenge even the most advanced skiers. (Taos Ski Valley, with its more difficult runs, draws a greater number of experienced skiers.) The ski basin originated in the 1930s when a Denver designer, Graeme McGowen, suggested that runs could be built along Indian trails and sheep trails. The Civilian Conservation Corps built a road to **Hyde Park** and a stone lodge that now houses the **Evergreen Restaurant** (★★$$$; Hyde Park Rd, 984.8190). The first chairlift was built at the present site in the 1950s, using surplus seats from a B-24 bomber.

Today there are four modern lifts and 39 downhill trails—20 percent for beginners, 40 percent for intermediates, and 40 percent for advanced skiers. The runs are protected from the winds by tree cover and the angle of the mountain and offer fine family skiing. The average annual snowfall on the slopes is 225 inches. Snowmaking equipment can supply about 25 percent of the slopes. Skis are available for rent at the base of the mountain as well as in town. Cross-country skiing is also plentiful in the area. Sledding and riding inner tubes—which is great fun for the kids— is permitted in **Hyde Park,** below the ski basin. In summer the ski lifts run to show people the scenic views. ♦ Snow permitting, the season runs from Thanksgiving to Easter. Ski Basin Rd (NM 475, 15 miles northeast of Santa Fe). 982.4429, snow report 983.9155

18 Bishop's Lodge $$$$ In the 19th century Archbishop Lamy, whose footprints seem to be everywhere in Santa Fe, had a private retreat, complete with a personal chapel, in the hills a few miles north of town. Years later Joseph Pulitzer bought the rolling parcel of land as a summer home for the family. In 1917 James R. Thorpe of Denver purchased it and laid the foundation for what was to become this thousand-acre full-service resort that offers four tennis courts, horseback riding (more than 60 steeds), swimming, and skeet-shooting amid rolling green hills. The lodge, which is still owned by the Thorpe family, offers 88 Southwestern-style guest rooms and suites. Some suites have fireplaces and terraces. The restaurant serves all three meals (jackets and dresses are required at dinner), and rooms can be booked on either the American or the European plan. Archbishop Lamy's chapel still stands on the property. ♦ Closed January-March. Bishop's Lodge Rd (NM 590, about 3.5 miles north of Santa Fe). 983.6377, 800/732.2240; fax 989.8739

M. BLUM

18 Shidoni Foundry For people who appreciate sculpture, a visit here is a must on any trip to Santa Fe. Large and small works in a variety of media, such as the castings by Jim Amaral illustrated above, are on display year-round in an outdoor sculpture garden set on green lawns against the backdrop of the Sangre de Cristo Mountains. A newer 5,000-square-foot indoor gallery features sleek contemporary works. Tommy Hicks, a sculptor, founded the place in 1971, on an eight-acre apple orchard in Tesuque, an upscale adobe suburb. It was begun as a foundry and still functions in that capacity. The pouring of molten bronze at a temperature of 2,000 degrees into ceramic shell molds can be viewed by visitors every Saturday, as sculptors transform miniature studies into larger bronze works. Mold making, sand casting, and lost-wax casting are also practiced on the premises. ♦ M–Sa. Bishop's Lodge Rd, Tesuque (5 miles north of Santa Fe). 988.8001

18 Rancho Encantado $$$$ In 1968 Betty Egan left her home in Ohio, moved to New Mexico, and purchased an old lodge in Tesuque. She turned her new home into a dude ranch and named it **Rancho Encantado** (Spanish for Enchanted Ranch). The secluded ranch is still flourishing and growing bigger. The main lodge was built in 1932 and contains Southwestern-style bedrooms. An assortment of cottages and casitas (bungalows) with bedrooms, living rooms, fireplaces, and refrigerators have been added to the property over the years, making a total of 56 guest accommodations. The 168-acre, year-round resort offers swimming, tennis, and horse-back riding. The restaurant serves breakfast, lunch, and dinner. Notables who've stayed here include Princess Caroline, Robert Redford, and the Dalai Lama. Betty Egan died in 1992, but her family, led by son John Egan, a former Santa Fe city councilor, continues to run things. A couple of years ago he sold a TV producer who stayed here on the idea of a series based on his mother's adventures when she created the ranch. La-La-Land liked the idea and immediately updated the story to the chic 1990s, which made no sense at all. A pilot movie was filmed in the region in 1992—under the title *Rio Shannon* (the family has Irish roots)—but had not yet been shown at press time, nor had a TV series been scheduled. ♦ NM 592, Tesuque (about 8 miles north of Santa Fe). 982.3537, 800/722.9339; fax 983.8269

19 Santa Fe Opera From early July to late August, the crystal tones of some of the world's best operatic voices pierce the night at this open-air amphitheater situated atop a hill seven miles north of the city. It is home to one of the best-known companies in the country. Founded in 1956 by general director John Crosby, the company has featured many top stars from New York's Metropolitan Opera and elsewhere. Young talents often perform here for modest pay to gain exposure and the chance to spend the summer in Santa Fe, then return here when they are major names. Five works are performed in repertory each summer—usually four classics, such as *Don Giovanni* or *Der Rosenkavalier,* and one world or US premiere of a contemporary piece; new works are also commissioned. Both the sight lines and the acoustics are excellent. The stage and some of the seats are beneath a curving roof; other seats are open to the elements, which are sometimes cold and wet. A heavy jacket or a blanket is always advisable, even in the covered sections, because the temperature drops quickly after dark. Many performances are sold out in advance, even though tickets are expensive. Much cheaper standing-room tickets are also available. Some folks use a night at the opera as a chance to air out their tuxedos; others attend in jeans. At press time, there were plans to add additional seats and to lengthen the roof in order to provide shelter for all the amphitheater's seats. **Polshek & Partners** of New York, the architects that handled the renovation of New York City's Carnegie Hall, were in charge of the refurbishment. ♦ July–late Aug. Hwy 84-285 (7 miles north of Santa Fe). 986.5955, box office 986.5900

19 Trader Jack's Flea Market One person's junk is another person's treasure. That's the theory behind all flea markets, and this huge outdoor garage sale operated since the 1970s by Jack Daniels (his real name) is no exception. Upwards of 500 vendors cram the dusty acreage every weekend, hawking everything from used paperback books and old magazines for a dime or a quarter to handmade furniture and antiques going for several hundred dollars. Old tools, cheap jewelry, and used boots and clothing abound in every direction while thousands of bargain hunters prowl and haggle. Situated on Tesuque Indian land across from the soaring Sangre de Cristos and just north of the **Santa Fe Opera,** this is a fun place to spend an hour or two—you never know what you might find. ♦ F–Su. Weather permitting, the market operates roughly from Easter to Thanksgiving. Hwy 84-285 (8 miles north of Santa Fe)

Many Native Americans living in the New Mexican pueblos say that water always tastes better when you drink it out of an *olla* (a clay water jar).

Restaurants/Clubs: Red   **Hotels:** Blue
Shops/ 🌿 Outdoors: Green   **Sights/Culture:** Black

Bests

Mark Miller
Owner/Chef, Coyote Cafe, Santa Fe

In Santa Fe:

Foreign magazines and newspapers at **Downtown Subscriptions.**

Hot tub and massage at **Ten Thousand Waves.**

Flamenco dancing by Maria Benitez at the **Picacho Plaza Hotel** in the summer.

The flea market on Saturday outside of Santa Fe.

Museum of International Folk Art—I love all the displays and colors. It's a great place to take children. A must!

Center for Contemporary Arts—Remarkably good foreign films, especially for a small town.

Sunset at the **Opera House**—Santa Fe has the best sunsets.

Lunch at **Escalera.**

Dinner at **Ristorante La Traviata**—Ask for extra red chile in the pasta.

Randolph J. Forrester
Operations Director, New Mexico Arts Division

Summer officially begins with Opening Night at the **Santa Fe Opera.** This is such a big do that the pre-opera activities—tailgate and parking lot dinners, champagne "on the house," and people watching—are carried live on the radio. This is the fashion get-up event of the year and the fact that it takes place at the most beautiful opera venue in the world makes this the hottest ticket in town. If you love waltzing, stick around after the performance. The set is cleared away and the symphony plays waltzes into the wee hours of the morning.

The following week pull out your cowboy boots and head to the Rodeo. Ty Murray and the best of the rest buck into town for four days of rodeoing. If you want to see the toughest women in the country, check out the All Women Rodeo that buckaroos into town two weeks later.

Each year the Santa Fe Chamber Music Festival and the **Desert Chorale** combine their talents for two joint performances. The progeny of this musical marriage is so beautiful that it is other-worldly. Order tickets early, as these are the second hottest tickets of the summer.

Santa Fe was voted the most romantic city in the United States a while back. And it's true. Have a romantic lunch in the enclosed courtyard at **La Casa Sena,** off East Palace Avenue. Or have a real New Mexican lunch at the mucho-colorful **Shed,** just a stroll away under the portal. Their mocha cake is one of the best desserts in town. Have margaritas at the **Casa Sena Cantina,** where your waiter sings Broadway tunes between servings. After this climb the steps to **Ten Thousand Waves,** where you can soak in Japanese baths under Coyote's stars.

Good eats are abundant in Santa Fe. **Tecolote Cafe** and **Pasqual's** get best marks for breakfast. While I generally boycott buffets, I go out of my way for the Asian-spiced foods at **India Palace,** on Don Gaspar.

You can tell fall is here when the green chile crop comes in from Hatch. These chiles are roasted in parking lots and roadside stands, coating the air with a tangy pungency that jump starts the salivary glands.

The week before Labor Day, Fiesta begins. If you want to see Santa Fe poke fun at itself, catch the melodrama put on by the **Santa Fe Community Theater.** For over 70 years, a secret committee of playwrights has gotten together to spoof the latest antics in the City Different.

For good old-fashioned pagan rituals, it's hard to beat the Burning of Zozobra. This closes Fiesta activities, and more people attend this event than live in Santa Fe. After much eating, drinking, and dancing, Zozobra, a 3-story giant representing gloom, is touched by the Little Fire People, with sparks and flames crackling and popping and people frolicking.

Christmas in Santa Fe is special. Snow blankets the adobe houses and hotels. Walk **Canyon Road** on Christmas Eve, when thousands of *luminaria* and *farolitos* line the streets and juniper and piñon fires perfume the night air.

Brown Town. The City Different. Santa Fe. These are just some of the monikers for our town's official name—*La Villa de Real de Santa Fe de San Francisco de Assis.*

Don Moya
Waiter

Any seat at the **Santa Fe Opera.**

Pasta and Chianti on the portal at **Ristorante La Traviata.**

Movies at the **Lensic Theatre.**

Eating corn cakes and squash blossoms at the counter in **Coyote Cafe.**

Watching the sunset from the **Bell Tower Bar** at La **Fonda Hotel.**

Watsu massage at **Ten Thousand Waves.**

Taking a motorcycle ride to view all of the aspens in the fall.

The Spanish Market on the **Plaza** in July.

Skiing at **Taos Ski Valley.**

The No. six, onion rings, and a root beer at **Bert's Burger Bowl.**

Dancing to the Lost Souls at **Luna.**

Foreign flicks at the **Center for Contemporary Arts.**

Eating massive burgers and steaks at **Bobcat Bite.**

Sipping Manhattans at **Edge.**

Martin L. Platt
Artistic Director, Santa Fe Stage Company

Breakfast at **Harry's Roadhouse.** Coffee that makes your hair stand on end, and creative, quirky cooking that gets the day off to a Santa Fe start.

A minimassage at **Wild Oats** market. The perfect oasis for mini-angst attacks—and you can get a great Hurry Curry sandwich as a treat afterwards.

A night at the **Santa Fe Opera,** under the stars or sometimes in the pouring rain. You may love it, you may get angry at the annoying staging by some of the German, English, and American directors hired by General Director John Crosby, but you'll never be neutral. Isn't that what art is all about?

Trader Jack's Flea Market, next to the Opera. We know it annoys John Crosby that it's his neighbor, but this is one of the great flea markets in America. Everything from dented pots and pans to the finest Indian jewels.

The cinema at the **Center for Contemporary Arts** (located behind the **Santa Fe Children's Museum**), which shows foreign films that even I have never heard of.

Looking up at the stars in the clear, high desert air every night.

Meat loaf and a pint of black and tan at **Zia Diner,** and if I'm feeling particularly flush, almost anything on the menu at **Santacafe.**

The Pet Parade on the Saturday morning of Fiesta de Santa Fe (held on the weekend after Labor Day).

Best sport in Santa Fe? Listening to residents (even those who just bought their house yesterday) complain about tourists and the influx of new residents.

Rand B. Lee
Writer/Intuitive Counselor/Psychic Consultant in Santa Fe

Bandelier National Park and the ancient **Puye Cliff Dwellings,** a short trip north of Santa Fe. Approach with reverence; Anasazi ghosts are everywhere.

The **Farmers' Market** at **Sanbusco Market Center** on Tuesday and Saturday from late spring to fall. Don't miss the chiles, flowers, honey, apricots, Jake's melons, homemade jams, excited laughter, fresh bread smells, and the neighborly Spanish and English mixed. "One hundred percent organic, ma'am!" Get there by 7:30AM.

The duck spring rolls at **Santacafe.** Heaven can wait. So will you, if you don't make a reservation.

Greg Darmont. In a city of massage therapist and "energy workers," he's a loving-hearted expert.

Flea markets on weekends from late spring to fall. The big one near the **Santa Fe Opera** and the little one on Cerrillos Road. Rich folks go to the big one; poor folks go to the little one; smart folks hit both.

Lamy, a small town that's 20 minutes south of Santa Fe. For peace and quiet and big skies; an old train station (**Amtrak** still runs through here); and a 19th-century whorehouse that is now a restaurant. Check out the wild hollyhocks come summertime.

The lobby of **La Fonda Hotel** on the **Plaza.** Delightful for people-watching; even we jaded locals enjoy dropping in now and again.

Watching them burn Zozobra at the fall Fiesta. A terrifying, exhilarating, cathartic, Christianized pagan scapegoat ritual. It's very easy to imagine the days when it wasn't effigies that were sacrificed.

The **Oldest House** and the oldest church, the **San Miguel Mission,** located off the Plaza. Spooky. Years of tourism have done nothing to drain these places of their numinous slumbering quality.

Alberto Calascione
Owner/Chef, Ristorante La Traviata, Santa Fe

Spring and especially fall are the best seasons to visit Santa Fe.

Don't miss New Mexico's national parks and monuments.

Santa Fe is indeed a wonderful town for culture.

Check out the great folk art and fine art museums.

Summer is a good time for chamber music and opera.

Ski here in the winter. Last winter Santa Fe had the best skiing in the country for well over a month.

Off-season the **Sangre de Cristo** and **Jemez Mountains** provide excellent hiking trails for people who enjoy nature.

A pungent tea made from osha, the root of a celery-like plant that grows wild in high valleys of the Sangre de Cristo Mountains, is widely used by New Mexicans as a cure for the common cold. The dried root is sold in most Santa Fe, Taos, and Albuquerque grocery stores and pharmacies.

The howling coyote, that ubiquitous symbol of Santa Fe style, may be cute to some, but to others, coyote art is the king of cliché. Stamped out by the thousands, coyote caricatures come in assorted pastel hues with Western kerchiefs around their necks and generally portray a seated coyote baying, presumably, at the moon. But in 1988, after seeing the kitschy critters in shops and galleries throughout Santa Fe, local artist Randy Bridgens founded the Santa Fe Society for the Prevention of Visual Cruelty to Humans. Claiming the coyotes are a blot on the landscape of the city's fine-arts scene, society members seek to put a muzzle on the proliferating critters and spend time plastering posters and bumper stickers about town. Their motto: "Just say no to coyote art."

Santa Fe Day Trips

No visit to Santa Fe is complete without at least one drive into the countryside. Only there can you get the feel of what the ancient Indians, the Spanish conquistadores, and eventually the Anglo artists saw in this region. Within easy reach of Santa Fe are small Hispanic towns, the landscape near **Abiquiu** that Georgia O'Keeffe loved so much, **The Downs at Santa Fe** racetrack, and six of the **Eight Northern Pueblos** (the other two are featured in the "Additional Highlights of Taos and Day Trips" chapter). Choose any of these destinations and you are likely to see piñon-studded hills, soaring peaks, and pine-covered mountains. If possible, make the return trip in the late afternoon or early evening, as the sun is sinking in the west—that's when the land is often illuminated with a special glow.

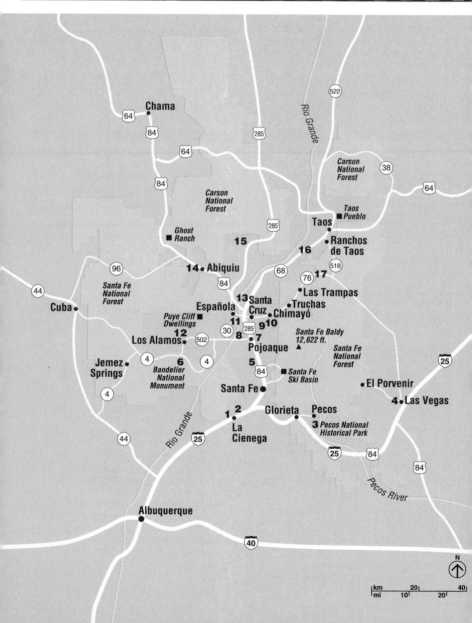

1 Las Golondrinas A 200-acre ranch in La Cienega, about 17 miles south of Santa Fe, **El Rancho de las Golondrinas** (the Ranch of the Swallows) is a time capsule of the region's Hispanic past. About 70 buildings, some original, some restored, indicate what life was like in the 18th and 19th centuries at this way station on El Camino Real. The hacienda was the first stop for wagons heading south from Santa Fe and the last one for those coming into town from Mexico. Several weekends during the year—at the spring, summer, and harvest festivals—volunteers dress up in traditional costumes and demonstrate to visitors the old ways of baking bread, making soap, drying chile, milling flour—in general re-creating a lifestyle long gone. This "living museum" is open from June through August for self-guided tours and in April, May, September, and October for guided tours. The place really springs to life on the festival weekends (call for schedules). The biggest of them, the Harvest Festival, coincides with the Albuquerque Balloon Fiesta in early October. ♦ Admission. W-Su Apr-Oct. Take I-25 south from Santa Fe to the Racetrack exit and follow the signs. 471.2261

2 The Downs at Santa Fe Not since 1980, when a big, gray, two-year-old colt named Pass the Tab was the premier horse at Santa Fe's grade III racetrack, has a horse as good as he run at Santa Fe. With pari-mutuel betting approved in several neighboring states, including Oklahoma and Texas, the quality of local racehorses has declined. Yet this is still an attractive small-town track, with the Sangre de Cristo Mountains forming a lovely backdrop for the mix of thoroughbred and quarterhorse races. It's very much a family track—not the least bit sleazy—with kids running around and carnival rides sometimes offered on the grassy infield. Ten or 11 races a day are held four days a week from mid-June through Labor Day. (From January through May, the track offers off-track betting and simulcasting of racing in Albuquerque.) Seating is divided between general admission, the **Turf Club** (with a concession stand and cocktail service), and the **Jockey Club** (★$$) (a full restaurant near the finish line). ♦ Fee. W, F-Su. Frontage Rd (take I-25 south to exit 599, about 20 minutes driving time from the Plaza). 471.3311

3 Pecos National Historical Park In a valley set among rolling green hills about 25 miles east of Santa Fe are the ruins of a once-flourishing Indian pueblo. The Pecos Indians traded with the pueblos along the Rio Grande—Santa Fe's Canyon Road was part of an Indian trail that led here—as well as with the Plains Indians farther east. Spanish explorer Coronado's men visited **Pecos Pueblo** in 1541. In the 1620s the Franciscans came and built a mission church to convert the Indians. The last residents abandoned the pueblo in 1838, for reasons not entirely clear; historians suspect that disease may have wiped out much of the population. Today the ruins, partly restored and partly in their original condition, are a national historical park. A separate, smaller unit of the park—between the villages of Pecos and Glorieta—preserves part of the Glorieta Battlefield, site of the westernmost military action of the US Civil War. ♦ Admission. Daily. Take I-25 to exit 299 or 307, 25 miles southeast of Santa Fe. 757.6414

4 Las Vegas If the chic development of Santa Fe begins to wear thin, the perfect antidote is an hour's drive to Las Vegas, New Mexico. There are no casinos here, no strip shows. This is an off-the-tourist-trail town, filled with wonderful old architectural relics, that is steeped in reality—the kind of reality symbolized by the state's mental hospital; a gritty, abandoned railroad area; bars for the drinking class; and the nonprestigious **New Mexico Highlands University.** In the 1880s the railroad that had bypassed Santa Fe ran through Las Vegas and made it a bustling commercial hub. It attracted at one time or another all the legendary bad guys of the era—not only Billy the Kid, but outlaws with names like Flapjack Bill, Rattlesnake Sam, Jimmie the Duck, and their attendant ladies, including Nervous Jessie, Careless Ida, and Lazy Liz. Hangings of such folks were not uncommon here. But time eventually passed the city by. Las Vegas now has 15,000 inhabitants who seem to be happy living in the past.

A visit here is worthwhile primarily because of the preservation of almost 900 buildings made of stone, brick, and wood in every color and architectural style; many are Italianate Commercial in design. The city is a welcome contrast to the stark adobe routine of most of Northern New Mexico. Among the attractions on the town plaza are the **Plaza Hotel** ($$; 425.3591, 800/328.1882), built in 1881 and renovated to preserve its historic look, and several cafes serving good New Mexican food. The excellent **Los Artesanos** bookstore (220 N Old Town Plaza, 425.8331)—run forever by

Diana and Joe Stein, who will be happy to pass the time with you—has an intriguing collection of old and new books on the Southwest. The shop (illustrated on page 73) is open Tuesday through Friday and Saturday morning. ♦ Take I-25 north to Las Vegas exit, 60 miles east of Santa Fe

5 Tesuque Pueblo This was one of the first pueblos to have contact with the Spanish settlers, and its members played a major role in the Pueblo Revolt of 1680. Two of the leaders who secretly notified other pueblos of the plan were betrayed and arrested by the Spanish. Originally at another location, the pueblo was established at its present site in 1694. While less picturesque than some, Tesuque does have a central plaza dominated by a Catholic church. The Tewa-speaking tribe operates a bingo parlor that is frequented by Indians and non-Indians alike, and a campground and RV park at **Camel Rock,** a local landmark located beside Highway 84-285. The Feast of San Diego is celebrated here on 12 November. ♦ Fees for photography, sketching, and painting. Daily. Hwy 84-285, 9 miles north of Santa Fe (the main village is 1 mile west of the highway). 983.2667

6 Bandelier National Monument The remains of one of the largest civilizations of the Anasazi (ancestors of the Pueblo Indians) —one of the most wondrous sites of the Southwest—can be viewed, photographed, and hiked among here. Named after archae-ologist Adolph Bandelier, who first explored the site, the monument contains more than 3,000 archaeological treasures, many of which are still unexcavated. The ruins, hidden in a deep canyon off the Pajarito Plateau, were home to perhaps thousands of Indians be-tween AD 1100 and 1500. Structures were built from volcanic rock. Crops of beans, corn, and squash were irrigated with water from Frijoles Creek. A fairly easy hiking trail that winds among the main ruins of Frijoles Canyon takes about an hour. Ladders can be climbed—much as the Indians used to do—to enter cliff dwellings. There are 70 miles of more strenuous, more remote trails that go to distant ruins among the area's 50 square miles. Free permits, obtainable at the visitors' center, are required for overnight hikes. Why the huge living center was

abandoned—whether because of drought, famine, or disease—is not known. ♦ Admission. Daily. Take Hwy 84-285 north to Pojoaque, then west on NM 502 and south on NM 4, 45 miles northwest of Santa Fe. 672.3861

7 Pojoaque Pueblo In the late 1880s the population of this pueblo was almost wiped out by an epidemic of smallpox, and today only small mounds of earth from the original pueblo remain. In 1932 a new pueblo was founded, and in recent years tribe members have made efforts to reestablish old customs: After more than a hundred years, the pueblo now celebrates a number of feast days with traditional dances, and the Tewa language is taught in classes, along with pottery and jewelry making. The **Poeh Center and Museum** (455.2489) exhibits pottery and jewelry, as well as vintage photographs, from the eight Northern Pueblos (**Pojoaque, Tesuque, Nambe, San Ildefonso, Santa Clara, San Juan, Pucuris,** and **Taos**). Although the pueblo lacks a central village (it is primarily a cluster of stores along the highway on pueblo land), it has an information center and a large tribally owned gift shop (455.3334). The pueblo unveiled plans a few years ago to build the largest Indian-owned gambling facility in New Mexico; at press time, a highly political and controversial battle raged and it was uncertain whether the casino would happen. ♦ Fees for sketching and filming. Daily. On Hwy 84-285, 15 miles north of Santa Fe. 455.2278

8 San Ildefonso Pueblo Visitors to this, one of the friendliest of all the New Mexico pueblos, are welcomed into the large, picturesque plaza. This spot is famous for the black pottery technique developed in the 1920s by Maria Martinez and her husband, Julian. Maria was one of the first potters to sign her work and is the most famous of all pueblo potters. The pueblo operates a museum and gift shop (check at the visitors' center for hours). ♦ Photography fee. Daily. Take Hwy 84-285 15 miles north of Santa Fe, turn left toward Los Alamos at NM 502, and go 6 miles; the entrance is on the right. 455.2273

The mission at San Ildefonso Pueblo

M BLUM

9 Nambe Pueblo Set in a valley of piñon and juniper, Nambe Falls, one of New Mexico's few waterfalls, is the site of this small pueblo in the Sangre de Cristo Mountains. Visitors come here for fishing, boating, and camping in and around Nambe Lake. On the Fourth of July the pueblo celebrates with dances at the falls. ♦ Fees for sketching, photography, and filming. Daily. Take Hwy 84-285 15 miles north of Santa Fe, then head 3 miles east on NM 503 to the sign for Nambe Falls; the pueblo entrance is 2 miles farther along. 455.2036

10 Chimayó One of those rare sites you won't soon forget awaits in this tiny Hispanic village. Situated off the plaza is the **Santuario de Chimayó** (no phone), an old adobe church that has sometimes been called the American Lourdes, after the Catholic shrine in France. In a small back room, there's a hole in the floor beside which visitors can kneel, scoop out dirt, and rub it on parts of their bodies that are ailing. According to legend, the dirt has healing powers. In a narrow room leading to the healing earth, crutches, wheelchairs, canes, and all sorts of other medical aids are hung on the walls, along with written testimonials from people who claim they were healed by the Chimayó dirt. If these are not provable tributes to miracles, they nonetheless are evidence of the human faith in divine intervention. The sanctuary is open daily.

Unlike Santa Fe and Taos, this small village has for the most part withstood the ravages of commercialism. If you can screen out the automobiles parked in the plaza, the scene resembles the New Mexican villages of centuries long gone.

This region is known as a weaving center. The Ortega family has been producing weavers for seven generations, going back to Gabriel Ortega in the 18th century. Their wool blankets, rugs, and apparel are for sale at **Ortega's Weaving Shop** (NM 76, across from the Santuario, 351.4215). The Trujillo family, which also claims seven generations of weavers and is now led by Irvin Trujillo, sells its products at **Centinela Traditional Arts** (NM 76, 1 mile east of Ortega's Weaving Shop, 351.2180). It's a fruitless debate over which family does better work, especially since there has been plenty of intermarrying.

Many people drive to Chimayó just to eat at **Rancho de Chimayó** (★★★$$; 351.4444). Set back from the road about a quarter-mile from the plaza, this atmospheric restaurant in a converted ranch house is run by the Jaramillo family. They offer quality New Mexican food on lovely outdoor terraces in warm weather and indoors year-round. The drive at sunset through New Mexico's back country, amid rolling high-desert hills, is memorable. ♦ On NM 76, about 25 miles northeast of Santa Fe

11 Santa Clara Pueblo With 2,600 tribal members, this is one of the area's larger pueblos. All are descendants of Indians who lived at the nearby **Puye Cliff Dwellings,** located west of the pueblo. The cliff dwellings are a national landmark, and walking tours—either self-guided or with escorts—can be made through the abodes. The original dwellings were carved out of the cliffs; structures were later built on the mesas and below the cliffs. The site was abandoned as a dwelling circa 1500. Atop the cliff dwellings are the ruins of a 740-room pueblo, from which is a stunning view of the surrounding mountain ranges. The road to the cliffs is closed during bad weather.

The Santa Clara artisans are known for their intricately carved pottery, including miniature etched pots. Tours of the pueblo are available on weekdays, during which potters can be seen at work. The tribe runs the **Santa Clara Canyon Recreation Area,** where camping, picnicking, and fishing are available. ♦ Admission to Puye Cliff Dwellings includes fee for photography; additional fee for videography. Free admission to Pueblo; fee for photography and escorted tours. Daily. Española; take NM 30 1.3 miles and cross to the west side of the Rio Grande; the entrance is on the left. 753.7326

12 Los Alamos In the early 1940s, physicist J. Robert Oppenheimer, who became familiar with the isolation of Northern New Mexico during boyhood vacations, chose the **Los Alamos Ranch School** as the site for the Manhattan Project, which would bring scientists together from all over the country to create the atom bomb. **Los Alamos National Laboratory** is still on the cutting edge of scientific research—most of it military, some of it civilian. The once-closed community known locally as "The Hill" is now an open, suburban-looking city, most of whose adult inhabitants work at the laboratory. The lab itself is not open to visitors, but the free **Bradbury Science Museum** (15th St and Central Ave, 667.4444) contains displays that depict simply how atomic energy works, as well as interactive exhibits on Manhattan Project history, among others. The **Los Alamos County Historical Museum** (2132 Central Ave, at Fuller Lodge, 662.6272) traces one million years of history in the region and reveals "Life in the Secret City" during the period the bomb was being built. Also on display is historic correspondence between President Franklin D. Roosevelt and the scientists, particularly Oppenheimer and Albert Einstein. Both museums are open daily; a donation is requested at the historical museum. ♦ Take Hwy 84-285 north about 16 miles, then head west on NM 502 about 20 miles

Restaurants/Clubs: Red		Hotels: Blue
Shops/ ♣ Outdoors: Green		**Sights/Culture:** Black

Custom Made: Indian Arts and Crafts

The first-time visitor to New Mexico is likely to be boggled by all the Indian merchandise that seems to be marketed everywhere. Most Indian arts were developed hundreds of years ago for practical, religious, or decorative uses. Kachina dolls (carved from dried cottonwood root) were created for religious instruction, pots and baskets were used to store grain and cornmeal, rugs were designed to warm and decorate hogans (a Navajo dwelling made of logs and mud), and jewelry was created for aesthetic purposes and to indicate status within the tribe. Today the same items are made primarily to sell to the public; it is one of the few ways Indians can live on the reservation and still earn a living.

Three variables determine the price of Indian art. The first is age; truly old pots and baskets created for practical use generally cost much more than new ones. The second, as in any art form, is the quality of the work. And the third is the nature of the materials. The following is a very brief guide to the more popular art forms:

Baskets

Nomadic Indians developed portable vessels made of straw or similar materials to transport goods. However, most Indian baskets for sale in Northern New Mexico come from Arizona or California—the Pueblo Indians live in stable villages and have no need for baskets. The Jicarilla Apache near the Colorado border make some baskets, mostly for the tourist trade.

Jewelry

Indian jewelry runs the gamut from bracelets and necklaces to rings, earrings, and *concho* belts (made of a series of silver ovals, known as *conchas,* strung on leather). Different tribes are associated with different specialties. The Zuni are best known for inlaying fine turquoise and other stones in silver; the Hopi specialize in silver overlay techniques; the Santo Domingo Indians string finely carved shell beads—*heishi*—into necklaces and earrings; and for centuries the Navajo have been creating elaborate pieces with silver and turquoise.

Turquoise is the stone most frequently used in Indian jewelry because it is indigenous to the area. But the quality of the stone varies greatly. Natural turquoise is the most valued. "Treated" turquoise is a low-grade stone that has been impregnated with resin to stabilize it so it doesn't crumble; in some cases the resin is also dyed to give the stone a brighter color. It is often difficult to tell if turquoise is natural or treated; your best bet is to buy from a reputable dealer or bring a knowledgeable friend along when you shop. Other stones the Indians trade for, such as coral or jet, are not treated. Old Pawn jewelry—made for the Indians' own wear decades ago and then pawned for cash—costs more than the new pieces made for tourist trade. (Beware of dealers who sell new jewelry as "Old Pawn," for it's usually junk.)

Kachina Dolls

These dolls are a form of religious art created primarily by the Hopi and to a lesser extent by the Zuni. They are small, elaborate wooden carvings that represent the men who dance in costume as kachina spirits during Hopi celebrations, and were initially used to teach Hopi children about the spirits. A dried cottonwood root is carved, then sanded and painted. The best dolls are chiseled from a single root, using no joints or glue, except to fasten on the symbolic items the dolls are holding. The Hopi have more than 400 kachina spirits, each with its own costume. Artistry varies greatly, and prices range from several hundred to several thousand dollars.

In recent years other tribes, particularly the Navajo, have begun making kachina dolls that tend to be larger, more brightly colored, and decorated with leather skirts. These particular dolls have no religious significance to the Navajo and are made strictly to sell to tourists. Some of the best kachinas can be found in Santa Fe at the **Kachina House** and at **Packard's Indian Trading Co.**

Pottery

Many different tribes use similar techniques to create the pottery found throughout New Mexico. Clay is gathered by hand and carefully rolled into coils, and the coils are shaped into pots. The pots are then fired in outdoor kilns. Some modern Indians buy commercially made pots and paint them with tribal designs, and these, of course, are worth less than the handmade pots. **Acoma Pueblo** specializes in distinctive black and white pottery designs that are often complex and exquisite. **San Ildefonso** and **Santa Clara Pueblos** are especially renowned for their solid black pottery.

The most famous Indian potter was Maria Martinez of **San Ildefonso Pueblo,** who began making black pottery in 1919. She revived an old style of pottery found in the ruins on the nearby **Parajito Plateau.**

Experiments to reproduce this style were encouraged by the **School of American Research** in Santa Fe; they were very successful, and the pottery became a good source of income for the pueblo. Pots made by Maria Martinez, who died in 1980, sell for thousands of dollars. Her descendants, as well as many others at **San Ildefonso**, continue to make the distinctive black pottery. Other types of pottery often feature animal designs and may include clouds, rain, the sun, and flowers. The most common design is the rainbird, because birds were considered carriers of prayers to the gods, and survival depended heavily on rainfall. Since pottery originated for the purpose of holding food and water (see the Zuni water vase on page 76), all pots were made with prayers to the gods for rain, sunshine, and good crops.

Rugs and Blankets

The Navajo are weaving specialists, in part because they have been shepherds for centuries and have access to plenty of wool. Their intricate and brilliantly colorful designs, such as "Two Gray Hills" (named after the site of a trading post), are famous. The finer the weaving, the better the rug or blanket and the higher the price. Many stores sell rugs with Navajo designs that are actually made by the Zapotec Indians in Mexico. These are of coarser quality and should cost much less. Two Gray Hills rugs in their best form have no dyed colors—only the natural colors of white, black, and gray. The "Chief's Blanket" has broad black and white stripes with three bands of contrasting color, usually blue or red, at each end. "Diamond Twill" or "Double Saddle" blankets feature a diamond pattern with variations, usually in red, white, black, and gray. Often there is a slight break in the border design of a blanket. This is created intentionally, so spirits don't get trapped inside the pattern. Navajo *yei* (divinities) are represented in the designs of the *Yei-bichai* blankets, also known as *Yei* blankets. They are typically made from brightly colored yarns and may be touted by dealers as Navajo ceremonial blankets. In fact, they are often made by Anglos or Anglicized Indians; most Navajos regard the blankets as a parody of their religion and find them offensive.

13 San Juan Pueblo In 1598 conquistador Juan de Oñate declared this pueblo the first capital of New Mexico; 11 years later the capital was moved to Santa Fe. It was a San Juan native called Popé who organized the Pueblo Revolt of 1680. Today this, the largest and northernmost of the Tewa-speaking pueblos, serves as the administrative headquarters of the Eight Northern Indian Pueblos Council, which was created in the 1960s to help the pueblos speak with a common voice in their own interests. The pueblo has two central plazas, where Catholic churches and ceremonial kivas stand beside one another. At the **O'ke Oweenge Arts and Crafts Cooperative** (852.2372) visitors can see and buy the red pottery that is a San Juan trademark, as well as crafts from many pueblos; it is open Monday through Saturday. Across from the cooperative the **Tewa Indian Restaurant** (no phone) serves fry bread (a puffy bread similar to sopaipillas), chile stews, and other dishes. The tribe runs bingo games, and tribal lakes are open in spring and summer for fishing (permits are available at the pueblo). The tribal Vespers and Evening Dances and Feast Day are held on 23 and 24 June. The Turtle Dance is held on 26 December. ◆ Fee for photography. Daily. Take Hwy 285 north about 15 miles to Española, drive a mile north on NM 68, then turn left onto NM 74 at the sign to San Juan Pueblo; the entrance is a mile farther. 852.4400

14 Abiquiu About an hour north of Santa Fe is a wonderland near the village of Abiquiu where the stony hills beside the road are striated in shades of pink and yellow. If you think you've been here before, you may have—in the paintings of Georgia O'Keeffe. When she visited Mabel Dodge Luhan in Taos in 1929, O'Keeffe wandered far and wide and discovered the hills here. Later she stayed at the nearby **Ghost Ranch,** which was then similar to a dude ranch. (The name is derived from the tale of the female spirits who allegedly haunted the place, crying over a man who was murdered there.) O'Keeffe began spending summers there painting and later bought two places of her own in the region. Her homes are closed to the public, but **Ghost Ranch** (Hwy 84, 685.4333)—now a conference center—is open daily; no admission.

In the old days, they used the skull of a steer to mark the turnoff to the dirt road to **Ghost Ranch.** Nowadays there's a sign bearing the outline of a steer's skull. Turn onto this bumpy dirt road and be patient for several hundred yards. Suddenly it will open onto a broad meadow surrounded by stunning mesa walls in purples and ochers and golden stripes. The sight is magnificent, and there are several hiking trails to choose from. Nearby is the **Ghost Ranch Living Museum** (Hwy 84; no phone), a small zoo that presents indigenous animals in their natural settings. Most of the animals were saved after being wounded by bullets or automobiles, and many are later returned to the wild. The museum is open daily and a donation is requested. If you can't afford to buy an O'Keeffe (who can?), seeing in person the stunning vistas she painted is the next best thing, maybe even better. ♦ Take Hwy 84-285 to Española, then take Hwy 84 (the road to Chama) for about 20 miles

15 Ojo Caliente While many people flock to the **Santuario de Chimayó** (see page 75) to try the holy mud, others prefer to be healed at **Ojo Caliente Mineral Springs** (off Hwy 285, 583.2233), which is billed as North America's oldest health resort. In the 1500s Cabeza de Vaca, a Spanish explorer, wrote: "The greatest treasure that I found these strange people to possess are some hot springs which burst out at the foot of a mountain that gives evidence of being an active volcano. So powerful are the chemicals contained in this water that the inhabitants have a belief that they were given to them by their Gods. These springs I have named Ojo Caliente." Five bubbling mineral springs contain iron, soda, lithium, sodium, and arsenic. A health resort at the springs offers mineral baths in the waters, as well as massages and herbal wraps. The village of Ojo Caliente (Spanish for "hot eye") has an adobe mission, a general store, and three cafes surrounded by desert slopes. Once a mecca for the sick, this region is now more of a place to go and relax. The proprietors claim the mineral waters offer the best results if you drink them as well as bathe in them in order to eliminate excessive acids from the body. ♦ Off Hwy 285, about 35 minutes north of Española

16 Taos via New Mexico Highway 68 The most direct route to Taos from Santa Fe follows NM 84-285 to Española—where you might see low-riders parading their fat-wheeled vehicles—and continues north on NM 68. The trip takes roughly 1.5 hours. About 40 miles into the drive, just past Velarde, the highway enters the twisting canyon of the Rio Grande and becomes a scenic drive that climaxes when it rises out of the canyon and Taos Mountain suddenly becomes visible on the plateau above. In late summer, fresh fruit stands along the way offer peaches, chile, and corn; in autumn they've got locally grown apples and pumpkins. The return drive is beautiful late in the day when the sun turns the river to molten gold. If you're hungry, watch for the short bridge across the river at **Embudo Station,** where an inexpensive restaurant (★$; NM 68, 852.4707) of the same name offers first-rate barbecue sandwiches and New Mexican food outdoors under tall cottonwood trees beside the river. Lunch or dinner at **Embudo Station** itself makes a relaxing getaway from the Santa Fe scene.

17 The High Road to Taos If you have the time for a leisurely drive to Taos, you might consider taking the high road. It takes approximately two hours to cover the same distance as the direct route, because the

second half is spent on looping switchbacks in the mountains. On the plus side, this route passes through some old-fashioned mountain villages that have a rugged appeal of their own. At Española, take NM 76 (there's a flashing light at the intersection), which leads to Chimayó (for more on this famous weaving center, see page 75), then northward to the village of Truchas, across from which the beautiful Truchas Peaks are covered with snow much of the year. In winter, if the roads are clear but snow is still on the ground, Truchas, with its snowy fields, wooden fences, and grazing horses in the foreground and the peaks behind, is a photographer's dream (but beware of unfriendly dogs). Robert Redford filmed some scenes for *The Milagro Beanfield War* in Truchas. Farther north in Las Trampas is a Spanish Colonial church built in 1763. At the village of Peñasco, take NM 75 east for a few miles, then go north on NM 518. This will join up with NM 68, the main road into Taos, just south of town. An alternate beginning to the high road out of Santa Fe is to take NM 503 east from Pojoaque and connect with NM 76 at Chimayó. Many people prefer to take the high road up to Taos and use the more direct Rio Grande route on the way back to Santa Fe.

Pride and Prejudice in the Pueblos

Nineteen Indian villages line the Rio Grande and its tributaries from the south of Albuquerque all the way up to Taos. The lives of these Indian residents are an uneasy combination of centuries-old customs and modern American ways. Traditional artistry and deep faith sustain a rich spiritual life among many, and the Indian ideal of living in harmony with nature has become more widely accepted, thanks to the growing political movement to protect the natural environment. But these ideals exist side by side in the pueblos with poverty and social dysfunction, especially alcoholism.

More than 12,000 years ago, nomadic peoples—forebears of the Pueblo Indians—roamed throughout Northern New Mexico, following grazing herds of bison and mammoth. With the passing centuries they began to settle the land and learned to gain sustenance by eating fruits and nuts and hunting elk and deer in the mountains. By about 5500 BC these hunter-gatherers had made their homes in natural caves found in the Santa Fe and Taos regions, and they began to plant and harvest corn on the fertile land. Gradually, groups of Indians splintered off into separate communities and built underground circular pit-houses to live in. They later developed techniques for constructing houses out of mud and stone.

A great civilization flourished at **Chaco Canyon** to the west and at **Mesa Verde** to the northwest of

Santa Fe between AD 900 and 1300. These ancestors of the Pueblo Indians are known as the Anasazi (a Navajo word meaning ancient strangers). The remains of large structures and extensive road networks can still be found in these areas. A sizable community of Anasazi also lived in **Frijoles Canyon,** about 30 miles northwest of Santa Fe, and their cliff dwellings can be viewed at **Bandelier National Monument** (see page 74). The fate of the Anasazi and why they abandoned their cliff dwellings is one of the abiding mysteries of the region. Some historians suspect flood or famine may have driven them away.

The Pueblo Indians were for the most part peaceful, although often they were victimized by raids of the more aggressive Navajo who were in search of food and horses. They cultivated crops, hunted, and performed dances that expressed their sense of unity with nature, and they spoke several languages. When the Spaniards arrived in the 16th century, there were more than 150 Indian pueblos in the area. The early Spaniards were missionaries who tried to convert the Indians to Christianity through persuasion or by force. Some Indians were murdered, many were enslaved. By 1680 the Pueblo Indians decided they had had enough and began to revolt. Led by men from **Taos Pueblo,** they attacked the Spanish settlers in Santa Fe and drove them all the way to El Paso, Texas. The Spaniards returned in force and reconquered the region 12 years later.

Catholic missionaries succeeded in constructing churches at most of the pueblos and converting many of the Indians in the following years. But Indian religion survived alongside Catholicism—in sacred meetings held in underground kivas forbidden to the white people and in ceremonial dances performed on feast days. For centuries the church and the government tried to discourage such traditional dances. This effort has stopped, and the dances are now recognized as a strong and powerful part of Indian religion (as well as a profitable tourist attraction).

In 1846 the Indians of **Taos Pueblo** joined local Hispanics in opposing the annexation of the region from Mexico by the US. When a Taos trader named Charles Bent was illegally appointed governor of the territory, a group of Hispanics and Taos Indians joined forces, broke into his home, and murdered him. US troops had to be sent in to restore order.

Here and throughout the West, the decades that followed were filled with broken promises to the Indians. Racial discrimination prevented Indians from getting jobs, and poverty on the reservations became endemic. Today some Pueblo Indians live in the cities, but most have remained in the pueblos, where centuries-old adobes and sacred underground kivas stand side by side with mobile homes and cinder block houses with TV antennas fastened to the roofs. Some of the pueblo dwellers work in the cities at everything from selling their traditional crafts to holding white-collar jobs; however, their unemployment rate is usually far higher than the rest of the country's.

Pueblo residents have their own independent governing bodies and tribal laws and police and cannot be taxed by the state. Special educational institutions have been established to meet the needs of the pueblos' young people; the **Santa Fe Indian School** instructs junior high and high school Indian students, and college-level students can enroll in Santa Fe's **Institute for American Indian Arts.**

Despite their stormy past with nonnatives, most pueblos welcome visitors on a daily basis. All have special feast days, when tribal members dress in traditional costumes and hold age-old dances to the throbbing pulse of drums. These dances and ceremonies—colorful affairs in which the entire tribe participates—are enactments of the Indian religious philosophy that human beings must live in harmony with the natural world. All but the most sacred dances are open to visitors. In most cases, permission must be obtained, and a small fee paid, before any picture taking, (photography is forbidden at some of the dances), sketching, painting, or filming at the pueblos.

Many of the Indians are friendly and welcome the constant flow of tourists, who fill the shops where jewelry and pottery produced by pueblo craftspeople is sold. However, there are some who harbor resentment, not only for past injustices, but for feeling as though they are regarded as living cultural exhibits. This latter ambivalence is most prevalent at **Taos Pueblo,** perhaps because its brilliant adobe architecture—five stories high and five centuries old—is the biggest tourist attraction among the pueblos, and **Taos Pueblo** more than any other survives by catering to the tourist dollar.

Indians have started to choose alternatives to this way of life by investing in projects off the reservations. One of the most notable examples of this is tiny **Picuris Pueblo**'s ownership of 51 percent of the large **Hotel Santa Fe** (see page 59). If such ventures continue to work, the Indians may begin to regain some of the economic independence that is needed to make their political autonomy more meaningful.

New Mexico State Senator John Morrow once suggested that the state try to lure new businesses by advertising heavily in California—right after an earthquake. In 1994, southern California residents and businesses began moving to New Mexico in record numbers following the 17 January 1994 earthquake that shook Los Angeles. As a result, California has surpassed Texas and New York as the place from which most emigrants come to New Mexico.

Like most Spanish Colonial cities, Santa Fe was built with slave labor. They first imported Aztec slaves from Mexico and later traded livestock for Hopi and Zuni captives that Navajo warriors brought from the west to the slave market at Taos.

Restaurants/Clubs: Red		**Hotels:** Blue	
Shops/ 🌴 Outdoors: Green		**Sights/Culture:** Black	

Taos

Beautiful as the setting of Santa Fe is, the natural location of Taos may surpass it. Upon arriving in Taos in the 1920s, D.H. Lawrence wrote: "I think the skyline of Taos the most beautiful of all I have ever seen in my travels round the world." The British writer made an isolated cabin in the region his home for several years, and his ashes are part of a shrine you can visit.

The drive to Taos almost equals the destination. Forty miles north of Santa Fe, at the apple-growing village of Velarde, the highway winds into the canyon of the **Rio Grande.** For 20 miles it twists and turns beside the river, climbing at last onto a broad plateau, at which point you see the majestic hulk of **Taos Mountain** looming in the distance. At the base of this brooding peak ancient Indians built the spectacular **Taos Pueblo** around 1450, more than 150 years before the Spanish settled Santa Fe. The pueblo, two large adobe apartment buildings five stories high, is a stunning creation of rooms, ladders, doorways, and primitive beauty, amid which men and women wrapped in colorful blankets move with the silence of shadows. Spanish settlers led by Frey Pedro de Miranda established a colony about two miles from the pueblo in 1617, which evolved into the modern Taos. The Pueblo Revolt of 1680 against Spanish occupation led to the flight or death of most of the Spanish settlers, but others returned to the area when an uneasy peace was restored in the early 18th century.

Like Santa Fe, Taos was discovered by Anglo artists from the east in the late 19th and early 20th centuries, and such painters as Irving Couse, Oscar Berninghaus, Robert Henri, and Ernest Blumenschein, among others, formed the basis of an art colony devoted to renderings of the landscape and the Indians. After New York socialite Mabel Dodge Sterne moved to Taos in 1918, divorced her painter husband, and married a Taos Indian, Tony Lujan, she played host in an adobe mansion (now a bed-and-breakfast), which she built into a cultural salon that attracted D.H. Lawrence, Georgia O'Keeffe, Ansel Adams, and others.

Taos today is a tidy little town of about 5,000 residents that easily could be tucked into one of Santa Fe's side pockets. It, too, looks like a Mexican town, all brown and beige adobes that are one and two stories high and filled with galleries and shops. And like Santa Fe, Taos is fighting the battle of controversial modernization. Because of its size, Taos can be explored casually in a single day, or more extensively in two. The central **Plaza** has been taken over by T-shirt shops, with the exception of a few genuine galleries such as the **Michael McCormick Gallery.** The city has only two main streets. On **Kit Carson Road**, which runs east from the Plaza, you'll find the **Total Arts Gallery**, the town's first-rate representational gallery, and the **Kit Carson Home**, former residence of the Indian fighter, now an Old West museum. On the north-south artery, **Paseo del Pueblo,** you can visit the **Stables Art Center,** housed in an old adobe in which the most puzzling unsolved murder mystery in Taos—the beheading of a wealthy rogue named Arthur Manby—took place in 1929; the **Fenix Gallery,** which shows the best in abstract art; and **Lambert's,** a four-star restaurant serving continental and American dishes with exquisite taste in all respects. For lunch in Taos you might want to try the **Bent Street Deli;** for the tastiest New Mexican fast food anywhere, stop at **Mantes' Chow Cart.** And be sure to walk over to **Ledoux Street,** a center of the original art colony, and browse the **Worth Gallery,** where craft becomes high art, and the **Harwood Foundation,** which has the finest collection of the early Taos painters.

Now you're qualified to join in an endless argument: Which is the more rewarding place to visit, Santa Fe or Taos?

1 Plaza Like most Hispanic towns, Taos grew out from a central plaza, which makes it the natural starting point for any tour. Once a meeting place for Indian, Spanish, and Anglo traders, this is now the modern equivalent—T-shirt, souvenir, and moccasin heaven. There are a few quality shops and galleries located on its perimeter. The center of the plaza is paved in brick. A large cross is dedicated to the men of Taos County in Battery H of the 200th Coast Artillery who died in the battle of Bataan and its aftermath. A band shell shaped like a gazebo is off to one side, and tree-shaded benches allow for people watching. ♦ Between Paseo del Pueblo Sur and Camino de la Placita.

2 La Fonda de Taos $$ This late-1930s hotel dominates the south side of the Plaza. The lobby decor exudes tradition: Elaborately constumed *muñeca* dolls (fancy Spanish dolls, often made of ceramic, for display only), toreador "suits of lights," a bullfighter's cape emblazoned with an image of *Nuestro Señora de Guadalupe* (Our Lady of Guadalupe), and old Navajo blankets. The walls are absolutely

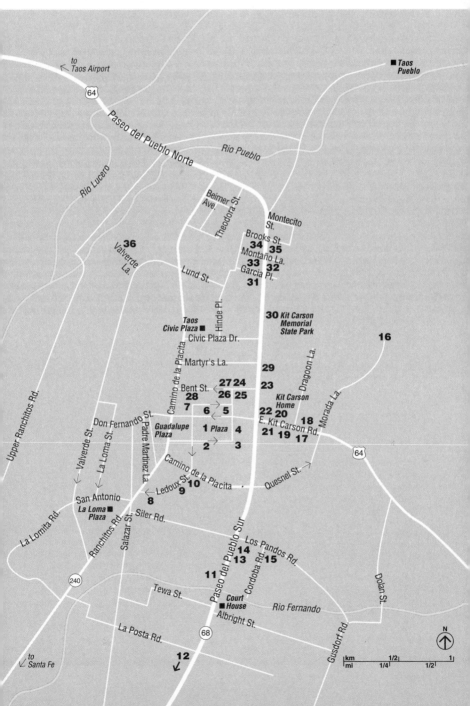

packed with dozens of paintings representing the Taos art community from the early days to the present. Most of the 24 rooms are small and charming; yet despite the vibrant Southwest decor, show signs of the passing years. For a fee nonguests can see a locked side room that contains erotic paintings by D.H. Lawrence which were banned in England in 1929. ♦ 108 South Plaza (between East Plaza and West Plaza). 758.2211

3 End of the Universe Cafe ★★$ Cross the Plaza to the southeast corner and you'll find a cul-de-sac known by some as Cantu Plaza and others as McCarthy Plaza. Perched up a sloping ramp on the second floor above some shops, this coffeehouse serves homemade bagels, salads, soups, and desserts at small wooden tables in a bright and cheerful space. A big draw is the bistrot bread—a round loaf with spinach and feta or chile and cheese—which is made on the premises and sold around the country. Music—everything from folk to rock to jazz—and one-act plays are performed in the evenings on a stage at one corner of the room. Lectures and storytelling are also highlights. ♦ Cafe ♦ Daily breakfast, lunch, and dinner. Cantu Plaza N (southeast of the Plaza). 758.7721

3 Maison Faurie Antiquités If you're looking to buy a dentist's drill from 1900, an instruction booklet from a turn-of-the-century embalming school, or a stethoscope used by a doctor who's long dead, this is definitely the place to shop. Owner Robert R. Faurie, who hails from France, has been in business here since 1980, collecting and selling anything that strikes his fancy—and just about everything does. In addition to cases filled with old medical objects, you'll find antique letter openers, inkwells, candlesticks, Art Deco lamps, straight razors, and a collection of US military wings from World Wars I and II large enough to supply a small air force. More intriguing than many museums, this shop stimulates the creative juices in most browsers. Focus on any object, imagine the person who first owned it, and you can create your own novel. ♦ Daily. Cantu Plaza N (southeast of the Plaza). 758.8545

4 Ogelvie's Bar & Grille ★$$ The main attraction of this restaurant and piano bar is its second-floor location overlooking the Plaza. On sunny afternoons, people sometimes wait hours for a table on the large, open balcony. The menu is eclectic and is big on appetizers and finger foods, making it a good place to eat light (the quesadillas are the best in town). Entrées include stir-fry, charbroiled rib-eye steak, and shrimp Hawaiian (stir-fried with pineapple), as well as more local fare such as fajitas and *carne adovada* (barbecued beef marinated in chile sauce) chimichangas. ♦ American/New Mexican ♦ Daily lunch and dinner. 103-I East Plaza (west of Paseo del Pueblo Sur). 758.8866

5 New Directions Gallery This modern gallery is owned by Cecelia Torres and often presided over by Ann Emory, a Taos native who remembers when Indian buckboards lined the Plaza, their horses tied to hitching posts. The Plaza's new direction is T-shirts, but in this gallery it is the abstract work of Taos artists such as Larry Bell, whose work has been acclaimed worldwide; Ted Egri, who makes modern sculpture; and Gloria Corbett, whose childlike paintings are inspired by such classic books as *The Magic Mountain* and classical music, including *Pictures at an Exhibition*. ♦ Daily. 107-B North Plaza (at Teresina La). 758.2771

6 The Garden Restaurant ★$ Doors gaping wide right on the Plaza, this restaurant is under the same ownership as **El Patio de Taos** (see page 83) but has an ersatz feel aimed at the passing tourist parade. It calls itself a cheerful hometown place, and the decor, including fake greenery, could come from Anywhere, USA. So could most of the food. You can slake your hunger here, but the sandwiches, salads, and New Mexican and Italian dishes are nothing you're likely to note in your journal. ♦ American ♦ Daily breakfast, lunch, and dinner. 115 North Plaza (at Teresina La). 758.9483

6 Michael McCormick Gallery When the Japanese-born artist Michio Takayama was 60 years old, he came to Taos on a sketching trip from his home in California. He and his wife fell in love with the place and moved here. The internationally renowned Takayama continued painting his delicate personalized landscapes through his late 80s, when he entered a nursing home. His work is one of the two anchors of this gallery run by Michael McCormick, whose personal contacts in the national literary scene are legion. The other anchor, and popular star of the gallery, is Taos painter Miguel Martinez, whose family has lived here for generations and whose stylized oils and oil pastels of women are rapidly gaining favor with collectors. When he began his woman series in the late 1970s, Martinez had a conscious goal: to create paintings that could be recognized as his from across the room, even without a signature. He has succeeded admirably. His women—a blend of Hispanic, Indian, and occasionally Asian—are strong, colorful, and evocative, proffering a mysterious silence that is an agreeable challenge to live with. ♦ Daily. 121-B North Plaza (in the North Plaza Art Center). 758.1372

7 El Patio de Taos ★★$$$ It is said that one wall of this building dates back to before the Spanish discovered Taos Valley. Now a popular restaurant and bar with a stone fountain in the main dining room located down a walkway at the northwest corner of the Plaza, in the 17th century the building housed a **Taos Pueblo** trading post, and for 200 years it was used by the Spanish government for administrative offices. The ambitious menu has separate pages for New Mexican, Italian, and French cuisine, and the portions are large. The duck chimichanga is quite good, as are most of the more traditional New Mexican dishes. The continental fare is more erratic. ♦ New Mexican/Continental ♦ Daily lunch and dinner. 125 North Plaza (at Teresina La). 758.2121

COURTESY OF KIT CARSON HISTORIC MUSEUMS

8 Blumenschein House Among the founders of the Taos art colony early in this century were Ernest and Mary Greene Blumenschein. They lived in this stunning Taos adobe built in 1797. The house (pictured above) is now a museum, which displays paintings by both Blumenscheins and their daughter, Helen, as well as those of other prominent Taos artists.

The house has been kept much the way it was when the artists lived here; the furnishings are a mix of rustic Taos furniture and European antiques, and the walls have been restored to the original adobe plaster. ♦ Donation. Daily. 222 Ledoux St (at Ranchitos Rd). 758.0505

8 Harwood Foundation About 550 paintings, drawings, and sculptures by the early Taos artists are in the collection of this museum, often overlooked in favor of the better-known **Millicent Rogers Museum.** Dating to 1923, this is the second oldest museum in the state. It's located at the end of Ledoux Street—a center of the artistic community in the early days—right next to the **Blumenschein House.** The first two-story building in Taos outside of **Taos Pueblo,** and the first to have electricity, it was a frequent gathering place for local artists when it was the home of Burt Harwood and Lucy Case Harwood. When Burt Harwood died in 1921, Lucy officially set up the foundation as a communal arts center. It has been operated by the **University of New Mexico** since 1935. A wide staircase leads to galleries on the second floor, where a major attraction is the 1932 oil *Winter Funeral* by Victor Higgins, which depicts a funeral in the village of Arroyo Hondo with Taos Mountain rising in the distance. Higgins appears to have poured into the painting his sadness at the death of his mother, who had died shortly before he saw this funeral. Other works in the collection range from paintings by Ernest Blumenschein and Andrew Dasburg to such contemporary artists as Fritz Scholder and Larry Bell. ♦ Donations accepted. M-Sa. 238 Ledoux St (at Ranchitos Rd). 758.3063

9 Navajo Gallery This is Taos painter R.C. Gorman's personal gallery. All those outlines of Indian women, who presumably do have fingers, toes, and personalities, make their first home here. Name the medium, Gorman works in it: drawings, lithographs, silkscreens, bronzes, ceramics, paper casts. Gorman books and videos are also sold here. ♦ Daily. 210 Ledoux St (between Camino de la Placita and Ranchitos Rd). 758.3250

10 Collins-Pettit Gallery Among the highlights in Karen Pettit's fine gallery, which opened in 1989, are sensual figure studies by Ron Barsano; lovely small albumen prints by Zoe Zimmerman that have an extraordinarily peaceful quality; colorful landscape and flower oil paintings by Robert Daughters; and monoprints of figures in landscapes by Joyce Stolaroff. ♦ Daily. 1 Ledoux St (at Camino de la Placita). 758.8068

10 Worth Gallery By far the finest crafts gallery in New Mexico, the works here have achieved the status of high art. The incredible, boundless range of the human imagination is amply represented by the works in proprietor Terri Illingworth's and director Kaaren Hardenbrook's lively space. The artists represented, from across the country, leave you feeling good about the human race in the ways they expand the bounds of their chosen media. Noteworthy among many pieces are the basket constructions that Michael Bailot makes out of dyed and knitted copper wire, the sculptures that David Bacharach fashions from woven copper and segments of steel wire, the bright aluminum constructions of John Garrett, and the two-faced tapestry figures of Hope and Phillip Holtzman. You can't help wondering what they'll think of next. ♦ Daily. 112-A Camino de la Placita (at Ledoux St). 751.0816

10 Jes Gordon Gallery This gallery presents some of the most original and unconventional art being created in Taos today. Owner Jes Gordon, who worked as a floral artist in New York City for many years before moving to Taos, shows her own work as well as that of several other up-and-coming local mixed-media artists, including Terrell Powell, Jeffrey Stolier, and Judith Shaw. Among the most unusual pieces here are those of James Scott Taylor, who glues driftwood, limestone, volcanic ash, and sand to his brilliantly colored textured abstract paintings. ♦ Daily. 118 Camino de la Placita (at Ledoux St). 751.0743

11 Mantes' Chow Cart ★★★$ Here's one of the little treasures of Taos that visitors are not likely to try unless a resident tips them off. In the early 1970s Mantes Chacon started a chow cart, or food wagon, on the Plaza (where **Ogelvie's Bar & Grille** now stands), from which he served tamales, *chalupas* (open-face tacos), and such. As the Plaza area was renovated, Chacon wheeled his food-filled wagon, a great local favorite, from one street corner to the next. Several years ago the roving restaurateur built a permanent drive-in space on Paseo del Pueblo Sur that looks like a 1950s-style drive-in without the neon. A waitress will come to your car and ask you to order from the menu posted on boards. Some of the concoctions are named after friends of Chacon: The Susie is a *chile relleno* (a whole green chile pod stuffed with cheese, breaded, and fried) rolled in a tortilla with beans and sour cream. The Lucero is even better—the same ingredients with meat added; it's a taste sensation. These tortilla-wrapped *rellenos* are something even Santa Fe—the big neighbor to the south—has never heard of. If the weather is nice, you can eat outdoors under shade trees on round stone tables, and in late summer and early fall you'll see, and smell,

the fresh chiles being roasted a few feet away If it's cold, eat in your car. You can call ahead for orders to go. ♦ New Mexican ♦ M-Sa breakfast, lunch, and dinner. 402 Paseo del Pueblo Sur (between Siler and Vocational School Rds). 758.3632

12 Sagebrush Inn $$ This Pueblo Revival–style motel was one of the few tourist accommodations in Taos when it was built in 1929. Georgia O'Keeffe lived here for six months when she first arrived in New Mexico. Today the inn's shady interiors evoke the Taos of a bygone era. The 81 guest rooms are dimly lit, cool, and romantic, and some have fireplaces. All are individually decorated with antiques that include original art by early-day Taos painters and authentic American Indian pottery and rugs. Guest facilities include a restaurant, tennis courts, a swimming pool, and hot tubs. ♦ 1508 Paseo del Pueblo Sur (2.5 miles south of the Plaza). 758.2254

13 Comidas del Mantes Restaurant ★★$ Across the road from **Mantes' Chow Cart** (and under the same ownership), tucked into a shopping strip a block closer to town, this casual restaurant serves very good New Mexican and American food in a family setting. ♦ New Mexican/American ♦ M-Sa dinner. 321 Paseo del Pueblo Sur (between Albright St and Los Pandos Rd). 758.9317

Lamberts

14 Lambert's ★★★★$$$ When Taos residents are asked to name the best dining spot in town, they almost always answer **Lambert's.** Opened in late 1989 by Zeke Lambert, formerly the head chef at the **Taos Inn,** this restaurant is set in a remodeled Victorian house with no frills—just plain white walls in several dining rooms. Some tables have a view of Taos Mountain. The food is excellent—the menu changes according to what's available fresh from the market—and in an unusually thoughtful arrangement, can be ordered in full or petite sizes. Prices of the petites are quite reasonable, and, combined with a shared appetizer, the portions are likely to fill you up. An appetizer of grilled shrimp with mango salsa is a treat to treasure and quite sizable. The pepper-crusted lamb with garlic pasta is also quite good. The service is casually impeccable without ever being intrusive. Good California wines are available, and some are surprisingly inexpensive. ♦ Continental ♦ M-F, Su lunch and dinner; Sa dinner. Reservations recommended. 309 Paseo del Pueblo Sur (at Los Pandos Rd). 758.1009

Restaurants/Clubs: Red	**Hotels:** Blue
Shops/ 🍴 Outdoors: Green	**Sights/Culture:** Black

15 Casa de las Chimeneas $$$ On a shady lane within walking distance of the Plaza, this bed-and-breakfast has four units; the largest is a suite with a separate living room, two fireplaces, and a study containing a library of local-interest books and magazines. The guest rooms are filled with antique furniture and little extra touches—like sheepskin mattress pads—and open onto a terrace and tastefully landscaped gardens. There's also a hot tub on the property. ♦ 405 Cordoba Rd (at Los Pandos Rd). 758.4777

16 Mabel Dodge Luhan House $$$ Back in 1918, when artist Maurice Sterne, who was painting Indians in Taos, urged his wife Mabel to join him, he could hardly know what he was setting in motion. Mabel was a prominent socialite in New York who liked to keep a salon of creative types around her. When she moved to Taos she quickly became the center of its artistic world. Mabel stayed in the **Arthur Manby House** while renovating and adding onto a 200-year-old adobe for her own use. She courted, and was courted by, a tall Taos Indian named Tony Lujan. Sterne returned to the East and Mabel, divorced, married Lujan, despite the fact that he already had a wife at **Taos Pueblo.** (Mabel's friends back East could never get the hang of pronouncing a *j* like an *h,* so Mabel spelled her new name Luhan.) When she moved into her renovated house—a three-story, 22-room hacienda—in 1922, she made it a gathering point for celebrities the world over. She induced D.H. Lawrence to move to Taos and supplied the Lawrences with a ranch out in the mountains. Lawrence painted the windows of the second-story bathroom in the "Big House," as it was called, which are still visible. Mabel invited Georgia O'Keeffe to visit from New York in 1929. After two summers, O'Keeffe could no longer abide Mabel's company, but she fell in love with New Mexico and never willingly spent another summer anywhere else, eventually making it her permanent home after husband Alfred Stieglitz died. Willa Cather and Aldous Huxley also came to visit at Mabel's house, and the outdoor patio was once the scene of a lecture by Carl Jung.

The huge house has adobe archways, vigas, *latillas* (wooden slats), flagstone patios, and pigeon roosts. The gates in the surrounding adobe wall were part of the original **San Francisco de Asis Church** in Ranchos de Taos. After Mabel died in 1962, the hacienda was purchased by actor Dennis Hopper, who

lived here while filming *Easy Rider.* The house, sometimes used for cultural seminars, is now a bed-and-breakfast inn. Visitors can stay in **Mabel's Suite,** which still contains her bed, or in **Tony's Bedroom.** There's also the **O'Keeffe Room,** where Georgia stayed for a time; the **Cather Room,** where the novelist visited; and **Spud's Room,** where Spud Johnson, Mabel's secretary, worked. You also can visit a glass room where Mabel sunbathed in the nude. Some guest rooms have shared bathrooms. A guest house nearby has private baths and fireplaces in each room. ♦ 242 Morada La (off Kit Carson Rd). 758.9456, 800/846.2235; fax 751.0431

16 Lumina Gallery Right next to Mabel's house is a beautiful, tree-shaded, multitiered adobe with mullioned windows that was the home of Victor Higgins, one of the most experimental of the early Taos painters. He also once ran for mayor of Taos. Felicia Ferguson, descendant of an old Taos family, and photographer Chuck Henningsen bought the Higgins house in 1981 and within a decade turned it into the most gorgeous gallery in town. The house remains furnished with Higgins's original sofas, beds, and chairs; and the art, most of it abstract, is displayed on the walls and tables as it would be in someone's home—definitely worth a visit. Henningsen's intriguing photographs—many of them symbolic, ghostlike montages, some with a religious content—are also on display, as are a few photographs by Ansel Adams and André Kertész. A number of Taos artists who work in abstract forms are represented, including the furniture of Jim Wagner, but the gallery doesn't yet demonstrate an exciting or unifying vision. A newly opened sculpture garden displays work from around the world. ♦ Daily. 239 Morada La (off Kit Carson Rd). 758.7282

17 Mission Gallery In 1962 Ivan and Rena Rosequist moved from New York to Taos and opened this gallery in a building that was once home to painter Joseph Sharp. (His fellow painter, Irving Couse, lived next door.) The Rosequists represented Andrew Dasburg from the time he was 75 until his death at 92, and Howard Cook, who was 60 at the time, until his death many years later. The gallery, still run by Rena, now shows aquatints by Doel Reed, watercolors by Mary Hoeksema, and photographs by Van Deren Coke and Eliot Porter, among others. ♦ M-Tu, Th-Su. 138 E Kit Carson Rd (at Dragoon La). 758.2861

18 Casa Benavides Bed and Breakfast Inn $$$$ Many people consider this place, just a block from the Plaza, the finest bed-and-breakfast in Taos. Most of the 30 rooms are spacious; all are furnished in Southwestern motifs with a different emphasis in each room, and feature antique and handmade furnishings, kivas, and down comforters. The **Georgia**

O'Keeffe Room, for instance, is decorated in her favorite pastel colors and has O'Keeffe posters on the wall and a book of her works on the coffee table. The accommodations are in a sprawling compound of restored historic buildings, including an early-day trading post and a former artists' studio, and two rooms in the house down the block where the owners grew up. There is a hot tub on the premises. The staff is friendly, and owners Barbara and Tom McCarthy make sure that their guests are well fed. The complimentary breakfast includes homemade granola, yogurt, fruit, muffins, eggs, tortillas, salsa, pancakes or waffles, and coffee. In the afternoon, tea and home-baked cake or pastries are served. ♦ 137 E Kit Carson Rd (at Dragoon La). 758.1772

19 El Rincón Trading Post Also known as "The Original Trading Post" (there's one in every city in New Mexico), **El Rincón** is filled with fine Indian crafts and jewelry, some of it Old Pawn, and all sorts of Old West memorabilia. It really is original, dating back to 1909, when it was founded by Ralph Meyers, who came from Germany to become one of the first traders in the area. Meyers was a painter, furniture maker, weaver, Indian trader, and general jack-of-all-trades who also taught jewelry making and pottery making to the Indians under WPA (Works Progress Administration). In his trading days he collected early Indian artifacts; many are on display, but not for sale, in a museum within the trading post. Meyers's wife still runs the well-stocked shop. ♦ Daily. 114-A E Kit Carson Rd (between Paseo del Pueblo and Dragoon La). 758.9188

19 El Rincón $$$ A 12-room bed-and-breakfast right beside the trading post goes by the same name and is run by Meyers's daughter, Nina, and Paul Castillo. Each guest room is furnished differently: the **Pioneer Room** has a Franklin stove and is decorated with a Winchester rifle and buffalo hides; the **Yellow Bird Deer Room** is brightened by Indian pottery and beadwork; the **Paisley Room** has Oriental rugs, teak woodwork, and a Balinese goddess of fertility giving her blessing over the queen-sized bed. Ten of the rooms have fireplaces, and five have whirl-

pools. You can't get more into the heart of Taos—or its ancient spirit—than this place. ♦ 114-B E Kit Carson Rd (between Paseo del Pueblo and Dragoon La). 758.4874

19 Total Arts Gallery Six rooms strung out in railroad-car style and separated by adobe archways make up the most agreeable representational gallery in town. Owner Harold Geller, who hails from Toronto, began the gallery in 1969 off a grassy courtyard and added more rooms as people left the adjoining spaces. His humanistic sensibility permeates the works shown. The variety of human personality shines through every painting, whether they be figure studies, still lifes, or landscapes. Each small room has its own feel yet they are all linked by a unifying taste, from the serene oil figures by Milt Kobayshi, to the more "hip" oil figures of Kim English, to the strong still lifes of Joan T. Potter, to the semi-abstract landscapes of Teruko T. Wilde, Gay Patterson, and Ovanes Berberian, to the nudes of Sherrie McGraw, the rich oil portraits by David A. Leffel, and the Mexican pastels of Albert Handell. ♦ Daily. 122-A E Kit Carson Rd (between Paseo del Pueblo and Dragoon La). 758.4667

19 Taos Book Shop The oldest bookshop in New Mexico (it was founded in the 1940s), this store (illustrated above) has the feel of an extended home library, complete with a few chairs. Under the current owner, Taos native Deborah Sherman, it specializes in Southwestern books and out-of-print titles, and Spanish and Indian tapes. There's a separate room full of children's books. ♦ Daily. 122-D E Kit Carson Rd (between Paseo del Pueblo and Dragoon La). 758.3733

Restaurants/Clubs: Red	**Hotels:** Blue
Shops/ 🌳 **Outdoors:** Green	**Sights/Culture:** Black

19 Caffe Tazza ★★$ A venerable old folkie such as Bob Dylan or Joni Mitchell is likely to be playing on the tape deck when you enter this place, the best feature of which is an outdoor patio beside a grassy courtyard. The menu offers homemade soups and locally made tamales as well as assorted espressos, cappuccinos, and desserts. Live entertainment is provided on weekend evenings. ♦ M-Th breakfast and lunch; F-Su breakfast, lunch, and dinner. 122 E Kit Carson Rd (between Paseo del Pueblo and Dragoon La). 758.8706

COURTESY OF KIT CARSON HISTORIC MUSEUMS

20 Kit Carson Home No name blankets the region more than that of this renowned frontiersman, scout, hunter, soldier, and Indian fighter (a phrase that has been dropped from the encyclopedias, but nonetheless remains the truth). The old home in which he lived during his years in Taos is now a museum, and the street it sits on—the second largest in Taos—bears his name; the park in which he is buried is also named after him, and tens of thousands of acres of surrounding greenery are known as the Carson National Forest.

A native of Kentucky, Carson ran off when he was 17 with a group of fur traders headed for Santa Fe. Adopting Taos as his soul's home in 1826, he bought this 1825 12-room adobe (pictured above) in 1843 as a wedding present for his bride, Josefa Jaramillo. Carson and his family lived here for 25 years, though he was often away months at a time fighting battles and blazing trails from New Mexico to California. In 1868 Carson and his wife died within a month of each other. Three of the rooms in the museum are furnished much the way they would have been back then. Other rooms

include gun exhibits and mountain-man lore. ♦ Admission. Daily. 113 E Kit Carson Rd (between Paseo del Pueblo Norte and Las Cruces Rd). 758.0505

21 Brooks Indian Shop In Margery Hanisee's modern Indian shop, almost all the work is signed by the artists. Fine pieces by Julian Lovato of **Santo Domingo Pueblo** are the standout in the jewelry case. Black pottery made by the grandchildren of Maria Martinez is another of the highlights of this shop, which opened in 1972. Also featured are intricate black-and-white Acoma pots by Geraldine Sandia and **Jemez Pueblo** pots by Lucy Lewis and her daughters, Emma and Delores. Drums and kachinas are also on display. ♦ Daily Memorial Day-Labor Day; M-Sa the rest of the year. 108-G E Kit Carson Rd (at Paseo del Pueblo). 758.9073

22 Horse Feathers Almost everything that has do with the Old West can be found here, including hats (the store's specialty), old spurs, boots, books, playing cards, a Lone Ranger board game, Western movie memorabilia, and assorted junk. Owner Lindsey Enderby presides in a cowboy hat and a friendly Western smile, beneath a sign that says: Where the West Lives On. ♦ M-Sa. 109 E Kit Carson Rd (at Paseo del Pueblo). 758.7457

23 Taos Inn $$$ A National Historic Landmark, this is probably the premier hotel in town. Parts of the building date to the 1600s, though it was renovated in the 1980s while retaining its historic charm. The lobby is a rustic orchestration of wood furniture, adobe archways, and walls adorned with rugs and artwork. The 40 guest rooms have the same Southwestern motif, with Indian-style wood-burning fireplaces; cable television brings guests into the late 20th century. Off the lobby is the **Adobe Bar**, a popular hangout for local artists, writers, and anyone else who wants to come. ♦ 125 Paseo del Pueblo Norte (between Kit Carson Rd and Kit Carson Park). 758.2233, 800/826.7466

Within the Taos Inn:

Doc Martin's ★★$$$ The home of Dr. Paul T. Martin from the 1890s to the early 1940s, today it's one of the city's best-known restaurants. Repeatedly honored for its extensive wine list by *The Wine Spectator* (the wines are also available for purchase in the inn's wine shop), it also offers friendly service and a selection of good New Mexican food and continental specialties, including seafood and game dishes. One popular choice is grilled venison medaillons with red-wine and cherry sauce. ♦ New Mexican/Continental ♦ Daily breakfast, lunch, and dinner. 758.1977

24 Governor Bent House Charles Bent was a prominent 19th-century trader who ran wagon trains along the Santa Fe Trail. When New Mexico became part of US territory during the Mexican War in 1846, Bent was named its first governor. But many local Indians and Hispanics did not care for the idea of US rule, and on 19 January 1847, they surrounded Bent's house and began to pound down the doors. When Bent asked what they wanted, he was told, "We want your head, gringo!" And they got it. Bent's family was permitted to leave, but the governor was killed and scalped in his own home. Today the house is a museum displaying frontier memorabilia. It also contains a gift shop and a gallery of Western art. ♦ Donation. Daily. 117 Bent St (between Paseo del Pueblo Norte and Camino de la Placita). 758.2376

25 Bent Street Deli and Café ★★★$ This centrally located deli serves first-rate food indoors and on heated patios. The menu is relatively small but is original and tempting; you won't have trouble finding just the sandwich you want. The Reuben, filled with lean corned beef, may be the best this side of New York City. The Taos (sliced turkey, fresh green chile, bacon, and guacamole rolled in a flour tortilla) is excellent. The kitchen will also create a sandwich mixing any of 14 ingredients. Breakfast is served until 11AM, and hot dishes are also served at dinnertime. A glass counter at the front offers meats, cheeses, and desserts to go. The service is faultless. This is one of those places that clearly aims to please—and does. ♦ Deli ♦ M-Sa breakfast, lunch, and dinner. 120 Bent St (between Paseo del Pueblo Norte and Camino de la Placita). 758.5787

26 Moby Dickens A clever name has helped put this bookstore on the Taos map. Founded in 1984 by Art and Susan Bachrach, it's a good, complete shop that rambles on down a series of narrow rooms, while a cat sleeping in a basket seems bored with the notion of literature. ♦ Daily. 124-A Bent St (between Paseo del Pueblo Norte and Camino de la Placita). 758.3050

26 G. Robinson, Old Prints and Maps The cartographer's art depicting every segment of the globe as it was recorded from the 16th to the 19th centuries hangs on the walls or is stacked for perusal at this shop. Old-fashioned prints and engravings offer variety. Perhaps to mix it up with the real world, George Robinson also serves as manager of the **Dunn House** (no phone), the two-story complex that houses Robinson's store, **Moby Dickens, La Tierra Mineral Gallery,** and about 20 other shops and galleries. ♦ M-Sa. 124-D Bent St (between Paseo del Pueblo Norte and Camino de la Placita). 758.2278

26 La Tierra Mineral Gallery Wonderful fossils in which whole schools of fish have been captured in a single rock are among the many natural wonders in this small gem of a shop run by Ellen Ross. "Made in the U.S.A. 75,000,000 Years Ago," says a sign, and Mother Nature was doing good work even back then. Fossil dinosaurs and sea scorpions, and mammoths' teeth are on display behind glass cases along with crystal formations and other natural treasures. This is a quiet, thoughtful resting place amid the surrounding myriad of art galleries. ♦ M-Sa. 124-G Bent St (between Paseo del Pueblo Norte and Camino de la Placita). 758.0101

27 Apple Tree Restaurant ★★$$$ One of the best-known restaurants in town is located in a historic two-story house that's painted yellow with white trim like a country cottage. The outdoor patio is dominated by an enormous apple tree, and the white-cheddar and green-chile hamburger is good, as is the chicken mole. The menu also features several vegetarian entrées. ♦ New Mexican ♦ Daily lunch and dinner. 123 Bent St (between Paseo del Pueblo Norte and Camino de la Placita). 758.1900

28 Tapas de Taos Café ★★$ Día de los Muertos (the Mexican holiday of the dead) is the decorative theme of this offbeat restaurant, with a collection of carved, wooden skulls set row after row on the walls of one room in a 300-year-old adobe. If you don't find that appetizing, there are pleasant outdoor patios in front and back. The choice of tapas on the menu is limited, but they are very good. One dish is satisfactory for a light lunch, and two should do nicely at dinner, when, happily, the prices remain the same. The shrimp and vermicelli pancake is superb, and the fried calamari is tasty. More robust Mexican dishes are also served. ◆ Tapas ◆ Daily lunch and dinner. 136 Bent St (between Paseo del Pueblo Norte and Camino de la Placita). 758.9670

29 Stables Art Center Once the grandest home in Taos, this lovely adobe building was the site of the city's most enduring murder mystery. In 1883 Englishman **Arthur Rochford Manby** came to New Mexico to get rich by speculating in ranching, mining, and other schemes in the newly opened American West. Schemes is the proper word, because that apparently was what he was best at. In 1898 he bought seven parcels of land just north of Kit Carson's home, and—trained as an architect—he designed and built a 19-room Spanish hacienda set in a square with three wings and stables in the rear. He laid out gardens in the English style, with sunken pools, trees, lawns bordered by roses, hollyhocks, and poppies. Within a few years it was filled with English furniture. In 1917, when New York socialite Mabel Dodge Sterne arrived in Taos, she wanted to rent the biggest and best home in town. She chose the **Manby** house, and he agreed to rent it to her for $75 a month. When she built her own home two years later, **Manby** moved back in. On 3 July 1929, his body was found in one room of the house, decapitated—his head was found in an adjoining room. The head was so mutilated that some said it was not **Manby,** that he had procured a body and faked his own death to escape people who were after him. (Others blamed his own mean dog.) For months the murder was the talk of New Mexico. To this day it has not been solved. Investigators found that countless people had motives, and the likelihood is that someone he bilked in one fraudulent scheme or another had taken revenge. According to some, his ghost still appears from time to time in the middle patio.

The house is now home to the **Stables Art Center,** a gallery run by the Taos Art Association. The group was founded in 1952 by Emil Bisttram and other local artists to promote art and help the artists show their work. They purchased the house, turned it into a museum, and converted the stables into a gallery. The museum project soon became unmanageable and was discontinued, and the art center moved to the front of the house (the **Twining Weavers** shop is housed in the former stables). In its early years the cooperative gallery existed to show the work of artists on the cutting edge who were denied space in the more conservative galleries in town. In recent years it has become merely one more local gallery.

The Taos Art Association has more than 700 paid members in a town of fewer than 6,000 residents. It sponsors the performing as well as the visual arts. In addition to the gallery, the building houses **The Stables Shop,** run for the art association by Vikki Madden, which sells fine art and quality crafts. Be sure to spend a few quiet moments in the lovely courtyard out back. ◆ Daily. 133 Paseo del Pueblo Norte (opposite Martyr's La, adjoining Kit Carson Park). 758.2036

29 Twining Weavers The long, low adobe stables behind the **Manby** house that used to house the gallery are now home to a large shop that features weaving and contemporary crafts. The old adobe bricks peek through the outer walls in spots. Huge skeins of wool in many colors are visible from the courtyard as you approach. Inside, owner Sally Bachman plies her craft and shows her handwoven rugs, tapestries, and pillows, as well as work by other gallery artists in fiber, basketry, and clay. ◆ Daily. 135 Paseo del Pueblo Norte (behind the Stables Art Center). 758.9000

30 Kit Carson Memorial State Park A few steps north of the stables that house **Twining Weavers** is the entryway to this welcome green space in the middle of town. As you move into the park away from the road a sense of solitude overtakes you, and with the rims of the mountains visible in the distance, you can see why a settlement arose here. This land was once part of the grounds of the **Arthur Manby House.** Toward the rear is a cemetery where Kit Carson is buried next to his wife. An iron fence surrounds the simple grave of the Indian fighter, who died on 23 May 1868 at the age of 59. A number of his descendants who were also named Kit are buried nearby. In a far corner of the cemetery, almost unnoticeable, is the grave of Mabel Dodge Luhan, Taos's famous hostess, who died in 1962. Also here is the grave of Padre Antonio José Martinez, who was defrocked and excommunicated by Bishop Lamy in 1856 over religious differences. The padre, who reportedly helped spur the 1848 Taos Indian revolt, founded his own church and had his own followers until his death in 1867. Just outside the cemetery fence, for some reason, is the grave of **Arthur Manby,** where his body and head are reunited. ◆ Paseo del Pueblo Norte (between Kit Carson Rd and Garcia Pl)

31 Patrick Dunbar A long rectangular enclave of grass divided by an unpainted boardwalk leads from the street to one of New Mexico's veteran antiques merchants. Old wagons, an adobe camel, and a gorgeous ornate garden swing fit only for the courting of a princess, preside over the lawns. Stacked against the outside walls are antique Oriental rugs, old wooden cabinets, and architectural relics.

Inside is a busy bazaar of rugs and antique treasures. ♦ Daily. 222 Paseo del Pueblo Norte (between Garcia Pl and Civic Plaza Dr). 758.2511

31 The Brodsky Bookshop Taos abounds with visitors who come here to go skiing, hiking, hunting, and fishing. The best place for them to get their bearings is in this shop, which specializes in all sorts of three-dimensional and topographical maps of the region. It is also a solid all-purpose bookshop and contains a throwback to the 1950s—a rental library. ♦ Daily. 218 Paseo del Pueblo Norte (between Garcia Pl and Civic Plaza Dr). 758.9468

32 Fechin Institute Renowned painter **Nikolai Fechin** was an architect from Russia who emigrated to Taos and became one of the leading lights of the village's art colony. This two-story house, which he designed and built in 1928, was long considered one of the marvels of adobe architecture. It contains hand-carved woodwork that combines Russian and Spanish traditions. The building, which contains **Fechin**'s own work and his art collection, is now used as a cultural and educational center. Tours are available. ♦ Admission. W-Su afternoon. 227 Paseo del Pueblo Norte (at Montaño La). 758.1710

33 Ten Directions Books In an enclosed room devoted to pre-owned literature within this used-book store, there's a small table with a large chess set on it, flanked by two chairs, and a sign that reads: "Chess fiend in residence." The fiend is Chris Clevenger, who owns and operates the store with his wife, Alice. The shop specializes in books on Eastern religions and the Southwest, including works by local authors, and will do special book searches. ♦ Daily. 228-C Paseo del Pueblo Norte (at Montaño La). 758.2725

33 The Fenix Gallery Named to conjure associations with the myth of the phoenix, this gallery represents 18 contemporary artists, all of whom live in Taos at least part of the year. The space is simple and bright, a no-nonsense place to show art. Opened in the late 1980s, this gallery is a must-see for serious collectors visiting the area. Gallery owner Judith Kendall says, "Anything original and

new, particularly when it comes from the archetypal—that's what I respond to." Among the things she has responded to recently are the bold mixed-media creations of Ginger Mongiello, the abstract oils and ceramics of Lee Mullican, one of her best-known artists, and the expressionist oils of Alyce Frank, as well as the paintings of Earl Stroh, among the last of the old-time Taos "Modernists." ♦ Daily. 228-B Paseo del Pueblo Norte (at Montaño La). 758.9120

34 Michael's Kitchen $ Owned by the Ninneman family, this casual place is one of the more popular low-priced restaurants in Taos. The food, especially at dinnertime, is somewhat pedestrian—the hamburger with green chile is a bit greasy, and their version of a Reuben sandwich is made with ham, not corned beef. Still, there is usually a waiting line, and the fellow in front folding huge stacks of colorful **Michael's Kitchen** T-shirts is sure evidence that it's the tourist trade they're after. The menu is enormous, however, and the breakfast items—eggs, pancakes, and waffles—are served all day. ♦ American/New Mexican ♦ Daily breakfast, lunch, and dinner. 304-C Paseo del Pueblo Norte (between Montaño La and Brooks St). 758.4178

35 Spirit Runner Gallery This gallery of Indian images, which is only open in the summer season (in the winter it becomes a ski rental place) is owned by Ouray Meyers, who must be the only offspring of a German immigrant named after a Ute Indian chief. Ouray is the son of the late Ralph Meyers, who founded the **El Rincón Trading Post** (see page 86) back in 1909. A photo taken by Ralph of Walter Ufer and Tony Lujan picnicking with Mabel Dodge Luhan hangs on the wall. The most evocative work in this uneven gallery is by Ouray himself, who paints airbrushed watercolors of spirit runners, both human and equine. His most moving piece in the gallery is an all-white paper cast of an Indian woman gazing longingly at **Taos Pueblo** in the distance. You can't tell if she is leaving for good or coming home after a long absence; it makes you want to know. Ross Lampshire fashions evocative pottery with three-dimensional pueblo ruins set into the sides. ♦ Daily Apr-Oct. 303 Paseo del Pueblo Norte (between Brooks St and Montaño La). 758.1132

Georgia on My Mind

In popular American iconography, two legendary figures have become the most prominent symbols of New Mexico. The southern, cattle-raising half of the state is the gunslinging, murderous province of William H. Bonney, aka Billy the Kid. But Northern New Mexico belongs, perhaps for all eternity, to a solitary woman who dressed all in black, her hair pulled back in a bun as severe as her personality. Like one of the ghosts of local lore, the image of Georgia O'Keeffe still stalks the land.

Born in Wisconsin in 1887, O'Keeffe became famous in New York City through the efforts of her husband and chief promoter, photographer Alfred Stieglitz, who featured her work in his 291 gallery. She was 41 years old and a fixture in the New York art scene before she fell in love with New Mexico.

Accepting an invitation from Mabel Dodge Luhan to visit Taos in 1929, O'Keeffe came west by train with her friend Rebecca Strand. She was immediately taken with the fierce desert beauty. She spent that summer, and the next, painting the landscape near Taos, the church at **Ranchos de Taos,** and huge crosses that she could see from Mabel's house. Roaming far afield, she discovered **Abiquiu,** a village 60 miles north of Santa Fe (for more on Abiquiu, see page 77). She decided at once that this was her soul's home. Beginning in the mid-

1930s she spent every summer at Abiquiu, apart from her husband, who refused to travel to the primitive, wild West. When Stieglitz died in 1946, O'Keeffe moved to Abiquiu permanently and lived there until her death at age 98.

To drive through that region today is to see the work of O'Keeffe come to life. The red hills she captured on canvas are there, along with the hills striped horizontally in pink, white, and yellow, and the hills tinted dark gray, where she often found solace, and where she walked alone in later life. She also painted the cow skulls she found in the desert, the dry bones, the wildflowers, the bright blue sky—everything except the people. For in the world of O'Keeffe, the land was the only star; there was little room for humanity. She never learned to speak Spanish, which was the language of the villagers all around her. She remained as aloof, tough, forbidding, and hostile as the landscape itself.

It is in a sense appropriate that her two homes in the region are not open to the public, that no museum in the region is dedicated to her work, that her only true monuments are those made by nature. Admiring her art, one might wish she had been a more sociable human being. But if she were, she might not have become as enduring as the stunning hills she chose to call home.

36 Orinda Bed & Breakfast $$$ This updated and enlarged adobe residence in a valley just outside of town, surrounded by pastures and woodlands, provides country-style peace and privacy within a 15-minute walk of the Plaza. The three guest accommodations, ranging from a single room with a queen-size bed to a large suite that can sleep up to six people, have kiva fireplaces, beamed ceilings, and plenty of Southwestern charm. Gourmet continental breakfast is served in a dining room decorated with Navajo rugs and paintings by local artists. Guests also have use of a living room with a library, fireplace, and media center. ◆ 461 Valverde La (off Valverde St, between Lund St and Martinez La). 758.8581

The artists' colony in Taos got its start in 1898 with American artists Bert Phillips and Ernest Blumenschein, who were on their way to Mexico on a painting expedition when their wagon broke a wheel outside of town. Stranded long enough to discover the charm of Taos, they decided to stay, and their paintings lured other artists from the East Coast and Europe.

"No man who has seen the women, heard the bells, or smelled the piñon smoke of Taos will ever be able to leave."

Kit Carson, Indian fighter and Taos resident for 42 years

The best-known artist in Taos, R.C. Gorman, is Navajo. He moved there in 1968. "I came as a tourist and refused to leave," he says. "Taos is the most beautiful place I know."

Restaurants/Clubs: Red   **Hotels:** Blue
Shops/ Outdoors: Green   **Sights/Culture:** Black

Additional Highlights of Taos and Day Trips

Some of the best things to see and do on a visit to Taos are on the town's perimeter or farther afield in the surrounding countryside. A visit to **Taos Pueblo** is the prime emotional reason for coming to Taos. The pueblo can be visually breathtaking, illuminating in its historical context, and depressing in its moody mixture of pride and subjugation—all at the same time. **Taos Ski Valley**, if you're so inclined, is 19 miles northeast and offers the most spectacular skiing in New Mexico, a challenge to world-class skiers as well as a safe haven for beginners. The largest ski area in New Mexico, Taos is the only place in the state with more visitors in winter than summer. The **Rio Grande Gorge Bridge**, where nature's handiwork and human ingenuity intersect between two steep cliffs, is sure to induce a moment of vertigo. A superb collection of Indian art is housed in the **Millicent Rogers Museum**. The church at **Ranchos de Taos**, one of the most painted and photographed in the world, will please any shutterbug.

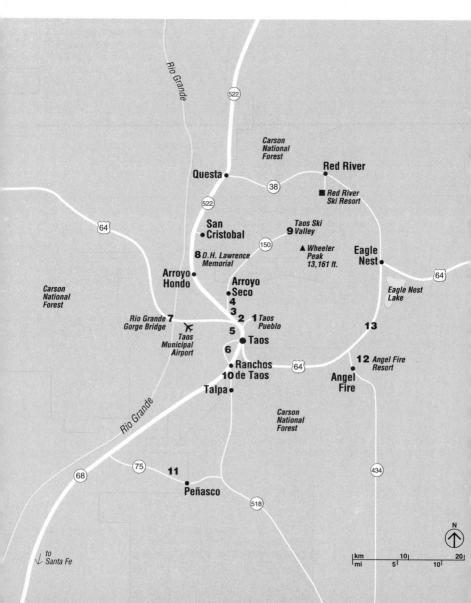

The town of Taos is surrounded by **Carson National Forest,** a 1.5-million–acre expanse of pine, aspen, and Douglas-fir woods on the slopes of the **Sangre de Cristo Mountains.** Several roadless areas of the forest have been set aside as federally protected wilderness areas, including **Wheeler Peak,** the highest mountain in New Mexico at 13,161 feet, and the northern part of the vast, alpine **Pecos Wilderness,** which extends all the way to Santa Fe, Pecos, and Las Vegas. The **Enchanted Circle,** a loop drive of about 100 miles of scenic views in the forest, offers photo opportunities galore. Unpaved roads off the drive suitable for four-wheel-drive travel into the forest expand touring, mountain biking, and hiking possibilities. The area also includes **Picuris Pueblo,** the smallest pueblo in the state, and **Angel Fire Resort,** a ski area with less advanced slopes than those at the Taos ski basin.

Taos Pueblo

ANTONIO COCILOVO

Additional Highlights

1 Taos Pueblo One of the most intriguing creations in the American West, this pueblo (illustrated above) is just a few miles north of town. Two huge multistoried brown structures (the tallest section is five stories high) built out of mud and straw rise from the plain on either side of the Rio Pueblo, which divides the plaza. Wooden ladders lead from one level to the next, and doorways are visible on every level. Men and women wrapped in blankets move about, some baking bread in outdoor ovens. This is the oldest continuously occupied apartment dwelling in the US. It existed in much the same form as far back as 1540, when members of the expedition led by Spanish explorer Francisco Vásquez de Coronado came upon it during their search for the Seven Cities of Cibola—the legendary seven cities of gold. If they happened to arrive at sunset, they surely must have thought this was one of them. (Some historians believe it was the Indian pueblos that gave rise to the legend.)

An Indian community existed at Taos more than 500 years before Columbus came to the New World. The pueblo, with its soft mud curves, was the forerunner of the architecture that is now symbolic of the entire region. And the people, though primarily peaceful, were the most rebellious of all the pueblos in their resentment against foreign intrusion. It was this pueblo that led the revolt that drove the Spanish from the region in 1680. Even when the southern pueblos were subjugated by Don Diego De Vargas in 1692, **Taos Pueblo** continued to rebel for another five years. A century later, when the Taos Valley was under repeated attacks by Plains Indians, many of the Spanish settlers took refuge in the pueblo's massive buildings. About 1,500 Taos Indians (who speak the native Tiwa language) now reside here.

A visit to the pueblo can be both inspirational and depressing. A certain exhilaration is sparked by the age and primitive beauty of the structures themselves. But a resentment that seems to hang heavily in the air itself can bring one back to reality. The pueblo derives much of its income from tourism. Visitors are charged for parking and charged again if they want to photograph, sketch, or paint the pueblo; if you want to photograph individuals, you are expected to ask permission and to tip them as well. Some ground-floor apartments house small shops where the residents sell jewelry and other crafts to visitors. They are a proud, independent people, as their rebellious history demonstrates, and pueblo residents do not wholly welcome the intrusion of tourism.

The pueblo feast-day celebration is held on 29 and 30 September. Other special days are the Turtle Dance, 1 January; Deer or Buffalo Dance, 6 January; Foot Races, 3 May; Corn Dances, 13 June and 24 June; the Powwow, second weekend in July; Santiago's Day, 25 July; and Deer Dance or *Matachines* on Christmas Day. Dances are open to the public, but (except for the Powwow) cannot be photographed. ♦ Admission. Daily. Paseo del Pueblo Norte (2 miles north of Taos). 758.9593

2 Laughing Horse Inn $$ This 1887 adobe hacienda became the home of Spud Johnson when he arrived in Taos in 1924. A writer and satirist, Johnson worked as secretary to Mabel Dodge Luhan while publishing from this adobe, on a handset press, *The Laughing Horse Press,* a sheet of satirical and literary works of the time. When D.H. Lawrence came to town, Spud gave him a bed, and that was the start of his open-door policy. Georgia O'Keeffe, Gertrude Stein, and Alice B. Toklas came to visit; frequently on the premises was Santa Fe poet Witter Bynner, who was Johnson's partner in life. Today, this colorful, ramshackle inn offers four small rooms that have a loft bed, six rooms with regular beds, two suites, and a penthouse. Only the penthouse and suites have private baths; the other guests share three bathrooms in the inn, although each room has a VCR and color TV set. There's a central hot tub and music and video libraries, and the whole place snuggles like a shaggy dog under shade trees on the banks of the Rio Pueblo. Across the road is an adobe double guest house (each with its own bathroom and fireplace) with redwood decks; one section sleeps four, the other six, and the door between them can be opened to accommodate a household of ten. Mountain bikes are available free for guests. There is no restaurant, but a full breakfast is served daily. ♦ 729 Paseo del Pueblo Norte (2 miles north of Taos). 758.8350, 800/776.0161; fax 751.1123

3 Brett House ★★$$$ Although D.H. Lawrence lived in Taos for only a short time, Lady Dorothy Brett, a British painter who came to Taos in 1922 as a traveling companion to Lawrence and his wife Frieda, became a central figure in the burgeoning local arts community and lived in this adobe house for 31 years until her death in 1977. Now a restaurant, its walls are graced with works by leading Taos artists and photographers. Picture windows afford a panoramic view of the Sangre de Cristo Mountains that makes sunset a magical time to dine here to the strains of classical Spanish guitar music. The menu emphasizes such continental fare with southwestern touches as poached salmon in hollandaise sauce and rack of lamb with mint sauce and piñon nuts. ♦ Continental ♦ Tu-Sa dinner; daily lunch June-early Oct. Reservations recommended. Taos Ski Valley Rd (at NM 522). 776.8545

4 Quail Ridge Inn $$$ This sleek, sprawling neopueblo-style resort four miles north of Taos on the way to the ski valley was designed with tennis buffs in mind. The central attraction is the six indoor and two outdoor tennis courts that are open year-round—in winter the outdoor courts are covered with a huge inflatable dome. The 110 guest rooms range from standard hotel rooms to individual 1,600-square-foot casitas. All have large fireplaces, and many have kitchenettes and patios or balconies. ♦ Taos Ski Valley Rd (off NM 522). 776.2211

Within the Quail Ridge Inn:

Carl's French Quarter ★★$$ Tired of spicy New Mexican food? For a change of pace you can enjoy equally spicy seafood and other Cajun and creole specialties at this softly lit, elegant restaurant. The menu is big on shrimp dishes and offers perhaps the only fresh oysters to be found in the Taos area. Also featured are less traditional offerings such as blackened prime rib and tempting desserts that include key lime pie. ♦ Cajun/Creole ♦ Daily dinner. Reservations recommended. 776.8319

5 Millicent Rogers Museum Millicent Rogers was a model and oil heiress who moved to Taos in 1947. She became interested in Indian and Spanish Colonial art and, in a few short years, acquired one of the best collections of such art in the country. When she died in 1953, her sons founded this private museum. Pottery, jewelry, baskets, and textiles fill the exhibit rooms, which include a strong collection of pottery by Maria Martinez of **San Ildefonso Pueblo.** The museum now also shows contemporary Indian and Hispanic artists. ♦ Admission. Daily. Off NM 522, 4 miles north of Taos. Turn left (west) just before the blinking light and follow the museum signs. 758.2462

Restaurants/Clubs: Red   **Hotels:** Blue

Shops/ 🌢 Outdoors: Green   **Sights/Culture:** Black

COURTESY OF KIT CARSON HISTORIC MUSEUMS

6 Martinez Hacienda Dating to 1780, this classic Spanish Colonial hacienda (pictured above) looks like an adobe fortress from the outside. It was built without windows in the exterior walls as protection against raids by the Apache or Comanche. Twenty-one rooms face out onto two courtyards. Now a museum, the hacienda features rooms illustrating life-styles of the colonial period, and exhibits depicting the history of trade on El Camino Real. The place is named after Severino Martinez, scion of a prominent family that built the hacienda two centuries ago. His son, Padre José Martinez, was a popular clergy-man who allegedly participated in the 1847 revolt against American occupation and was later excommunicated by Bishop Lamy. ♦ Admission. Daily. NM 240 (Ranchitos Rd), 2 miles south of Taos. 758.1000

7 Rio Grande Gorge Bridge For millions of years the Rio Grande—which in truth does not appear very grand in this region—has been cutting its own canyon into the ancient lava flows that formed this area. In 1965 a steel bridge spanning the gorge was completed. Park beside the bridge and walk out to its center, and you are almost certain to experience a moment of vertigo as you look down the steep canyon to the river, which flows like a tiny ribbon far below. The bridge, 650 feet above the river, is the third highest in the US, after the Royal Gorge Bridge in Colorado and the Glen Canyon Bridge in Arizona. The reality is awesome, but photos cannot capture it. ♦ On Hwy 64, about 12 miles northwest of Taos

8 D.H. Lawrence Memorial Driving north on State Road 522 there is a well-maintained dirt road on the right that wends into the mountains for another 4.5 miles until it reaches the ranch that Mabel Dodge Luhan tried to give to D.H. Lawrence in the 1920s. Lawrence did not want to be beholden to Mabel and declined the ranch, but his wife, Frieda, accepted it in exchange for the original manuscript of *Sons and Lovers*. In one of the wooden cabins clustered together here, Lawrence wrote parts of *The Plumed Serpent*. The Lawrences lived here for several years before returning to Europe, where the writer died in France in 1930. Some years later Frieda had his body exhumed and cremated, and she returned to Taos to bury his ashes in the mountains he loved. Fearful that the covetous Mabel would steal the ashes, Frieda had them mixed into the cement of a small shrine, which looks like a miniature white cabin, built on the ranch. (Frieda is buried just outside the shrine.) Visitors from all over the world now come to pay homage to the author and sign the guest book. The shrine is located up a zigzagged walkway from the ranch buildings. The ranch is now owned by the **University of New Mexico** and is maintained as a scholarly retreat. ♦ Free. Daily. Call ahead in winter for road conditions. NM 522, about 11 miles north of Taos. 776.2245

9 Taos Ski Valley Serious skiers from all over the country come to the Taos ski basin. Its stunning alpine setting—the peak elevation is 11,819 feet, base elevation is 9,207 feet—gets more than 26 feet of snow annually. There are 71 ski runs: 51 percent are classi-fied expert, 25 percent intermediate, and 24 percent beginner.

New Mexico ski pioneer Ernie Blake, who took up residence in Santa Fe after World War II, founded the resort. While he was manager of the Santa Fe ski basin in 1949, he began to implement his dream of creating his own ski resort. A native of Switzerland, Blake made repeated flights over the Sangre de Cristo Mountains looking for a spot in which to re-create the Alpine retreats of his youth. He chose a valley north of Taos with stunning views of the Carson National Forest, and the resort has been booming—and expanding—ever since. About 20 lodges located at the ski valley, in the alpine village, and on the road to the valley provide rooms for more than one thousand skiers. Many offer ski package rates exclusively. At others you can book rooms alone. ♦ Thanksgiving weekend-early Apr. 18 miles northeast of Taos via Hwy 64 and NM 150. 776.1111, 800/776.2916, snow report 776.2916

So numerous were Indian pueblos and cliff dwellings on the Pajarito Plateau around Los Alamos and Bandelier National Monument that the plateau's population was larger in AD 1300 than it is today. Of the 7,000 known archaeological sites on the plateau, many are still used for secret ceremonies today by Pueblo Indians.

"The moment I saw the brilliant, proud morning shine high up over the desert of Santa Fe, something stood still in my soul, and I started to attend. There was a certain magnificence in the high-up day, a certain eagle-like royalty. . . , Ah, yes, in New Mexico the heart is sacrificed to the sun and the human being is left stark, heartless, but undauntedly religious."

D.H. Lawrence

Ranchos de Taos Church

M. BLUM

10 Ranchos de Taos Church Although the proper name of this church is **San Francisco de Asis Church,** it is more widely known as "Ranchos de Taos Church" because Georgia O'Keeffe named it thus in numerous paintings. In 1929 and 1930 O'Keeffe painted the rear of the church, with its sweeping mud walls that look like natural creations, omitting the crosses in the front and any other sign of the human touch. The church (illustrated above) has been open since 1815 and is still used for masses, weddings, and funerals. The curving rear supports face west, and the changing light and shadows have made this one of the most painted and photographed churches in the country. A slide show depicting the history of the church is given several times a day at the church office across the street. ◆ St. Francis Plaza, Ranchos de Taos, 4 miles south of Taos. 758.2754

Day Trips

11 Picuris Pueblo The smallest pueblo in New Mexico is tucked into Hidden Valley, about 20 miles south of Taos. It was first settled around AD 1200 and over the next two centuries grew into a multistory adobe structure. The pueblo was abandoned after the Pueblo Revolt of 1680 but was reestablished in the 1700s. Ruins of the original pueblo are still visible and can be toured. If hunger strikes, stop in at the pueblo's **Hidden Valley Restaurant** (★$; 587.2957), which serves traditional pueblo food as well as American fare. The tribe also runs a gift shop/museum and offers fishing in two stocked lakes. Business ventures have expanded to the capital—the pueblo is 51 percent owner of the **Hotel Santa Fe,** which opened in 1991. The tribal feast day is 10 August. ◆ Fees for photography, sketching, and filming. Daily. Off NM 75, about 28 miles southwest of Taos. 587.2957

Andrew Dasburg, a prominent American cubist, moved first to Santa Fe and then to Taos early in this century. "I felt as though I had come upon the Garden of Eden," he said.

12 Angel Fire Resort Founded in 1967 by Texan Roy Leubus, this ski resort offers families affordable lodging and ski programs for kids. The slopes are mostly for beginning and intermediate skiers, though there are a few runs that challenge the experts. Off-beat events, such as the world shovel race championships, in which contestants shoot down the mountain at high speeds on scoop shovels, are also available to guests. And when there's no snow, you can fish, hike, bicycle, golf, and camp. ◆ Take Hwy 64 to NM 434, 24 miles east of Taos. 377.6661, 800/446.8117, snow report 377.6401

13 Enchanted Circle North of Taos, this one hundred-mile loop of highways offers spectacular views. If you have the time, do not miss it, and be sure to take your camera. You can drive in either of two directions, pass beyond New Mexico's highest mountain, Wheeler Peak, which tops off at 13,161 feet, and not have to return to your starting point along the same route. The drive alone takes less than two hours, but chances are you'll want to take in some side sights along the way.

If you head east out of Taos to Highway 64—out Kit Carson Road—you'll switchback through forestland and come to a turnoff to **Angel Fire.** For the Enchanted Circle, however, proceed on Highway 64. You'll quickly arrive at the **Disabled American Veterans Memorial Chapel** (377.6900). Built in the shape of wings, it peers down from a hill overlooking the Moreno Valley. The chapel was built by Dr. Victor Westphall in memory of his son David, a marine who was killed in action during the Vietnam War. An emotional video is shown in the chapel daily at 9AM.

The next stop along the way is Eagle Nest, nestled in a valley beside a lake of the same name. You can stop and fish here along 15 miles of shoreline, or rent a boat. At Eagle Nest, the Enchanted Circle continues on NM 38, which will bring you to Elizabethtown, an Old West ghost town with a long-deserted mining camp. Look for a cattle guard on the left to find it. Continuing north on 38, you sta a long ascent over Bobcat Pass (check the road conditions in winter). Behind you is an incredible view.

As you bottom out of the pass you'll be in the town of Red River. In the 19th century gold was discovered in the hills, and Red River became one of the wildest towns in the West. By 1905 there were 3,000 people in the village. There were four hotels, 15 saloons, and a red-light district. But by 1925 the mines had played out. Today the population is down to 350, and the hell-raising is mostly a memory. The wild life offered now is mostly hiking and fishing, though country music swings in the nightspots.

Whether you stay overnight or keep going, your next stop on NM 38 is Questa. High on a hill, this village offers stirring views of the valley below. Hiking, fishing, and camping are available at the nearby **Wild and Scenic Rivers Recreation Area** (758.8851), where the Red River and the Rio Grande come together just northwest of town.

Heading south on NM 522, you'll pass the turnoff to the **D.H. Lawrence Memorial** (see page 95) on your left. Then it's past the village of Arroyo Hondo, where artist R.C. Gorman lives in the big house on the left, and back into Taos.

Bests

Judy Buck
Real Estate Broker, Taos

Apple Tree Restaurant—Fabulous casual spot with an outside patio perfect for summer dining. The staff is very friendly.

Shopping on **Bent Street** and the **Dunn House** shops area—With their carnival atmosphere, it's much more exciting than the Plaza.

Total Arts Gallery—This is a standout among the many other good galleries and consistently has the highest quality art.

Sagebrush Inn—There's a unique Taos two-step band atmosphere in this bar. Come here to see and be seen.

Taos Inn—They have a great meet, greet, and hangout bar, plus an excellent restaurant.

Taos Pueblo—This is what makes Taos special. Go for some of the ceremonial dances, the Powwow, or on Christmas Eve.

Jess Williams
Editor, Taos News

Rio Grande Gorge Bridge—A great view for those undaunted by heights. Be sure to check out the graffiti on the underside. Holy cow!

Taos Pueblo—A living museum (with friendly people) where the past meets the present and gives hope for the future. A must.

Adobe Bar at the historic **Taos Inn**—Live music frequently, killer margaritas consistently, and always the world's best nachos.

West Mesa (Petroglyph National Monument)—At night, under a clear sky, you can see stars to the edge of the universe.

Taos Ski Valley—If you ski, you'll fall in love with this resort immediately; if you don't ski, you'll soon find plenty of rationalizations for learning.

Natalie Goldberg
Author

Mabel Dodge Luhan House—Bathroom windows painted by D.H. Lawrence, on the edge of Pueblo land.

Lumina Gallery—Old Victor Higgins's house.

Lambert's

Ouray Meyers
Artist/Owner, Spirit Runner Gallery, Taos

I was born across the street from Kit Carson's home in Taos and grew up playing in the shadows of **Taos Pueblo**. I love the spirit and magic of this valley and its mountains. The town's character is a unique blend of old Spain, Mexico, and American Indian. Visit for just two days, and you won't even begin to experience it.

Michael's Kitchen for breakfast—In the winter, skiers form a line at the door; in the summer, tourists queue up. The pancakes and burritos are worth the wait.

Apple Tree Restaurant for lunch—Try the shrimp burrito and blue-corn tortillas (and be sure to call for reservations).

El Patio for dinner—Don't miss the buffalo roast chimichangas served with black beans and *posole* (dried corn kernels treated with mineral lime), and topped with red or green chiles.

Sagebrush Inn for country and western dancing.

The **Taos Pueblo** anytime, but try visiting for the Powwow in July, San Geronimo Days in September, or the Christmas Eve procession.

Taos—Spring and fall arts festivals and our 70-plus galleries.

Kit Carson's home, the **Martinez Hacienda** (the only active Spanish hacienda left in the country), and the world-renowned **Millicent Rogers Museum.**

R.C. Gorman
Artist/Owner, Navajo Gallery in Taos and Albuquerque

Because of its excellent restaurants, **Taos** is a marvelous place to get fat and sloppy yet remain exceedingly happy. Ties and jackets are not required for men, but you can't tell a lady not to look her best because she will do it anyway.

One must eat at the **Brett House** and **Lambert's.**

Albuquerque

On 23 April 1706 New Mexico Governor Francisco Cuervo y Valdes took a seat within his dimly lit palace in the capital of Santa Fe and composed a formal letter to his sovereign, the Duke of Alburquerque, viceroy of New Spain. He wrote: "I certify . . . to the most excellent señor viceroy that I founded a villa on the banks and in the valley of the Rio del Norte in a good place as regards land, water, pasture, and firewood . . . and named it the *Villa de Alburquerque*." There, Cuervo y Valdes continued, in accordance with the laws under which Spanish colonial towns were founded, some 35 families had taken up residence, a church had been built, government buildings erected, and irrigation ditches streamed nourishment to newly sown crops of beans, squash, and corn. Finally, he boasted, "I do not doubt . . . that in a short time this will be the most prosperous villa. . . ."

But Cuervo y Valdes had lied. When he first arrived in this remote, arid valley stretching along a broad bend of the **Rio Grande**, he found fewer than 20 families here, and they were plagued by disease and floods. True, the location was ideal: the river was a good irrigation source and the *bosque* (wooded area) and nearby mountains produced ample wood. But the governor's erroneous claim that 35 families inhabited the area was made only to skirt Spanish law, which required a minimum of 30 families to charter a villa. The governor, however, was a politically ambitious man eager to gain the good graces of the viceroy; thus, by naming the new

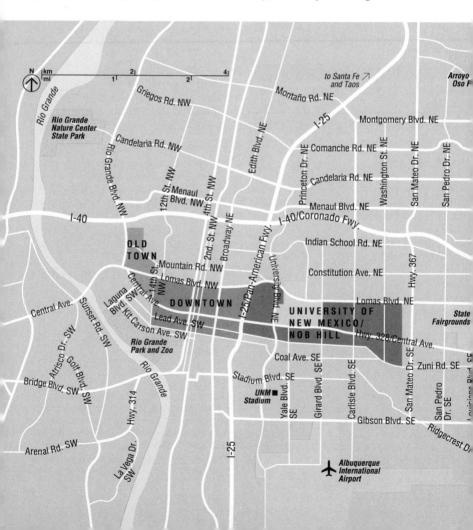

settlement "Alburquerque" (the first "r" was dropped later on) in the Duke's honor, he felt assured of his superior's approval. He won it, and in the midst of his political maneuvering, the tiny Villa de Alburquerque was born.

Nearly three centuries later, Cuervo y Valdes's unscrupulous actions are legendary, but to some, his assertion that the faraway frontier outpost would one day be a "most prosperous villa" has proved no less than visionary. Indeed, with a population nearing a half-million, Albuquerque today is the biggest city in New Mexico and home to one-third of the state's residents. A major center of transportation, science, education, and technology, the city is the state's economic and industrial core. Tourism is big business, too, and an estimated six million people visit the city each year. As home to a multicultural mix of Hispanics, Native Americans, Anglos, and more, the city is also a nucleus for centuries of ancient regional culture, history, and lore.

From its humble adobe beginnings beside a plaza on the city's southwest side, Albuquerque has survived several incarnations. In the late 1800s, the arrival of the railroad two miles east of the original town site brought droves of new people, spurring a shift in population and commerce that resulted in the creation of a vital "New Town" beside the tracks. Later, as the city began to spread out around it, New Town became **Downtown**, the city's central business district. There in 1926, **Route 66,** the historic highway of legend and song, sliced through the downtown area along **Central Avenue**, transforming the provincial "Duke City," as the city is commonly called, into a burgeoning neon strip of hotels, diners, truck stops, and more.

World War II made the city a major national center for military research and production, and a new influx of arrivals wasn't far behind. By the mid-1950s, however, residents old and new began shifting their buying power from downtown to the new **Northeast Heights**, a modern and rambling residential quarter with strip malls at practically every turn. Downtown fizzled as the city continued to sprawl in all directions. And during the next 30 years, as Albuquerque slowly came to terms with its urban identity, the city settled into the vast metropolis that exists today.

Map labels:
Osuna Rd. NE
to Sandia Peak Aerial Tramway
Montgomery Blvd. NE
Comanche Rd. NE
Candelaria Rd. NE
Menaul Blvd. NE
Wyoming Blvd. NE
Eubank Blvd. NE
Indian School Rd. NE
Juan Tabo Blvd. NE
Chelwood Park Blvd. NE
Hwy. 556/Tramway Blvd. NE
Los Altos Park
Lomas Blvd. NE
I-40/Coronado Fwy.
Wyoming Blvd. SE
Central Ave.
Eubank Blvd. SE
Albuquerque Chapter Boundaries:
Old Town
Downtown
University of New Mexico/Nob Hill
F St. SE
H St. SE

Sitting in central New Mexico at the crossroads of Interstate 25 and Interstate 40, the modern Albuquerque stretches 12 miles east from the Rio Grande to the towering **Sandia Mountains,** 3.5 miles west to the rugged remnants of ancient volcanoes, and 14 miles north and south through the lush agricultural **Rio Grande Valley.**

Commanding the view on the city's eastern edge are the Sandia (Spanish for watermelon) Mountains, massive granite outcroppings that blush shades of watermelon at sunset. **Sandia Crest,** the cool 10,678-foot-high mountain summit, is reached via an 18-minute aerial tramway ride, which is the world's longest. Climbing almost three miles from the northeastern outskirts of the city to the rocky crest, the tram passes above craggy cathedral cliffs and forests of aspen and pine, providing a stunning view of the entire city. To the far west are the lava-crested mesas that serve as reminders of the city's volcanic past. There, along miles of volcanic escarpment, you can glimpse into the world of early Indian inhabitants, who as long ago as AD 1300, etched some 15,000 petroglyph drawings into the dark basalt. The city's rural North and South valleys provide a meandering mix of farms, orchards, chile fields, and fruit and vegetable stands.

Albuquerque hosts the state's two largest annual events: the New Mexico State Fair, a down-home celebration of exhibits, entertainment, and regional cuisine held in September, and the October International Balloon Fiesta, the largest gathering of balloonists in the world. It's home to the **Albuquerque Dukes,** the Triple-A Pacific Coast League farm team of the **Los Angeles Dodgers;** to Kirtland Air Force Base and Sandia National Laboratories, major centers for defense, high technology, and science; and to the **University of New Mexico,** the state's largest educational institution. It's surrounded by the homes of ancient Pueblo Indian tribes— Acoma, Cochiti, Isleta, Jemez, Laguna, Sandia, San Felipe, Santa Ana, Santo Domingo, Zia, and Zuni—who continue to practice their traditional ways of life. Albuquerque's wide open spaces, stunning vistas, and magical natural light also provide an inspirational home to scores of artists, photographers, writers, nature lovers, and more.

Due to its size, the city is best toured by automobile, with walking tours in the most historic sections of town. **Old Town,** the site of the city's original settlement, retains the architectural charm and cultural spirit of its Spanish founders. Today, as the city's top tourist draw, Old Town enjoys the most foot traffic. Other popular walking spots include Downtown, the **University of New Mexico,** and the **Nob Hill** district, all of which feature a mix of the historic and the contemporary and lend a more modern appeal to ancient Albuquerque.

Divided into north and south by Central Avenue, and east and west by the Downtown railroad tracks, the city is comprised of four quadrants—NE, NW, SE, and SW. Unlike the more compact cities of Taos and Santa Fe, Albuquerque is often accused of being infected by urban sprawl. But that's fine with the city's down-to-earth residents, who claim they'd rather be "infected," than as affected and expensive as its trendier northern neighbors. Better yet, they boast, no one would ever dare call Albuquerque quaint.

Old Town

Sitting squat and unassuming in a southwest corner of the sprawling city of Albuquerque, Old Town, with its ancient adobe architecture and serene village ambience, might appear to be no more than a quaint reminder of days past. Yet **Plaza Vieja,** as the area's Spanish founders called it, remains the heart of Albuquerque's centuries-old Hispanic heritage.

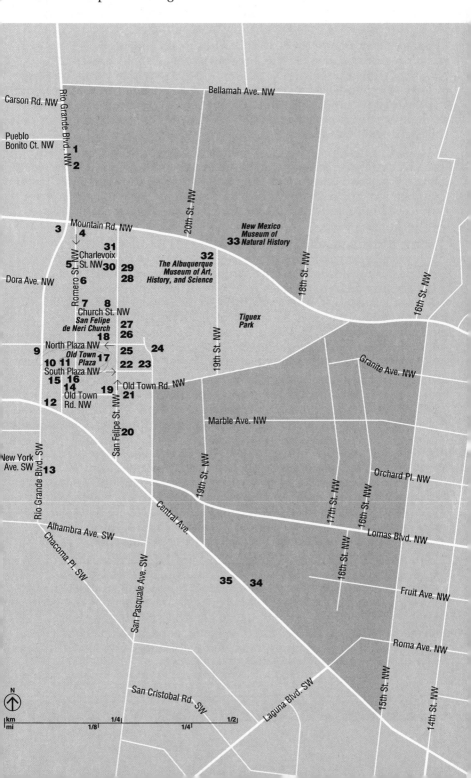

Established in 1706, along the winding banks of the **Rio Grande,** Old Town is the prized site chosen by Provincial Governor Don Francisco Cuervo y Valdes to become the *Villa de Alburquerque,* in honor of the Duke of Alburquerque, viceroy of New Spain. It began as a scattering of small farms and a simple adobe church, and the new settlement drew nourishment from the waters of the Rio Grande and a deeply rooted Catholic faith.

By about 1780 a traditional Spanish town had taken shape: A central plaza was surrounded by rows of humble earthen homes, shops, and civic buildings, while a newer and larger New Mexican–style church—**San Felipe de Neri**—loomed peacefully overhead. Within a century, the town was firmly established as a burgeoning center of commerce, a community of nearly 2,000 residents where traders traveling the Santa Fe and Chihuahua trails met to sell and exchange their wares.

The arrival of the railroad in 1880 spurred new opportunities for growth and trade, along with an influx of Anglo-Americans to the region. But the location of the railroad two miles east of the established town caused a dramatic shift in population. The result of the birth of a booming "New Town"—today's Downtown—alongside the railroad tracks, and the demise of Old Town as the area's economic hub.

Now more than a hundred years later, even as a bustling city of nearly 400,000 has grown up all around it, Old Town hasn't died. Though the area declined during the initial post-railroad era, it was rediscovered in the 1930s by artists inspired by its timeless architectural beauty and merchants who believed the arts, cuisine, and traditions of the Hispanic residents held tremendous tourist appeal. During the next 20 years, Old Town was transformed as original buildings were restored in the Pueblo Revival style. And by the 1970s, a delightful mix of shops, galleries, and restaurants had sprung up to make Old Town one of Albuquerque's top tourist attractions.

Although it's now geared primarily to tourists, Old Town retains an air of history and charm. Ancestors of many of the original settlers still live in the area, and significant buildings and sites are now listed on state and national registers of historic places. Its secluded patios and winding brick paths harbor hidden gardens and other interesting finds, while the tree-shaded **Old Town Plaza** (known to locals as the "Plaza") is the perfect place for people watching or enjoying an occasional performance of music or dance. Wild West gunfights are staged on **Romero Street** on Sunday afternoons. And on Christmas Eve, those willing to brave the winter chill bask in the golden glow of some 500,000 *luminarias* (small candles set in sand at the bottom of a small paper bag) that cover Old Town from sidewalk to rooftop, an age-old tradition symbolizing a lighting of the way for the Christ child.

Concentrated within an area of approximately four square blocks, Old Town can be explored easily on foot. In fact, parking opportunities are few and far between, so walking is usually unavoidable. The downside is that with nearly 200 shops, restaurants, and galleries in the area—most of them specializing in Southwest something or other—your chances of encountering one too many wooden howling coyotes and machine-made "ancient" Indian artifacts are pretty high. The suggestions included here will guide you to some of the most authentic and intriguing spots.

1 Sheraton Old Town $$$
Larger-than-life-size *bultos* (traditional Hispanic hand-carved images of saints) flank the lobby of this modern 11-story structure. The giant statues are part of the annual April Founder's Day procession commemorating Albuquerque's establishment in 1706, and they lend an air of Southwest tradition to this otherwise contemporary inn. The 190 large guest rooms are adorned in desert hues with simple handwrought furnishings and Southwest-style crafts, and the south-facing rooms, which overlook Old Town, have private balconies. **Old Town Place,** the hotel's gallery/gift shop row sells Southwestern goods. The hotel is within walking distance of the historic sites and shops of Old Town, as well as the **Albuquerque Museum of Art, History, and Science** and the **New Mexico Museum of Natural History.** ♦ 800 Rio Grande Blvd NW (between Mountain Rd and Bellamah Ave). 843.6300, 800/237.2133; fax 842.9863

Within the Sheraton Old Town:

The Rio Grande Customs House ★★$$
Set in a rustic atmosphere reminiscent of early seafaring days (very non–New Mexican), this restaurant and pub specializes in beef, seafood, and New Mexican cuisine, as well as combinations of the above. Try the red chile–dusted shrimp or the guacamole hamburger (green chile is optional). The prime rib is also a favorite, and Sunday features an excellent champagne brunch. ♦ New Mexican/American ♦ M-F lunch and dinner; Sa dinner; Su brunch and dinner. Reservations recommended. 843.6300

Cafe del Sol ★★$ This hotel coffeehouse is a casual breakfast and lunch spot offering everything from snacks to full meals. The menu includes a variety of New Mexican dishes as well as soups, salads, and sandwiches. Liquor service is also available. ♦ New Mexican/American ♦ Daily breakfast and lunch. 843.6300

Albuquerque Children's Museum Shops line the indoor walkway that connects the dignified lobby area of the **Sheraton Old Town** to this children's museum full of hands-on exhibits. There's a bubble zone, a giant loom, a dress-up area, a capture-your-shadow wall, a giant camera, and make-it, take-it art activities. ♦ Admission. Tu-Su. 842.5525

New Mexico, famous for its high altitudes and dry climate, was covered by shallow inland seas teeming with marine life 75 million years ago. At that time, Albuquerque's Sandia Crest, now towering above the city at an elevation of 10,678 feet, was hundreds of feet *below* sea level.

2 Maria Teresa Restaurant & 1840 Bar
★★★$$$ Salvador Armijo, a prominent merchant and politician, built this sprawling adobe hacienda for his family more than a hundred years ago. Constructed with 32-inch-thick adobe bricks and few windows, the structure is a classic example of 19th-century New Mexico architecture—when defense was as big a consideration as aesthetics—and is listed on the National Register of Historic Places.

Today, the building houses one of the city's most elegant restaurants. Seven of its 12 rooms are now individual dining areas that bear the names of Armijo family members and are decorated in a mix of Victorian antiques and early Spanish-American furnishings, including a wine press and a piano belonging to the original family. The lounge features an 1840 bar that hails from an old-time saloon in the southern part of the state. Outside, a beautiful courtyard and garden is a favorite place for warm-weather diners.

An innovative dinner menu features steak, chicken, seafood, and a host of classic New Mexican specialties. Recommended are raspberry chicken, *carne adovada* enchiladas (cubed pork marinated in a rich red-chile sauce on a blue-corn tortilla), and lamb fajitas. Lunch always includes some excellent fish dishes, and Sunday brunch offers a good mix of New Mexican dishes and traditional breakfast fare. Weekday Happy Hours are a good excuse to try the fresh lime margaritas. ♦ Steak/Seafood/Southwestern ♦ Daily lunch and dinner. Reservations recommended. 618 Rio Grande Blvd NW (between Pueblo Bonito Ct NW and Mountain Rd NW). 242.3900

3 Plaza Don Francisco Cuervo y Valdes
Dedicated on 23 April 1988, this site is highlighted by a massive bronze sculpture of Albuquerque's founder, Don Francisco Cuervo y Valdes, created by artist Buck McCain as part of the city's Arts in Public Places program. Looking dashing and noble, like any good Spanish conquistador should, the sculpture depicts a triumphant Cuervo y Valdes, in flowing cloaks and armor, trotting on horseback into the tiny village he founded on the banks of the Rio Grande on 23 April 1706. Native landscaping completes this picturesque point of interest, a popular spot for taking tourist pics. ♦ Mountain Rd NW and Rio Grande Blvd NW

Restaurants/Clubs: Red	Hotels: Blue
Shops/ ♣ Outdoors: Green	**Sights/Culture:** Black

4 The Candy Lady Take just one step inside this house of sweets and you'll be hard put to decide which is more sinful: entering the room to your right marked with a sign that reads "This Room Rated X" or moving straight ahead to counters chockablock with chocolates and other candy treats. After 15 years in Old Town, owner Debbie Ball knows how to lure visitors of every ilk.

Whatever your pleasure, fudge fans revel in the 15 to 20 varieties offered daily, including a special red-chile recipe mixed with bits of the spicy stuff. The piñon, New Mexico's buttery native nut, is deliciously combined with toffee, chocolate, or caramel, and has become a favorite replacement for the peanut in brittle. Jalapeño jelly beans are another fiery favorite, and the chocolate-dipped strawberries are always fresh. The shop also boasts the city's best selection of "diabetic" chocolate sweets, up to 30 types of hard and soft candies made with all-natural sugars.

The X-rated section features such explicit sweets as candy panties, chocolate male members, and protuberant pink mint-candy breasts. Anatomically correct cakes can also be special ordered. ◆ Daily. 524 Romero St NW (at Mountain Rd). 243.6239

5 Adobe Gallery Once the site of the **Old Town Post Office,** this 1879 Territorial-style home is the perfect setting for a gallery specializing in historic Southwest art. Emphasizing works of the Southwest Indians, the 16-year-old gallery features a high-quality, handpicked selection of pre-1940 Navajo textiles; pueblo pottery dating from 1860 to 1930; pre-1940 Navajo and Zuni jewelry; plus a fascinating array of Hopi kachina dolls and some contemporary pueblo pottery. Shop owners take credit for bringing to popularity the now-famous Storyteller doll—the open-mouthed pottery figurine who spins legendary Indian tales to piles of children on its lap. On display is a select collection of the dolls created by the master Storyteller-makers of **Cochiti Pueblo,** who still use strictly traditional materials and techniques, as well as beadwork and dollhouse-size kachinas, baskets, and pottery. The gallery's east end is

a showcase for works by deceased artists, including Carl von Hassler, dean of the early Albuquerque art colony. There's also a fascinating library of more than 500 titles on everything you've ever wanted to know about Southwest Indian art. ◆ Daily. 413 Romero St NW (south of Mountain Rd). 243.8485

6 Tanner Chaney Gallery Weekend Navajo weaving demonstrations are just one of the highlights to be found in the spacious adobe showrooms of this fine gallery of American Indian art. The collection includes one of the city's most impressive displays of quality Indian jewelry as well as historic and contemporary pottery, weaving, sculpture, kachinas, baskets, and fetishes (objects said to have the power to protect their owner)—all handmade by Indian artists from around the country. Equally impressive is the historic gallery space (one of the oldest haciendas in Old Town), which provides some fine examples of early New Mexican architecture and spills out onto an airy outdoor patio awash in hibiscus and bougainvillea. The owners also run **Native Gold** (Native American gold jewelry; 400 Romero St NW, between Charlevoix and Church Sts, 247.4529, 800/255.5425) and **Legends** (classic Native American arts; 2047 South Plaza, between Romero St and Rio Grande Blvd, 243.7300, 800/243.7302). ◆ M-Sa; Su noon-6PM. 410 Romero St NW (between Charlevoix and Church Sts). 247.2242, 800/444.2242

7 The Christmas Shop One of Old Town's old-time merchants, this shop specializes in all things Christmas all year-round. Stocking everything for tree and trim, they feature an international hodgepodge of handmade holiday crafts hailing from as far away as Russia, Poland, and Germany, as well as the Southwest. How about red-and-green-chile lights and ornaments for your tree? Or a pueblo pottery nativity scene? And cactus cookie cutters come in your choice of saguaro or prickly pear. ◆ Daily. 400 Romero St NW (at Church St). 843.6744

8 Sunbird Southwestern Fashions This out-of-the-way women's clothing store, tucked behind the historic **San Felipe de Neri**

Catholic Church, features natural fibers in simple, casual styles. The shop emphasizes Out West wear you can actually wear: hand-embroidered and fine art T-shirts; back-to-basic blouses; denim, cotton, leather, and rayon skirts; and even cowboy boots. There's also a wide assortment of accessories: belts, bags, hats, and jewelry all made by local artisans. ◆ Daily. 2113 Church St NW (between Romero and San Felipe Sts). 243.5909

9 Esperanza Fine Furniture Fortunately, woodworker Mark Gonzales didn't lose *esperanza* ("hope" in Spanish) when a fire destroyed his furniture factory and showroom (pictured above) just outside of Albuquerque some years back. Instead, the sixth-generation New Mexican relocated to Old Town, where he rebuilt his business into the area's only exclusive collection of fine hand-crafted furnishings. Using Spanish, Indian, and country motifs, Gonzales fashions all of his pieces after the historical designs of the Southwest, combining ponderosa pine and red oak with hand-forged iron hardware. A local stable of master craftspeople then hand-carve his interpretations into finely detailed dining room, living room, and bedroom collections that echo the simple functional furnishings of the past. The collection fits right into the beautiful adobe showroom (circa 1912). Don't miss the other showroom upstairs. Best of all, there's ample parking in the rear. ◆ M-Sa; Su 12:30-6PM. 303 Rio Grande Blvd NW (at N Plaza). 242.6458

10 Santo Domingo Indian Trading Post Though it may look a little dark and dusty, this small shop offers some of the best bargains in Albuquerque on traditional turquoise-and-silver Indian jewelry. A few years ago, in a misguided attempt to improve the image of Old Town, a coalition of art gallery owners succeeded in persuading the city to pass an ordinance prohibiting Indians from selling their crafts in the Plaza area. One of the Indian vendors, **Santo Domingo Pueblo** native Manuelita Wagner, responded by renting this shop space in which to sell her work and that of her friends. After public protests, the city eventually repealed the law and let the vendors return to the Plaza; Manuelita's shop flourished, and she has opened a second location on the other side of Old Town. ◆ Daily. 2049 S Plaza NW (at Rio Grande Blvd). 766.9855. Also at: 401 San Felipe St NW (between Church St and Mountain Rd). 764.0129

11 Santa Fe Store Owner d'Alary Dalton hails from Santa Fe, and her shop is better than most you'll find there. The spotlight is on traditional and contemporary Hispanic folk art from Northern New Mexico to Ecuador to Peru. Especially notable are the traditional *retablos* (painted images of saints), *bultos* (three-dimensional carvings in the round), *colcha* (bedspread or counterpane) embroidery, and tinwork of New Mexicans Anita Romero Jones and Monica Halford, whose fine work embodies the artistic traditions that have been at the heart of the state's Hispanic culture for centuries. But the best part is Dalton's large collection of folk art animals: multicolored monkeys, leopards, snakes, iguanas, bears, elephants, penguins, giraffes, and more inhabit her whimsical animal kingdom. A special Oaxacan collection features brightly painted dragons and other mystical critters, while the graceful hand-crafted creatures of New Mexico artists Joe Ortega and Max and David Alvarez exemplify some of the finest woodworking in the state. ◆ Daily. 2041½ S Plaza NW (between Romero St and Rio Grande Blvd). 242.4707

11 The Last Straw Art & Gift Gallery An Old Town favorite since 1975, this tiny shop of collectibles is a showcase for more than 40 of New Mexico's Hispanic, Anglo, and Indian artists. Exclusive to the shop are the works of internationally known Robert Rivera, whose unique hand-painted gourds have inspired a new American art form. Rivera tailors classic Indian motifs to the natural shape of gourds, often embellishing them with rare stones and other natural touches. Also featured here are the exquisite hand-painted eggs of Ruben Gallegos, the traditional *retablos* of Irene Martinez Yates, watercolors by Noami Slater, **Acoma Pueblo** pottery miniatures, and a sleepy cat that's usually lounging in the window. ◆ Daily. 2039 S Plaza NW (between Romero St and Rio Grande Blvd). 243.2175

12 Smiroll's International Cuisine ★★★$$$ This understated dining spot offers a quaint Old World setting and a menu that's quite different from the typical New Mexican cuisine that's so popular in these parts. It bills itself as the House of Veal, and the tender calf is indeed the specialty here: Decide among veal francese, veal piccata, veal cordon bleu, veal parmigiana, veal scallopini, and a delightful Wiener schnitzel. The duck and Cornish game hen are tasty, too, and the homemade Italian sausage or prosciutto with melon are super starters. An extensive selection of seafood, pasta, and fine wines rounds out the international repertoire. ◆ International ◆ Daily dinner. Reservations recommended. 108 Rio Grande Blvd NW (at Central Ave). 242.9996

Restaurants/Clubs: Red	**Hotels:** Blue
Shops/ 🌳 Outdoors: Green	**Sights/Culture:** Black

13 Casas de Sueños $$$ A scant two blocks south of Old Town, these little "houses of dreams" are situated amid 2.5 acres of intricate English gardens abloom with hollyhocks and roses. Built in the 1930s by J.R. Willis, the cluster of 12 adobe casitas was created as a haven for artists and writers who came to work and relax inside its private environs. But since 1990, when Albuquerque native Robert Hanna took over, this charming bed-and-breakfast has been the choice of visitors who want privacy plus the convenience of having the pleasures of Old Town nearby.

Dwellings range in size from a single bedroom that comfortably fits two people to a two-bedroom suite with a drawing room that's suitable for four. House interiors also vary from an elegant English and Oriental antique decor to a classic Santa Fe–style motif with brick floors, exposed adobe, and kiva fireplace. Another of the old artist's studios is now a dining room with a fireplace and French doors leading to an outdoor eating area that's enveloped by a lush rose garden. A gourmet breakfast is served daily and includes exquisite dishes such as asparagus cheese soufflé and baked curried fruit as well as home-baked pastries and bread, fresh juice, and gourmet coffee. Lunch and dinner are not served, but afternoons feature a traditional English tea service complete with scones, wine, and real English tea.

A small gallery within the main office frequently features readings and exhibits by local artists. Even the office itself (unusually built in the shape of a snail) was created by the well-known local architect **Bart Prince,** whose strangely shaped structures have brought him international acclaim. Inside the "snail" is an extensive concierge service to help you plan your stay. ♦ 310 Rio Grande Blvd SW (between Central and Alhambra Aves). 247.4560, 800/242.8987; fax 842.8493

14 The Moccasin Shop You'll find more than 200 styles of authentic Native American footwear to choose from here. Popular leather and suede slip-ons, ankle-high "squaw boots," and over-the-calf boots by moccasin makers from the historic **Taos Pueblo,** as well as tribes in Minnesota and upstate New York, are available in adult and children's sizes. ♦ Daily. 106 Romero St NW (between S Plaza and Old Town Rd). 243.7438

14 Antiquity Restaurant ★★★★$$$ Originally built as a honeymoon cottage almost a century ago, this ancient adobe still has romance lingering in the air. The secluded restaurant provides two intimate dining areas lined with traditional brick floors and bordered by walls clad in regional art. These rooms look out upon an open kitchen and grill, whence comes an exquisite filet mignon; *crêpes de poulet* (chicken and mushroom crepes in béchamel sauce); and the special chateaubriand for two, charcoal-broiled and carved tableside. Other beef, seafood, and pasta entrées and appetizers are equally delicious, and dessert—*Polyczenta* (ground walnuts, cream, and rum wrapped in crepes and drizzled with hot chocolate sauce)— doesn't get any better than this. ♦ Continental ♦ M-Sa dinner. Reservations recommended. 112 Romero St NW (between S Plaza and Old Town Rd). 247.3545

MARIPOSA GALLERY

15 Mariposa Gallery Providing a wonderful change of pace from the local Indian art galleries, this adobe art space features an extensive (though not necessarily expensive) selection of fine contemporary American crafts. Exhibiting works primarily by New Mexican crafts artists since 1974, owners Fay Abrams and Peg Cronin emphasize traditional craft media—wood, glass, clay, metal, fiber, and mixed media—"that tends toward the whimsical." The wire sculpture, ceramic bolo ties, and hand-painted leather purses are just a sampling of the fun, while hand-painted silk scarves, hand-crafted tableware, and spectacular jewelry exhibit the finer side of things. Don't miss the Día de los Muertos (Day of the Dead) pieces—functional ceramics with skeletal images—by Steve Kilborn. The changing gallery exhibits feature works by some of the area's most innovative emerging artists. ♦ M-Sa; Su noon-5PM. 113 Romero St NW (between S Plaza and Old Town Rd). 842.9097. Also at: 303 Romero St NW (in Plaza Don Luis, at N Plaza). 842.9098

16 John Isaac Antiques A second-story nook overlooking the Plaza is where folk-art fan John Isaac found his niche when he brought his antique pieces here from back East and settled in Old Town in 1985. Isaac's collection has grown considerably since then, evolving into an impressive display of antique folk and Native American art works that would intrigue any serious collector and could convince even the casual admirer to start buying.

Isaac has divided his simple studio into display areas that spotlight various artistic genres and historical periods. One fascinating room is devoted to the devotional materials of the Spanish Empire, and includes *retablos,* ex-votos (offerings of thanks for miracles performed), and other religious objects from

18th- to early–19th-century Guatemala, Ecuador, Mexico, and the Philippines. Another room houses pre-1930 Pueblo and Hopi pottery, baskets, and textiles, while the Latin folk art display highlights traditional Mexican works, including an incredible collection of jewelry dating from the 1920s to the 1960s.

His even rarer collection of religious works by renowned early New Mexico *santeros* (traditional Hispanic folk artists) can be viewed by appointment only. And his recently added **Antigua, Arts of the Americas** gallery showcases a specialized selection of Mexican painted furniture, pottery, ironworks, and tin. ♦ M-Sa. 2036 S Plaza NW (between Romero and San Felipe Sts). 842.6656

17 Old Town Plaza The hub of activity in traditional Spanish Colonial village life was always centered around a plaza, a town square of sorts where residents could gather to talk, take a break from a hard day's work, or simply sit and enjoy the scenery. Thus this plaza, built in 1780, has for centuries served as a social center for scores of local denizens whose families have inhabited the area for generations.

Most recently, however, the Plaza, with its towering cottonwoods, winding brick paths, wrought-iron benches, and graceful white gazebo, has provided a shady haven for visitors who wish to take a respite from their sight-seeing and shopping jaunts. Situated across the street from the **San Felipe de Neri Catholic Church,** the Plaza still forms the core of the original Albuquerque and is surrounded by many of the same adobe structures built by the first settlers, which now house Old Town's popular galleries, shops, and restaurants. At the Plaza's east end stand two reminders of a Civil War skirmish that took place in Albuquerque on 8 and 9 April 1862. The pair of cannons are replicas of those buried behind the **San Felipe de Neri Catholic Church** by retreating Confederate troops. The originals can be seen a few blocks away at the **Albuquerque Museum of Art, History, and Science.** And on Christmas Eve, visitors marvel as Plaza sidewalks are set aglow with some 500,000 traditional *luminarias* that light up the night. ♦ Bounded by N and S Plazas NW, and Romero and San Felipe Sts NW

18 San Felipe de Neri Catholic Church The 16th-century Florentine saint Felipe de Neri, for whom Albuquerque's oldest church (illustrated below) is named, was known as a fastidious man who avoided religious dispute. But the church that has served as the anchor of village faith and the focal point of the Old Town Plaza for nearly three centuries has certainly seen its share of change—and the controversy that often comes with it.

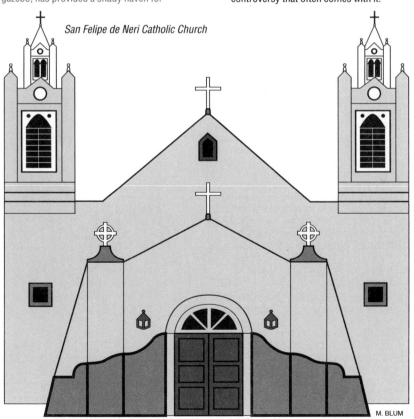

San Felipe de Neri Catholic Church

M. BLUM

Beginning as a small adobe structure among a group of farms on the banks of the Rio Grande, the church was established by Franciscan friars at the same time Albuquerque was founded in 1706. By 1793, the village populace was burgeoning, but years of erosion had taken its toll on the tiny earthen church, and it collapsed. Following a decree by then Governor Fernando de la Concha, a new church was erected. That building, dedicated in honor of San Felipe de Neri, was designed in the traditional New Mexican architectural style, with a flat roof, ceiling vigas, and hand-carved wooden corbels. Today it forms the heart of the present church.

Two centuries later, the church has grown into a massive and curious combination of architectural styles, bearing Spanish Colonial, Gothic, Pueblo Revival, and modern motifs that are far from its simple beginnings. This is due to the culturally diverse group of priests who have overseen the structure through the years, including those of Spanish, Mexican, New Mexican, French, and Italian descent. Each managed to leave his personal mark on the church, but all had to endure the grumblings of their parishioners in the process.

The gradual transformation that eventually would cover up the traditional New Mexican character of the church began in the 1850s when it was redecorated under the supervision of the French priest Father Joseph Machebeuf. The major change was the addition of the ornate Victorian bell towers that still loom above the entrance. Then in 1868, Italian Jesuit priests refurbished the interior, covering the vigas and corbels in tin, adding nontraditional woodwork throughout, and applying trompe l'oeil painting to various surfaces to give the appearance of polished marble. Finally, as recently as 1978, a veneer of artificial stone was applied to the facade and other portions of the church, lending it the look of a suburban ranch house. By this time, the church had been listed on both the state and national registers of historic landmarks, and Father George Salazar, the priest who ordered the stonework, was cited for an infraction against a city ordinance protecting such landmarks. Father Salazar went to court, where the judge ruled the ordinance unconstitutional.

Despite the changes, today the church sits regally amid a crush of Old Town tourist shops and restaurants and still serves an estimated 800 local families. Picture taking is allowed, but be considerate of those who may be at prayer. For an extra special taste of local culture, attend the Spanish Mass on Sunday. ♦ Museum daily. 2005 N Plaza NW (between Romero and San Felipe Sts). 243.4628

19 Anitra's Old Town Poster Company and Gallery After 11 years in business, this small family-run poster shop and gallery still offers the only complete selection of Southwest posters and limited edition prints in Old Town. Included are posters by Amado Peña, R.C. Gorman, Doug West, and naturally, Georgia O'Keeffe. Also featured are original artworks by Oklahoma Cherokee artist Bill Rabbit and the official posters of the annual Albuquerque International Balloon Fiesta. ♦ Daily. 201 San Felipe St NW (at Old Town Rd). 842.1858

20 Böttger Mansion $$$ Built in 1912 by a German immigrant known as Mr. Böttger, this pale-blue Victorian-style home was obviously a blatant departure from the surrounding adobe earth tones and architectural styles that have long characterized the area. Today, run by the Garcia family as the only bed-and-breakfast in Old Town proper, the quaint two-story building is still considered unique to the area and is listed on the National Register of Historic Landmarks.

Situated in a quiet southeast corner of Old Town, the mansion offers a choice of three guest rooms. All are drenched in Victorian-era decor, with delightful floral motifs bouncing off of original tin ceilings and large brass beds. One room features a comfortable sunroom overlooking the patio garden; the second an elaborate hand-painted mural created by an original Böttger family member; while the third boasts glossy marble floors and a private patio. A smattering of pottery and other regional art adds a tasteful Southwestern touch.

Outside, an enclosed grassy courtyard with marble patios shelters guests from the area's tourist bustle. Breakfast is served in the patio garden during the warmer months. Innkeeper Frances Maldonado whips up two New Mexico favorites: homemade *bizcochitos*—honored as New Mexico's official state cookie—and red-chile tortillas, a spicy twist on the plain flour variety. Maldonado's marvelous morning meal might include scrambled eggs smothered in green chile or fabulous apricot French toast and always features fresh fruit, coffee, juice, and tea.

The management happily picks up the tab for parking across the street. ♦ 110 San Felipe St NW (between Old Town Rd and Central Ave). 243.3639

21 American International Rattlesnake Museum There are more than 20 rattlesnake species on display in this specialty "museum" of natural history. The tiny museum (with two aisles of some 28 rattlers enclosed in natural settings) is billed as the largest multispecies exhibit in the country and features snakes from North, Central, and South America. Such interesting oddities as the albino Marilyn and the only patternless Western diamondback rattlesnake in known captivity are popular draws. The display was mounted in 1990 by one-time biology teacher Bob Myers, who wants to dispel the myth of the ferocious rattler. "Rattlesnakes don't attack; they only defend," Myers says, "and they're essential to the ecological balance of the hemisphere." Thus, he strives to educate visitors with an interesting mix of videos and rare artifacts—fangs, skeletons, skins, and the like—dating from as far back as 15 million years. An adjacent display area features unusual and entertaining memorabilia, and a gift shop offers rattlesnake-related souvenirs. No petting, please. ♦ Nominal admission. Daily. 202 San Felipe St NW (at Old Town Rd). 242.6569

21 Montoya's Patio Cafe ★★$ Veronica Montoya's homey New Mexican cafe is a winner in the warmer months, when diners sit outside on the patio munching on the massive Montoya burger (a half-pound burger heaped with green chile and guacamole) and watching the world go by. The beef or chicken fajitas are famous here, too, and the Mexican combo (enchilada, taco, tamale, beans, rice, chile, and tortillas) should satisfy all your cravings for Southwestern food. Some American fare is served, too, and kids have their own menu. Indoor seating is also available. ♦ New Mexican/American ♦ Daily breakfast, lunch, and dinner. 202½ San Felipe St NW (at Old Town Rd). 243.3357

La Placita

22 La Placita Dining Rooms ★★$$ Directly facing the Old Town Plaza, the rambling hacienda now named for Don Ambrosio

Armijo dates back to the city's founding in 1706. Besides housing the prominent Armijo clan, it later served as the family mercantile, where women's lace gloves sold for 10¢ a pair and men's linen underwear went for a buck. During the tumultuous settlement years, the house was also used as a military fort, where soldiers sought refuge behind its three-foot-thick adobe walls. In peacetime, however, the house was alive with music and revelry as Don Ambrosio, known for his love of parties, hosted some of the most lavish balls in town. In 1872, when his daughter, Teresa, married, Don Ambrosio added a second floor to the house and a rich walnut staircase that ran the length of her wedding train. Later, the house fell into disrepair, but was restored to its original state in 1930.

Today guests dine in six spacious rooms clad in fine regional art and furnishings that echo the warm, rustic ambience of early New Mexico. One room, formerly an outdoor patio, has a great tree growing through its roof. Upstairs, **La Placita Gallery** is a showcase for classic Native American and other Southwest art. And strolling Mexican troubadours entertain nightly. Both lunch and dinner feature a selection of traditional New Mexican dishes, such as plump *chile rellenos* (whole green chiles stuffed with cheese), flat and rolled blue-corn cheese or chicken enchiladas, scrambled eggs with green chile and spicy homemade Mexican sausage, and fluffy sopaipillas drenched in honey. The house favorite is a whopping Mexican dinner that includes a red-chile cheese enchilada, *chile relleno,* beef taco, beans, Spanish rice, salad, and sopaipillas. Other entrées include beef, chicken, and fish, and there's a children's menu, too. ♦ New Mexican ♦ Daily lunch and dinner. Reservations recommended. 208 San Felipe St NW (east side of Old Town Plaza). 247.2204

Outside La Placita Dining Rooms:

La Placita Portal Beneath the wooden portal that runs the length of **La Placita Dining Rooms,** Native American artists and craftspeople sell jewelry, pottery, and other wares to passersby. This colorful way of doing business continues a longstanding Old Town tradition. ♦ San Felipe St NW (east of Old Town Plaza)

23 Perfumes of the Desert and Candle Shop Follow your nose through the unusual smells of the Southwest in this family-owned house of fragrance. Located in Old Town since 1948, three generations of perfumers from the Mollenkopf family have created an original array of rare desert scents inspired by the aromatic mountainsides, deserts, and canyons of New Mexico, Colorado, and Arizona. The Mollenkopfs' secret formulas are derived from select native plants of the Southwest and are formulated for the region's dry climate by containing more oil than most perfumes. Yucca, purple sage, ginger blossom, desert mistletoe, and cactus flower are just some of the savory scents you'll find here. Women's perfume and cologne are featured, although men may be tempted by an exotic piñon aftershave. Candles, incense, and other fragrant sundries are available, too. ♦ Daily. No. 4 Patio Market NW (behind La Placita). 242.1745

24 The Old Town Card Shop An Old Town staple since 1957, this shop specializes in richly colored silk-screened cards of your favorite Southwest vista or theme. Hundreds of other greeting cards, postcards, and note cards from more than 75 independent makers (there's not a Hallmark card in sight) also boast regional motifs from the likes of Ansel Adams and Georgia O'Keeffe. Or if you're tired of the Southwest, the rare collection of European paper models of famous castles, cathedrals, and other landmarks might make you dream of a vacation abroad. ♦ M-Sa; Su noon-5PM. 1919 Old Town Rd NW, Plaza Hacienda No. 1 (between San Felipe and 19th Sts). 247.9634

25 La Hacienda Restaurant ★★$$ A charming mural on the outer wall depicts the founding of the city of Albuquerque and the building of this traditional adobe home at the turn of the 18th century. Today, the house has been transformed into a casual New Mexican restaurant where a shady front patio looks out onto the activity of the Old Town Plaza. Inside, the atmosphere is cozy and intimate. The most unusual items on the menu are Mexican-style seafood dishes such as *chimichangas de pescado* (fried burritos made with fish) and tacos Monterey (stuffed with shrimp, crabmeat, and whitefish). Other specialties are regional and include *carnitas asada* (pork marinated in red or green chile), *tostadas compuestas* (deep-fried corn tortillas topped with meat, beans, guacamole, and sour cream), and a savory chile-tortilla soup, as well as delicious homemade desserts such as flan, blueberry piñon ice cream, and tequila lime sherbet. Speaking of tequila, margaritas here are made for a variety of tastes and include melon, Kahlua, apricot, raspberry, and peach. ♦ New Mexican ♦ Daily lunch and dinner. Reservations recommended for large parties. 302 San Felipe St NW (at N Plaza). 242.4866

26 Delmonico's Leslie and Bob Delmonico concentrate on casual Southwest wear in denim and suede and the accessories to go with it. Most notable is their selection of traditional Navajo skirts: Crushed velvet styles come in deep, rich shades of earth and sky, while the cotton quarter-inch pleated "broomstick" design is created by tightly pleating the skirt around a broomstick. The hundred-percent cotton boots and shoes are

another Southwest classic. ♦ Daily. 304 San Felipe St NW (between N Plaza and Church St). 243.9500

SCHELU

26 Schelu Decorative and functional items for hearth and home are featured in this Southwest interiors gallery. Showcasing the works of more than 65 area artists, the six-room space is crammed with everything from handmade lamps, pillows, and place mats to tableware, canisters, pitchers, and pottery. Traditional territorial New Mexican ponderosa pine furniture is also scattered throughout, as well as textiles, designer sculpture, and scores of Southwest knickknacks. ♦ Daily. 306 San Felipe St NW (between N Plaza and Church St). 765.5869

27 Nizhoni Moses, Ltd. *Nizhoni*, in Navajo, means "beautiful," and the Moses family has been bringing some of the area's most beautiful fine Indian art to Old Town for more than 10 years. With pieces from most of the state's 19 Indian pueblos, this small gallery has amassed an incredible collection of Pueblo pottery, including the renowned black pottery of the late Maria Martinez and her great-granddaughters, Barbara Gonzales and Kathy Sanchez. **Acoma, Isleta, Zia,** and **Santa Clara** potters are also represented, as well as Navajo potters Alice Cling and Sue Williams. A few contemporary artists are shown here as well, notably sculptor Dennis Andrew Rodriguez of **Laguna Pueblo.** Pieces of rare Zuni and Navajo jewelry from the famed Egeland Collection are featured along with works by Navajo jeweler Thomas Singer. Also from Navajo land: a select display of weavings (from transition rugs circa 1900 to contemporary textiles), plus fun, one-of-a-kind "mud toys," the whimsical play ornaments of Navajo children. ♦ Daily. 326 San Felipe St NW (between N Plaza and Church St). 842.1808

28 La Crêpe Michel ★★★$$ Finding a French bistro in the heart of Old Town is kind of like finding green chile in Paris: a happily unexpected surprise. This intimate little cafe offers impeccable French classical cuisine, with an emphasis on an inventive array of chicken, seafood, beef, vegetarian, and dessert crepes. The onion soup, escargots, and fresh-baked bread are also classically French, while the luscious chocolate mousse is just plain classic. Diners have their choice of the indoor cafe, an enclosed patio, or an outdoor patio, all of which are equally romantic. Bring your own booze: City law dictates that the restaurant's proximity to the **San Felipe de Neri Catholic Church** makes it ineligible for a liquor license. ◆ French ◆ Tu-Su lunch and dinner. Reservations recommended. 400 C-2 San Felipe St NW, in Patio del Norte (between Patio Escondido and Pueblo Don Gaspar). 242.1251

28 V. Whipple's Mexico Shop Old Mexico meets New Mexico here in Virginia Whipple's exotic Mexican market. Once yearly, Whipple travels to southern Mexico to handpick her specialty stock of Mexican folk art, furniture, dinnerware, jewelry, and glass by artists hailing from places like Oaxaca, Guerrero, Jalisco, Michoacán, and Guanajuato. Highlights include hand-blown glassware in aqua, cobalt, and amber hues; lead-free dinnerware; hand-punched tin; *milagro* charms (traditional offerings for good health); terra-cotta patio furniture; and such traditional Día de los Muertos artifacts as pop-up coffins and sugar skulls. A small selection of Huichol Indian art is also featured, and the bronze door knockers (in the shape of gargoyles, lizards, frogs, and the like) are truly bizarre. ◆ Daily. 400-E San Felipe St NW, in Patio del Norte (between Patio Escondido and Pueblo Don Gaspar). 243.6070

29 Chapel of Our Lady of Guadalupe Though it looks like it could have been erected by original Old Town settlers, this small secluded chapel was built in 1974 under the direction of Sister Giotto Moots, a colorful and controversial figure who once ran a school of religious art on the site. Dedicated in honor of Our Lady of Guadalupe, the patroness of the indigenous peoples of the Americas, the picturesque adobe chapel boasts traditional New Mexican woodwork and a brilliant large-scale image of Our Lady of Guadalupe painted in flaming colors on a prominent inside wall. The chapel is a symbol of the deeply entrenched Catholic faith of the area and provides a nice opportunity for a moment of quiet reflection in the midst of Old Town's tourist flurry. ◆ 404 San Felipe St NW, in Patio Escondido (between Mountain Rd NW and Patio del Norte)

Pitching great Orel Hershiser and first baseman Pedro Guerrero are two Los Angeles Dodgers' superstars who played with the Albuquerque Dukes, the Dodgers' Triple-A farm team (a minor league team that's one step below the majors).

Fiesta in the Sky

Since 1972, when 13 balloons ascended from the parking lot of a local mall, the city has been home to the Albuquerque International Balloon Fiesta, today's largest gathering of balloonists in the world. Every year during the first weekend in October, the city's azure skies and wide open spaces are the backdrop for a nine-day aerial extravaganza featuring some 650 of the world's most talented balloonists, who fly their hot-air and gas balloons through a number of eye-dazzling events.

Pilots from around the planet flock to the fiesta to enjoy some of the best flying conditions in the world. Flanked by mountains on all sides, the city's unique wind and weather patterns create what is known as the "Albuquerque Box Effect," a phenomenon that allows balloonists to traverse the city in different directions and at varying altitudes. With an estimated 1.4 million spectators—plus pilots representing numerous countries including the United States, Switzerland, England, Germany, Canada, Russia, Australia, France, and Japan—the event ranks as New Mexico's biggest, and Albuquerque proudly wears the title "Balloon Capital of the World."

Held on the city's northwest side at the 77-acre **Balloon Fiesta Park,** the event features amazing mass ascensions on the first and last weekends. Balloonists gather at dawn and take to the skies in droves just as the sun rises above the horizon. Then, on the first Sunday of the fiesta, the breathtaking "Balloon Glow" takes place after the sun has set again. Remaining tethered to the ground, the balloons are illuminated, lighting up the night like giant light bulbs.

Throughout the week, pilots compete in a number of events, including the difficult "Key Grab," in which they attempt to steer their balloons from more than a mile away toward a 30-foot-high pole, where a set of shiny new car keys waits to be snatched from the top. On two weekday afternoons, the "Special Shapes Rodeo" takes place, and pilots parade their balloons in such outrageous forms as Santa Claus, the Cow Jumping Over the Moon, Broom Hilda, and a very large tennis shoe. Meanwhile, a number of the city's commercial balloon pilots are on hand during the week to take visitors up, up, and away.

The **Balloon Fiesta Park** is located between Paseo del Norte and Alameda Boulevard, approximately a half-mile west of Washington Place NW. For more information on the Albuquerque International Balloon Fiesta, call 821.1000.

29 Stern's Leatherback Turtle New York refugee Steve Stern has been selling leather goods in Old Town for more than 20 years. Featuring fine leathers from around the world, his collection is all handmade in New Mexico and caters to tastes that range from the briefcase-toting executive to the Southwest-style aficionado seeking a traditional hand-beaded Native American deerskin dress. Other clothing and accessories include skirts, jackets, wallets, handbags, luggage, and belts, many of which feature such fun Southwest touches as fringe or Western-style hand-tooling. ♦ M-Sa; Su noon-5PM. 404 San Felipe St NW, in Patio Escondido (between Mountain Rd NW and Patio del Norte). 842.8496

30 The Good Stuff Richard Hulett offers a large and diverse collection of Southwest antiques and memorabilia at this shop. From the Old West comes his stock of antique cowboy collectibles—bits, spurs, saddles, hats, chaps, and branding irons—dating from the turn of the century to 1940. From Indian country comes vintage pots, baskets, and Navajo rugs plus a prime selection of aged Old Pawn Indian jewelry. From the Hispanic world comes antique textiles, Mexican masks, and religious relics from Old and New Mexico. You might also find that ox yoke you've been yearning for in the "primitives" section, next to the old cheese boards and worn wooden doors. ♦ Daily; evenings by appt. 2108 Charlevoix St NW (at San Felipe St). 843.6416

31 High Noon Restaurant & Saloon ★★★$$$ Located on the corner of a block of former brothels and saloons, this 1750 former woodworking shop mixes a 19th-century saloon atmosphere with a touch of upscale class. The setting is traditional New Mexico territorial, with ceiling vigas (exposed wooden beams), brick floors, and handmade Southwest-style tables and chairs. An interesting blend of Native American and New Mexican art dots walls, ledges, and windowsills, while a skylight in the roof surrounds diners with subtle plays on light and dark, depending on the time of day. Steaks are a specialty here, with choices of rib eye, T-bone, filet, and a hot and hearty pepper steak cooked with cracked black pepper, red peppercorns, and a cream-and-cognac sauce. The high-noon red trout (dusted with blue-corn flour, panfried, and served with avocado margarita salsa) is another favorite, as are the rack of lamb (oven roasted with fresh herbs) and the chicken à l'orange (grilled chicken ast in a zesty sauce of oranges, lemons, glazed leeks, and brandy). Seafood, veal, and a host of New Mexican favorites round out the entrées, and the potent margaritas complement any dish. ♦ New Mexican/Steaks ♦ Daily lunch and dinner. Reservations recommended. 425 San Felipe St NW (at Charlevoix St). 765.1455

32 The Albuquerque Museum of Art, History, and Science Documenting 400 years of New Mexico history, this huge museum houses the largest collection of Spanish Colonial artifacts in the US. Anchoring the collection are two life-size bronze models of Spanish conquistadores, which symbolize the earliest arrival of the Spanish in New Mexico in 1540. Other artifacts include ancient maps from as early as the 15th century (when the Rio Grande spilled into the Pacific), arms and armor used during the Hispanic conquest, and coins and domestic items traded from the 16th to the 18th centuries. A permanent exhibit, *Four Centuries: A History of Albuquerque,* charts the city's evolution from the earliest Hispanic presence to its current existence as the state's industrial center, while a multimedia audiovisual presentation chronicles the development of the city since 1875. Other highlights include permanent and changing exhibits of traditional and contemporary works by New Mexico artists, an extensive photo archive, special children's exhibits, and an outdoor sculpture garden. The museum also hosts hourlong walking tours of Old Town. ♦ Museum: free; tours: fee. Museum: Tu-Su; tours: M-W 11AM, Sa-Su 1:30PM; call for reservations. 2000 Mountain Rd NW (at 19th St). 242.4600

33 New Mexico Museum of Natural History "Spike" the pentaceratops and "Alberta" the albertosaurus greet visitors at the front door to this state museum, and they are just two of the natural wonders in this treasure-trove of New Mexico natural history. Strikingly modern, the museum entices adults and children alike to bone up on 12 billion years of history with some of the most interesting, innovative, and entertaining educational exhibitions anywhere. Indeed, a good part of this world of wonders was designed by professional Disneyland artists who know the meaning of the word adventure.

The adventures here include the *Evolator,* an impressive high-tech video ride through 35 million years of New Mexico geologic history and time; an active volcano that oozes hot lava beneath a see-through glass floor; a cool Ice Age cave; and a 3,000-gallon shark tank that evokes the New Mexico of 75 million years ago, when Albuquerque and most of the state were covered by an inland sea. Today, there's a lot less water in the state, and the museum's 85-foot-long replica of the Rio Grande educates visitors about the state's most precious water resource. Another permanent exhibit charts the evolution of the horse.

The museum is also home to the incredible **Dynamax Theater,** whose two-and-a-half-story-tall screen magically transports viewers into the vast natural land- and seascapes the earth has to offer. The theater is a favorite for kids, who are also encouraged to participate at the **Naturalist Center,** where they can touch snakes and frogs, buzz about beehives, and make tracks of New Mexico's indigenous animals in the sand. ♦ Admission. Daily. 1801 Mountain Rd NW (between 18th and 20th Sts). 841.8837

Within the New Mexico Museum of Natural History:

Museum Cafe ★★★$$ Dine in the shadow of a giant pterodactyl and choose from a diverse menu that ranges from tuna salad to French country pâté at this memorable spot. The chef's salad and the chicken salad (with bacon, lettuce, and tomatoes) are particularly good. Desserts are also wonderful, as is the view of the Sandia Mountains from the outdoor terrace. ♦ New Southwestern ♦ Daily lunch. 841.8837 ext 59

34 Duran Central Pharmacy Established in 1912 by Pete Duran a few blocks west of its current location, this pharmacy quickly rooted itself in the hearts and stomachs of local residents by featuring some of the finest *remedios* (traditional herbal remedies) and one of the most popular luncheon counters in the city. Two moves and more than 80 years later, its present owner, Albuquerque native Robert Ghattas (he bought the pharmacy in 1964), hasn't messed with Duran's formula for success; good personal service and good local grub are still the standards here.

In addition to its established collection of more than a hundred medicinal herbs, such as *osha* (good for colds and flu) and *yerba buena* (good for upset stomachs), today's spotless, sprawling pharmacy includes a huge selection of sundries ranging from cosmetics to candy, greeting cards to gift wrap, coffeemakers to comic books. Some unexpected finds include imported soaps and colognes as well as a number of discontinued products (when was the last time you found Monkey Shine toothpaste at your local drugstore?). The pharmacy is still a family-run business—Mona Ghattas oversees the pharmacopoeia—and prescriptions are still delivered to your door, free of charge. ♦ Daily. 1815 Central Ave NW (between San Pasquale Ave and Laguna Blvd). 247.4141

Within the Duran Central Pharmacy:

Duran Central Pharmacy Restaurant ★★★$ From this simple, 48-seat restaurant tucked at the pharmacy's south end, one hears hungry customers say, "I'll have the *huevos rancheros,* please. And make that

Christmas." That's New Mexican for two eggs swimming in cheese and both red and green chile (hence the "Christmas"). The dish, which comes with beans, potatoes, and a tortilla, has been a breakfast favorite here for years. The Torpedo (potatoes, chile, and cheese wrapped in a flour tortilla) is another popular option. Or just forget all the extras and order a steaming-hot bowl of red or green chile straight up. Take-out orders are available except during the busy lunch hour. ♦ New Mexican ♦ Daily breakfast and lunch. Smoking is prohibited. 247.4141

35 Garcia's Kitchen ★★$ Move over, Wheaties. The breakfast of champions in this local hot spot is *menudo,* a hearty portion of beef tripe topped with a thick layer of red chile, which New Mexicans-in-the-know swear will cure the most horrendous of hangovers. Andy Garcia (no relation to the actor) and family have been serving the stuff in this kitschy New Mexican kitchen for decades, but if the thought of stomaching stomach is too much to take, the Garcias are famous for lots of other traditional New Mexican dishes, too. Most notable are the *carne adovada,* the green chile stew, and bottomless baskets of hot and fluffy homemade tortillas. ♦ New Mexican ♦ Daily breakfast, lunch, and dinner. 1736 Central Ave SW (between San Pasquale Ave and Laguna Blvd). 842.0273

Bests

Rudolfo Anaya
Author

In my 1992 novel I used the original spelling of the city. *La Villa de Alburquerque* was founded in 1706. If visiting here, a stop in **Old Town** to visit the church, eat, and shop is a must.

The **Alburquerque [sic] Museum** is near by. So is the **Indian Pueblo Cultural Center.** From there it's a short drive to the **University of New Mexico,** the **Nob Hill** area where you find excellent bookstores and restaurants.

If time permits, the tramway ride takes you to the top of **Sandia Mountain,** 10,000 feet high. On the west side there's the **Petroglyph National Monument** to see.

The city is brimming with art galleries and good Mexican food. Check the phone book.

Restaurants/Clubs: Red   **Hotels:** Blue
Shops/ 🌳 Outdoors: Green   **Sights/Culture:** Black

Downtown

When the railroad whistled its way into New Mexico in 1880, Albuquerque was still a small adobe village huddled around a traditional Spanish plaza on the banks of the Rio Grande. But eager to cash in on the economic gains that the dawn of modern transportation was predicted to bring, merchants and residents packed up and moved closer to the tracks. The original settlement—the site of today's Old Town—was practically abandoned. And "New Town," two miles east of the original town site, quickly picked up where it left off.

As the population grew, New Town blossomed into Downtown, the city's central business, government, and social hub. By the turn of the century, as businesses bustled, saloons and gambling houses flourished, and tourists arrived in droves, Albuquerque began to lose its small-town feel. **Route 66** came to Albuquerque in 1926 and cut a swath through Downtown along **Central Avenue.** Dubbed by John Steinbeck as the "Mother Road," the highway linked Chicago with the West Coast and transformed Central Avenue into a neon haze of motels, truck stops, diners, and more.

During the next 20 years, Downtown thrived as restaurants, stores, and movie houses multiplied, and major companies moved in. But in the mid-1950s, appealing new residential and commercial developments in the northeast quadrant of town caused the city's business and population center to shift to the sprawling neighborhoods and shopping centers of Albuquerque's Northeast Heights—and it sent Downtown downhill.

Like many of America's once thriving downtown areas, Albuquerque's central business district became dormant for nearly 20 years, although it continued as the seat of city government. Then, in the late 1970s, residents longing for the nostalgia and charm of Downtown's golden age began to revitalize the area. Slowly, old buildings were restored, new businesses settled in, and shoppers appeared again on the sidewalks of Central Avenue.

Although a few cheap motels, greasy-spoon diners, and old-fashioned gas stations inspire sentimental thoughts of Route 66, Downtown today leans more toward the contemporary: 20-story buildings stretch skyward, first-rate restaurants feature innovative combinations of native and nouvelle cuisines, nightclubs pulse with new and alternative sounds, and galleries tout contemporary painting, sculpture, photography, and other fine art.

But Downtown hasn't snubbed all of its roots. A delightful mix of old adobe and Victorian-style neighborhoods still borders Downtown on all sides, and architectural wonders such as the Pueblo Deco–style **KiMo Theatre**, a one-of-a-kind 1927 picture palace, and **La Posada de Albuquerque**, Conrad Hilton's 1939 Spanish-style showpiece hotel, are well-preserved landmarks. Strolling through the "new" Downtown presents visitors with an interesting blend of sights and sounds that range from the upscale to the casual, the corporate to the funky, and the ultraconservative to the downright weird.

STEPHENS

1 Stephens ★★★$$$ This Southwestern/American cafe packs in the let's-make-a-deal lunch crowd but also draws folks from throughout the city seeking a much less stressful dining experience. There are three elegant areas in which to eat: an enclosed patio, a large Santa Fe–style room with a view of the open kitchen, and a formal dining room with an exposed brick wall dating from the original 1915 building in which the restaurant stands. Chef Jeff Perry is classically oriented but offers a little bit of everything. The menu ranges from a delectable rack of lamb and roast duckling to excellent grilled fish, chicken, veal, seafood, and pasta. The special spa menu offers dishes low in cholesterol, sodium, and calories, including an incredible veal schnitzel. If it's fat grams you want, the baked brie or bread pudding should suffice. The service is notable, as is Albuquerque's only award-winning list of more than 340 fine wines. ◆ Southwestern/American ◆ M-F lunch and dinner; Sa-Su dinner. Reservations recommended. 1311 Tijeras Ave NW (at Central Ave). 842.1773

2 El Rey Theatre Once a popular movie house, and long owned by a great-niece of famed opera composer Giacomo Puccini (Virginia Puccini Doyle), this renovated 1941 theater now bustles as a house of spirits with live music and dance. With its huge screen, red-velvet curtains, and classic 1940s decor, the **El Rey** (The King) reigned as the monarch of Downtown movie houses until the modern theaters of the 1960s moved into the city. After falling into disrepair, the **Puccini Building,** as it was known then, was renovated in the early 1970s, and 15 years ago reopened as a neighborhood nightclub and bar. Today, the stage spotlights live musicians at least three times weekly—with many of the biggest national and international acts to pass through the state—in performances that include blues, rock, alternative, jazz, metal, and country sounds. The high ceilings provide great acoustics, while dance floors are featured on both levels of the two-story space. If you don't want to dance, head over to the **El Rey Liquor Establishment** (242.9300), the corner bar. Once one of the most popular soda fountains in the city, the tiny one-room tavern is now an equally famous watering hole. Free movies are shown in the theater on Sundays. ◆ Cover for shows. Call for show times; bar daily. 624 Central Ave SW (between Sixth and Seventh Sts). 243.7546; Ticketmaster 884.0999

3 Golden West Saloon Just like **El Rey Theater,** this swinging nightclub and bar is owned by Puccini's great-niece. It's named after one of the composer's famous operas, *Girl of the Golden West,* but it doesn't cater to opera fans (the walls, however, are plastered with original posters of famous Puccini opera pics). Featuring loud live music every night (with at least two national acts a week), club managers Anton Vanas, Ric Hurff, and Jason Thomas concentrate on making their casual night spot a center for live music (in the 1950s, it was a lively saloon). A small indoor grill and ornate wooden bar offer affordable food and drink specials, including 19 beers on tap, while a huge hardwood dance floor provides plenty of room for moving to different musical styles every day. ◆ Cover for shows. Daily. 620 Central Ave SW (between Sixth and Seventh Sts). 243.7546; show tickets through Ticketmaster 884.0999

4 Lookie Loos Named after the slang term for book lovers who browsed—but never bought—in bookstores in the 1920s and 1930s, this hodgepodge of quality antiques and modern-day collectibles offers lots to look at and prices so affordable a "lookie loo" might actually be tempted to buy. John Gallegos's fascinating selection (it's the only antiques store in Downtown) includes furniture, glassware, jewelry, and art plus an impressive array of vintage hats, clothing,

and accessories. He also offers local artists free exhibit space on store walls; if their work doesn't sell, they just come and take it down. ◆ M-Sa. 519 Central Ave NW (between Fifth and Sixth Sts). 242.4740

5 CAFE Albuquerque's largest gallery, the two-story space here features nontraditional works by New Mexico artists, including contemporary painting, photography, printmaking, sculpture, and collage. Carlos Quinto Kemm, Valerie Arber, Rudy Verhoever and Beverly Magennis are just a few of the major names exhibited here, and owner Bill Graham boasts that his spacious site continues to attract new-to–New Mexico artists. The result is an interesting cross-section of work that provides a nice change of pace from the state's traditional art scene. The venue is also frequently packed for readings and other "live art" performances. ◆ M-Sa. 516 Central Ave SW (between Fifth and Sixth Sts). 242.8244

5 Richard Levy Gallery Owner Richard Levy has been collecting prints for years. In 1992 he made his passion public with the opening of a gallery dedicated exclusively to modern and contemporary prints and works on paper Representing artists of regional, national, and international standing, this large, well-lit space is home to one of the most diverse collections of prints anywhere, including works by Clinton Adams, Patrick Nagatani, Steven Sorman, Christopher Brown, Wes Mills, Lorna Simpson, and James Casebere. A staunch supporter of new printmaking styles, Levy's focus is on the unusual, and his displays of waterless lithographs are both new and unique. ◆ Tu-Sa, and by appointment. 514 Central Ave SW (between Fifth and Sixth Sts). 766.9888

6 Skip Maisel Wholesale Indian Jewelry & Crafts "No one in town can beat my prices," says wholesale dealer Skip Maisel, and maybe he's right. The large, warehouselike store may not be incredibly attractive, but it's packed with quality Indian arts and crafts at genuine wholesale prices. Gigantic **Taos Pueblo** drums, for instance, go for at least half the price of those found elsewhere. Other main attractions include authentic **Zuni, Navajo,** and **Santo Domingo Pueblo** jewelry, some crafted in-shop; pottery from the pueblos of **Jemez, Acoma,** and **Santa Clara;** kachina dolls, rugs, painting, sculpture, and more. ◆ M-Sa. 510 Central Ave SW (between Fifth and Sixth Sts). 242.6526

7 KiMo Theatre Built by Italian immigrant Oreste Bachechi, this architectural masterpiece (illustrated below) fulfilled his dream of bringing a unique picture palace to his adopted city. The year was 1925: Art Deco was in and picture palaces were all the rage. Bachechi, a film buff who had come to Albuquerque in 1885 and made his fortune as a grocer, wanted to repay the city with a premier theater. Native American themes had appeared in only a handful of theaters thus far, so Bachechi chose "Pueblo Deco," a flamboyant but short-lived architectural style that fused the spirit of Southwest Indian culture with the exuberance of the Roaring '20s.

Bachechi hired Hollywood theater architect **Carl Boller** to design a building that would evoke the arts, culture, and traditions of New Mexico and the American Indian. Boller traveled extensively throughout the state, visiting the Indian pueblos of **Acoma** and **Isleta** as well as the Navajo reservation. Back in Albuquerque, he then created an outrageous rendering that combined traditional Indian motifs and Spanish-mission styles with such garish touches as garlanded longhorn steer skulls with eerie, glowing amber eyes. Bachechi loved it, and one year and $150,000 later, his peculiar picture palace opened. On 19 September 1927 the theater was christened the **KiMo,** a Pueblo Indian expression meaning "King of Its Kind."

As opening night visitors poured into Bachechi's two-story dreamworld, they must have thought they were the ones who were dreaming. The outside facade was covered in terra-cotta Indian shields, and inside, door handles took on the shape of Indian kachina dolls, air vents were painted to look like Navajo rugs, and stylized wrought-iron waterfowl descended the stairs. Overhead, plaster ceiling beams were decorated with thunderbirds, rain clouds, and other geometric designs, all of which were illuminated by chandeliers in the shape of war drums and glowing steer skull sconce lights. All of the Native American symbols had precise historical significance, and even the color scheme was based on abstract Indian meanings: yellow stood for the setting sun, white the approaching morning, and black the darkening northern clouds. Crowning the lobby ceiling were seven murals by Carl von Hassler, dean of the Albuquerque art colony. In trompe l'oeil style, the murals represented a panoramic view of low mountains, cloud-filled skies, and peaceful Indian pueblos.

An elaborate $18,000 Wurlitzer organ was also purchased to accompany silent films. In addition to movies, the theater became home to weekly bingo games, vaudeville acts, and other live performances. Several up-and-coming talents got their start here, including Vivian Vance, who played Ethel Mertz in the "I Love Lucy" TV series. Other stars to grace the stage included Ginger Rogers, Tom Mix, Gloria Swanson, and Sally Rand.

Bachechi died just one year after the theater opened, but it remained a popular entertainment venue until the late 1960s. By that time, however, the original building had been altered several times to keep up with current architectural trends, and modern movie houses were in full swing. The **KiMo** was closed as a picture palace, and during the next 10 years was used for office space and occasional live performances. Then in 1977 the City of Albuquerque purchased the theater and restored it to its original flamboyant elegance. The theater is now a thriving performing arts center for local and national acts and is listed on the National Register of Historic Places. ♦ Tours: M-F. 423 Central Ave NW (at Fifth St). 848.1370

KiMo Theatre

BLUM

Adobe Abodes

Along with the desert landscapes and the mystical light of this region of the country, the adobe architecture of Santa Fe, Taos, the older sections of Albuquerque, and all of the surrounding smaller villages gives Northern New Mexico its truly distinctive look. Most homes and commercial buildings are either constructed of adobe or painted in shades of brown to look like adobe. They typically stand a story high, the roofs are flat, and all of the structure's corners are rounded, with small windows spaced carefully arround the building. The doors and windowsills are usually painted turquoise, bright blue, or white. Adobe walls surround many homes, and larger, older residences have been built around courtyards in the traditional Spanish manner. No place else in the US looks like this—and most visitors find it a fascinating change.

In Santa Fe and Taos this look is preserved by law— no building in Santa Fe can stand more than 65 feet high (about five stories), and that maximum is only permitted in a small area downtown. Throughout most of the city, commercial buildings are limited to heights of 36 feet and residences to 24 feet. In the historic districts, even the trim color and the roof shape are strictly regulated to preserve the traditional style, and all buildings are painted in brownish hues to match the colors of the surrounding landscape; this follows the Indian tradition of blending in with nature rather than warring with it.

Adobe construction was initiated by the Pueblo Indians long before the Spanish arrived. Stiff, damp sections of mud, about eight or 10 inches high, were laid one on top of another, and each layer was allowed to dry before the next was applied (this construction method is called "puddling"). The Spaniards achieved the same effect by drying the mud in wooden molds. Details introduced to the Indians by the Spanish were the corner fireplace, which replaced the "smoke hole" in the roof, and the *horno* (a beehive outdoor oven of Moorish origin). Some homes also have garden areas enclosed by coyote fences (unpainted vertical tree limbs used to keep animals in or out; see illustration above).

Most early adobe homes in the region were built around a central courtyard in the Spanish tradition. Windows often were small to keep heat in during the winter and out in the summer, and the roofs were supported by protruding vigas (wooden beams). In the 19th century many structures were designed in the squarer-looking Territorial style, in which brick was placed atop adobe walls, and more decorative woodwork was added to the doors and windows. Though builders still use handmade adobe bricks, many modern structures are constructed of cheaper cinder block covered with adobe-colored stucco instead.

The architect best known for adapting ancient adobe building methods to modern needs was **John Gaw Meem**, who died at the age of 88 in 1983. Born in Brazil to American parents and raised there and in the eastern US, **Meem** came to Santa Fe on doctor's orders at the age of 26 because he had contracted tuberculosis and needed to live in the clean environment found in the West. For six decades thereafter he designed much of the adobe architecture of Northern New Mexico. Among his best-known buildings are the **Cristo Rey Church** (see page 52) and the **Santa Fe Public Library** (see page 29)

ANTONIO COCILOVO

8 Her Majesty's Secret Record Shop
"Corporate Rock Sucks" is the motto in this specialty underground music shop. Created by local musicians Stacy Parrish and Steve Anthony as an alternative to the mainstream music scene, the dark and funky music space is stocked with records, tapes, and CDs of British pop, techno-rave, and other hard-to-find underground sounds by independent record companies. The duo also puts music by Albuquerque bands on their shelves and makes some of their own recordings in a back-room studio. Besides weird music, you'll find weird clothes, weird plant stands in the shape of guitars, plus weird (and rare) British rock posters. ♦ M-F 11AM-8PM; Sa-Su noon-midnight. 315 Gold Ave SW (between Third and Fourth Sts). 246.9726

9 Beyond Ordinary This small, progressive nightclub and gallery spans the musical realm from alternative to country to Top 40 and is a little like visiting the nightclub twilight zone. Live entertainment is featured nightly in one downstairs room, while a DJ spins tunes in the next. Upstairs, gallery browsers get a mix of music from both rooms while poring through the contemporary works of local artists. All sounds converge on the compact dance floor, where black strobe lights set a diverse crowd of dancers aglow, including representatives of the executive set, the college clique, and the hard-core punk corps. Anything but ordinary. ♦ Cover. W-Sa. 211 Gold Ave SW (between Second and Third Sts). 764.8858

La Posada

10 La Posada de Albuquerque $$$ Hotel mogul and New Mexico native Conrad Hilton chose this spot to become the highlight of his hotel chain and the hospitality hub of Downtown Albuquerque. The 10-story hostelry was built to ooze Southwestern architectural charm and featured a lavish two-story lobby with whitewashed arches, Mexican tile floors, ceiling vigas (exposed wooden beams), and hand-carved corbels.

It was the first air-conditioned building in New Mexico as well as the 1949 honeymoon spot for Hilton and his famous bride-of-the-moment, Zsa Zsa Gabor.

Restored as **La Posada de Albuquerque** under new ownership in the 1980s, the 114-room hotel today is listed on the National Register of Historic Places and has retained its original charm. The lobby floor has an ornate brass and mosaic fountain, while ceilings are anchored by old-fashioned etched glass and tin chandeliers. A hand-carved wooden balcony circles overhead, and murals of Native American war dancers grace the downstairs halls. Southwest and Indian themes are carried over into the large earth-toned guest rooms, which feature hand-crafted furniture and Mexican tile, and wood-shuttered windows (some have fireplaces). Limited-edition prints by R.C. Gorman and Amado Peña hang on whitewashed walls, while Hopi pottery dots tables and shelves. Health club facilities are available adjacent to the hotel, and complimentary shuttle service is offered to and from the **Albuquerque International Airport.** ♦ 125 Second St NW (at Copper Ave). 242.9090, 800/777.5723; fax 242.8664

Within La Posada de Albuquerque:

Conrad's ★★★$$$ This recently renovated restaurant feels like springtime with its white walls and table linen, large windows, and bird of paradise plants. Specialties include *chuletas de cordero y camarones* (lamb chops and shrimp) and *salmon con salsa de mango* (salmon fillet with a sweet mango salsa). Three paellas are served, including a vegetable-only version. In the evenings, classical Spanish music is played by resident guitarist José Salazar. ♦ New Southwestern ♦ Daily breakfast, lunch, and dinner. Reservations recommended for lunch and dinner. 242.9090 ext 25 or 26

Lobby Lounge A favorite local hangout for weekday Happy Hour, this is one of the only places in town to hear live jazz. ♦ Happy Hour: M-F; live music: F-Sa. 242.9090

11 Hyatt Regency $$$ Open since 1990, Albuquerque's newest major hotel towers 20 stories above Downtown in understated desert tones. Boasting Neo-Classical decor with a Southwest flair, this modern and luxurious facility offers 395 spacious guest rooms and suites decorated in mixed shades of mauve, burgundy, and tan, with mahogany furnishings and all the standard Hyatt amenities. The lobby features a palm-shaded fountain bathed in natural light, while original Frederic Remington sculptures and other classic Southwest art are spotlighted throughout the hotel. Also included are a full-service health club, spa, outdoor pool, three lounges, and a shopping promenade.

♦ 330 Tijeras Ave NW (at Third St). 842.1234, 800/233.1234; fax 766.6710

Within the Hyatt Regency:

McGrath's ★★★★$$$ This award-winning establishment—considered by many to be the best hotel restaurant in Albuquerque—was named after Lizzie McGrath, the madam of a "parlor house" on this site from 1880 to 1914 who became one of Albuquerque's most influential businesswomen of the era. The emphasis is on traditional dishes made with a Southwestern touch: filet mignon is brushed with red-chile butter; the rack of lamb is made with garlic and Mexican oregano; and the seared Norwegian salmon is served with an avocado-and-lime relish. Other wild and wonderful dishes include Texas blue crab cakes, roast-duck quesadilla with sweet potato and black-bean puree, and a tangy Caesar salad that just may be the best in town. There's also a *cuisine naturelle* menu that offers great low-fat, low-calorie items including breast of chicken with mixed greens, followed by a fresh fruit basket served in a baked, crispy shell with a strawberry coulis for dessert; calories, carbohydrates, and percent of calories from fat are all given. Those who don't mind high-calorie splurges can choose from such items as tequila key lime pie and crème brûlée. Kids get an activity book and crayons along with pizza, burgers, and fries. The restaurant's cherry wood appointments add to its intimate atmosphere. ♦ New Southwestern/Continental ♦ Daily breakfast, lunch, and dinner. Reservations recommended. 766.6700

12 Civic Plaza The "front yard" of Albuquerque City Hall, this wide-open landscaped space is the centrally located site of downtown arts-and-crafts fairs, musical events, and other outdoor performances. The highlights of these events include the big annual Cinco de Mayo celebration and the annual Summerfest series—weekly Saturday night celebrations held from June through August that feature food, entertainment, and arts and crafts from one of Albuquerque's many ethnic communities. Greek Night, Italian Night, and of course, New Mexico Night are always hits. ♦ Bounded by Marquette and Tijeras Aves NW, and Third and Fourth Sts NW. Event information 768.3490

13 Albuquerque Convention Center In addition to nearly 168,000 square feet of exhibition space (106,000 square feet is column-free), a 2,500-seat auditorium, and 30 meeting rooms, this windowed complex has a two-story central atrium and a landscaped park area. ♦ 201 Second St NW (between Marquette and Tijeras Aves NW). 268.6060

Restaurants/Clubs: Red	Hotels: Blue
Shops/ 🌳 Outdoors: Green	Sights/Culture: Black

DOUBLETREE

14 Doubletree Hotel of Albuquerque $$$ Located next to the **Albuquerque Convention Center,** this hotel boasts a convenient location and a friendly staff. The 15-story structure features 294 comfortable guest rooms clad in pastel hues with custom-made Southwestern furnishings and other regional touches. The pillared lobby is drenched in marble elegance and includes a two-story waterfall that cascades down a marble backdrop. Visitors can also take a dip in an outdoor swimming pool or forge their way through a fully equipped fitness room. Courtesy shuttle service is available to the airport and Old Town and complimentary chocolate chip cookies await visitors in every room. ♦ 201 Marquette Ave NW (at Second St). 247.3344, 800/528.0444; fax 247.7025

Within the Doubletree Hotel of Albuquerque:

La Cascada Restaurant ★★$$ Sitting at the foot of a streaming waterfall, this restaurant is an airy, intimate dining space serving Southwestern specialties, fresh seafood, soups, and salads. The patio is ideal for casual dining while the adjacent **Bistro Bar** also offers light snacks. ♦ Southwestern ♦ Daily breakfast, lunch, and dinner. Reservations recommended. 247.3344 ext 1605

15 First Plaza Galeria Located in the heart of Albuquerque's business and government district, this seven-story retail mall covers an entire block and is conveniently located next to the **Albuquerque Convention Center** and two of Downtown's finest hotels. Courtyard fountains, native landscaping, and a two-story lobby and atrium greet visitors, while escalators and elevators provide easy access to shops and covered parking lots. The award-winning building, designed by **Harry Weese,** boasts contemporary geometric motifs and includes an exclusive athletic club, restaurants, galleries, gift shops, hair care and beauty services, and upscale clothing boutiques. Of particular note are **La Esquina Restaurant and Bar** (★$$; 242.3432), which features good New Mexican food and great margaritas in a relaxed Southwestern ambience, and the eclectic collection of Southwest traditional and fine art at **Concetta D. Gallery** (243.5066). ♦ Most shops: M-Sa. 20 First Plaza NW (at Tijeras Ave NW and Second St NW). 242.3446

Within First Plaza Galeria:

¡Explora! Much of First Plaza Galeria's lower level is taken over by this colorful, kids-oriented 9,000-square-foot science museum that is full of such hands-on exhibits as a flight simulator, a Bernoulli ball (a big ball suspended by air currents that demonstrates a theorem by mathematician Daniel Bernoulli), and lots of computers. During the week it can be crowded (and noisy) with youngsters from rural schools throughout New Mexico, thanks to a state program that provides the transportation. Open since 1993, the museum will relocate in 1996 to a $5-million facility near the **New Mexico Museum of Natural History** in Old Town. ♦ M-Sa. 842.6188

16 The Artichoke Cafe ★★★★$$$ One of the best things about this upscale, intimate restaurant is that dining can be as fine or as casual as you like: Ordering a full meal or a mix of appetizers is equally acceptable to the friendly, unpretentious staff. Given the marvelous modern American menu, however, sampling a little of everything is highly recommended. At both lunch and dinner, head chef Patty Keene (and co-owner, along with her husband Bob) alternates beautifully between the classic and the experimental with dishes that range from hearty and heavy to heart-healthy. Appetizers include roasted garlic with goat cheese and grilled red pepper; grilled rabbit, sausage, and pancetta in a red-wine, demi-glaze sauce; and steamed mussels and clams in a light broth of white wine, garlic, leeks, tomatoes, and herbs. A particularly good main course is the baked free-range chicken breast with wild mushrooms in a pesto of fresh basil, parsley, garlic, and olive oil served in a sea of fresh crushed tomato concasse sauce garnished with gorgonzola and walnuts, as is the egg fettuccine with a sauce of sautéed lobster, rock shrimp, shiitake mushrooms, shallots, brandy, cream, tarragon, and chives. The ingredients are organically grown, which explains why everything tastes so incredibly fresh. And while the wine list is not large, it's more than adequate. Specials are offered on weekends. The enclosed patio adds to the art-filled atmosphere. ♦ American ♦ M-F lunch and dinner; Sa dinner. Reservations recommended. 424 Central Ave SE (between Edith Blvd and Walter St). 243.0200

17 Star Dust Inn $ Offering a clean, comfortable alternative to the more expensive Downtown accommodations, this basic 48-room motel (there's no restaurant or coffee shop) features budget rates and a great location that is convenient to Old Town, the **University of New Mexico,** and Interstate 25.

The extras: free doughnuts and coffee 7-11AM in lobby, courtesy airport shuttle, and an outdoor swimming pool. ♦ 817 Central Ave NE (at Locust St). 243.1321

Bests

Robert Spiegel
Publisher/Owner, *Chile Pepper Magazine*

La Luz Trail—It takes you to the top of the **Sandia Mountains** above Albuquerque. Seven miles of high desert beauty, overlooking the city.

Rio Grande Nature Trail—A walk along the Rio Grande, a beautiful river running through the desert.

Rio Grande Zoological Park—It's not a big zoo, but it's sweet.

Monte Vista Fire Station restaurant—The best in Southwestern food, with strange combinations of native mushrooms and native peppers. Meals here are always interesting and excellent.

Prairie Star—North of Albuquerque, this restaurant has great scenery and wonderful Southwestern food.

G.D. Nash
Professor of History, University of New Mexico

National Atomic Museum, Albuquerque—It's a blast about the past.

Sandia Crest—Best view for 50 miles.

Old Town, Albuquerque—A trip back in time.

Albuquerque Museum of Art, History, and Science—Explains the region.

New Mexico Museum of Natural History, Albuquerque—Dinosaurs and prehistoric views of the Southwest.

Indian Pueblo Cultural Center—A must for Eastern Tenderfeet.

University of New Mexico, Albuquerque—Unique Southwest architecture.

Albuquerque Sports Stadium (Dukes Baseball Stadium)—For the sports fans.

Palace of the Governors, Santa Fe—Oldest capital building in US.

Santa Fe art galleries—unmatched.

Plaza de Santa Fe—a bit of Old World charm.

Museum of International Folk Art, Santa Fe—unique.

Bishop's Lodge, Santa Fe—Western hospitality.

St. Francis Cathedral, Santa Fe—Historic significance.

When New Mexicans talk about being "addicted" to chiles, the pungent green and red peppers that are a staple of their cuisine, they're not kidding. Scientists have determined that capsicum, the ingredient that makes chiles hot, stimulates production of endorphins in the brain, which is thought to give runners a "high."

University of New Mexico/Nob Hill

In the 1880s a new generation of Albuquerque businesspeople shared a vision that would chart the economic future of the city and state. Looking to ensure Albuquerque's long-term growth and profits, they appealed to the territorial legislature to establish a university in their town. But New Mexico had yet to become a state, and public education was rare; thus, legislators nearly laughed the entrepreneurs out of the capital of Santa Fe. Still, money was on the minds of even the harshest critics in the poverty-stricken territory, and in the waning hours of the 1889 legislative session, the **University of New Mexico (UNM)** was born.

UNM took root two miles east of the Downtown railroad tracks on a sandy, yucca-studded tableland, where a three-story redbrick Romanesque building—today's **Hodgin Hall**—was erected as the school's first hall of academia. In 1901 university president William Tight initiated the transformation of the desert campus into "the pueblo on the mesa," a shady oasis of native plants and trees dotted with adobe buildings that reflected the architectural styles of surrounding Indian villages. But when he decided to integrate the original Romanesque structure into the distinctive campus design—ordering laborers to plaster over the red brick with earth-colored stucco and replace gables and chimneys with vigas, corbels, and a flat roof—he was run out of office by those who considered his architectural vision too primitive for their up-and-coming town.

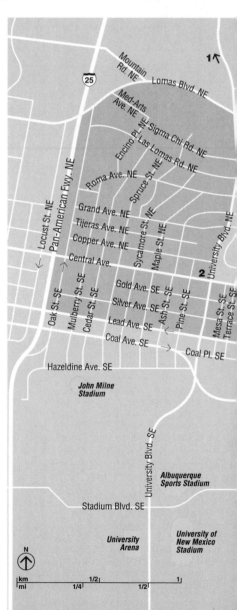

More than a century later, it is **UNM**'s unique architectural character, along with noted programs in anthropology, medicine, and Latin American and Southwest studies, that attracts nearly 25,000 students from around the globe to make it the state's largest university. Ironically, the Pueblo Revival style that led to William Tight's professional demise was later adopted as the official campus design; the total transformation of the campus to the Pueblo Revival style began in the mid-1930s and was headed by famed Santa Fe architect **John Gaw Meem**, who served as the university's architect for 25 years (for more on **Meem**, see "Adobe Abodes" on page 118). Today, the beautifully landscaped 700-acre campus is filled with some of the finest examples of Pueblo Revival architecture in the state, including the **Zimmerman Library**, **Scholes Hall**, **Alumni Memorial Chapel**, and the once-controversial **Hodgin Hall.** A series of plazas and pathways woven throughout the central campus makes these structures easily accessible by foot.

Beyond the university's borders is the usual college landscape of coffee shops, bookstores, pizzerias, and other cheap places to eat, drink, and study. While many of these spots are appealing to some visitors, others prefer to head farther east along Central Avenue to the trendy specialty shops, restaurants, and galleries of the historic Nob Hill district.

When it was built in 1947 at what was then the edge of town, the **Nob Hill Business Center** was the city's first car-oriented shopping center. The **Central Avenue** stretch of clothing and variety stores flourished until the early 1960s, when the arrival of the interstate drove shoppers to new outlying malls. Then in 1985, the district was one of eight commercial areas in the nation chosen

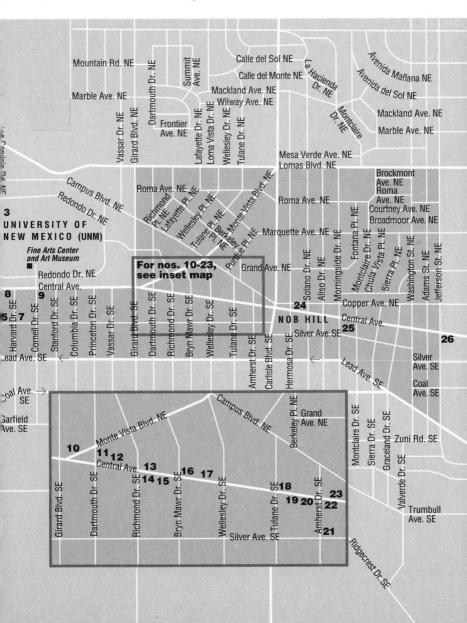

for a government-funded redevelopment project. Galleries, restaurants, and boutiques sprung up along Central Avenue again, and those who once sought the enclosure of the glossy mall scene returned to a renewed Nob Hill.

Today's Nob Hill is a seven-block strip that stretches along Central Avenue from **Girard** to **Washington;** new Art Deco–style arches will soon straddle the strip to designate the district borders. Neon signs and eye-catching store facades encourage foot traffic, and the area's budding gallery and music scene brings Nob Hill hobnobbers out after dark. The district attracts trendsetters and trend-haters alike—from middle-aged yuppies to the college crowd to teenaged neo-hippies—and is commonly referred to by Nob Hill residents as Albuquerque's Melrose Avenue. A stroll through Nob Hill is still the best way to witness the increasing urbanization and ever-changing character of Albuquerque.

1 Albuquerque Hilton $$$ This 253-room chain hotel lies beyond the university's borders, but offers probably the best contemporary lodgings in the immediate area. The large rooms are pastel shaded and decorated with regional art and wooden appointments. Interiors throughout the rest of the hotel feature Native American and Western motifs—the white stuccoed corridors are clad in petroglyph-style paintings—while the high ceilings and arched doorways echo regional architectural styles. Indoor and outdoor swimming pools, plus a sauna and whirlpool offer relaxing options. The hotel provides free transportation to and from the airport, bus, and train stations. ♦ 1901 University Blvd NE (at Menaul Blvd). 884.2500, 800/HILTONS; fax 889.9118

Within the Albuquerque Hilton:

Ranchers Club ★★★$$$ Built in the style of a British hunting lodge, this cozy, elegant restaurant is the quintessential steak house: The fireplace is always blazing and a buffalo head looms above the mantel. Lunch features excellent salads and such pastas as the spicy Southwest pasta with green-chile cream sauce. Dinner, however, is the restaurant's forte, with offerings of gigantic steaks, as well as other prime meats, poultry, and seafood, grilled over aromatic woods that customers select themselves. Exotic woods include piñon, hickory, apple, cherry, sassafras, and mesquite. Grilled items are complemented by grilled vegetables and one of more than 20 gourmet sauces. The wine list is extensive, and the bar features live entertainment.
♦ Steaks/Southwestern ♦ M-F lunch and dinner; Sa dinner. Reservations recommended. 884.2500

Casa Chaco ★★$$$ At breakfast and lunch, this casual eatery serves standard coffee shop fare. But at dinner, its original Southwestern cuisine served by tuxedoed waiters at candlelit tables draws raves. Try the grilled Rocky Mountain lamb with dijon mustard and seasoned breadcrumbs served over green chile with a shallot beurre blanc sauce. ♦ Southwestern ♦ Daily breakfast, lunch, and dinner. 884.2500

2 66 Diner ★$ Take a nostalgic trip back to the days of soda jerks, hopscotch, and jukebox tunes that spin for 25¢ a pop in this thoroughly 1950s diner. Once a transmission shop on the old Route 66, the fun Art Deco establishment now features such blue plate specials as liver and onions, meat-loaf sandwiches, and chicken-fried steak. The old-fashioned burgers with a touch of grease are great, and the milk shakes and sundaes are rich and gooey. ♦ American ♦ Daily breakfast, lunch, and dinner. 1405 Central Ave NE (between Pine St and University Blvd). 247.1421

In 1902 Albuquerque's celebrity hot spot was the Alvarado Hotel. Hotel magnate Fred Harvey built the magnificent $200,000 Spanish-style structure beside the railroad tracks after the iron horse snaked its way into New Mexico in the late 1800s. Soon it was considered the "finest railroad hotel on Earth," with scores of the trademark "Harvey Girls" serving all-you-can-eat meals for a dollar. Rudolph Valentino, Joan Crawford, Jack Benny, Charles Lindbergh, and Albert Einstein were among the many celebrated guests. A number of US presidents also lodged there, including a portly William H. Taft, who reputedly got stuck in the bathtub. Later, as more hotels sprung up nearby, the Alvarado fell on hard times and was abandoned. And though it was one of the city's finest architectural masterpieces, the building was demolished in 1970.

Restaurants/Clubs: Red   **Hotels:** Blue
Shops/ 🌳 Outdoors: Green   **Sights/Culture:** Black

Hodgin Hall

COURTESY OF SUSAN SELIGMAN

3 University of New Mexico (UNM)

The 700-acre campus of the state's largest university features some of the finest examples of Pueblo Revival architecture in New Mexico, and is studded with native flora, grassy knolls, and large-scale sculptures by internationally renowned artists. The university is known for excellence in anthropology, medicine, and Southwest and Latin American studies. Its outstanding museums and galleries—which are free to the public—shouldn't be missed. And its array of performing arts venues play a major role in the city's thriving arts-and-culture scene. ♦ Central Ave NE (between University and Girard Blvds, east of I-25). 277.0111

Within the University of New Mexico:

Hodgin Hall Erected in 1892 as the first building on the campus, **Hodgin Hall** (pictured above) was transformed from its original redbrick Romanesque design to the flat-roofed Pueblo Revival style in 1908. Named after former faculty member Charles Hodgin, the three-story structure underwent an extensive renovation in 1983. Its traditional architectural elements of ceiling vigas and hand-carved wooden corbels make it one of the jewels of the **UNM** campus. ♦ M-F. South Campus

Alumni Memorial Chapel Designed by renowned Santa Fe architect **John Gaw Meem** and completed in 1962, this small chapel (pictured below) sits in the shade of tall cottonwoods and is patterned after the pueblo mission churches erected by Franciscan friars throughout the state during the 17th and 18th centuries. The eastern tablet on the chapel's south wall is etched with the names of alumni killed in World Wars I and II and the wars in Korea and Vietnam. ♦ South Campus. 277.5808.

Jonson Gallery Located on the north side of campus in the former home and studio of the late modernist painter Raymond Jonson, this intimate space presents changing exhibits of more than 2,000 of his works, as well as those of the Transcendentalist painters and other contemporary artists. Retrospectives of Jonson's work are presented each summer, and gallery talks are held on the first Tuesday evening of the month. ♦ M-F. 1909 Las Lomas Rd NE (near University Blvd). 277.4967

Maxwell Museum Founded in 1932 as the first public museum in Albuquerque, this incredible museum of anthropology is a renowned repository for more than 2,500,000 artifacts from the United States, the Arctic, Mexico, Central and South America, Africa, India, Pakistan, Southeast Asia, New Guinea, Australia, and Oceania. Located in the **UNM Anthropology Building** on the campus's west side, the museum's two galleries give a special emphasis to the native cultures of the Southwest. The *Ancestors* exhibit chronicles four million years of human emergence, while *People of the Southwest* documents 11,500 years of art, life, and culture in the American Southwest. The **Maxwell's Photographic Archive** houses more than 250,000 images, including many of the earliest photographs of

Alumni Memorial Chapel

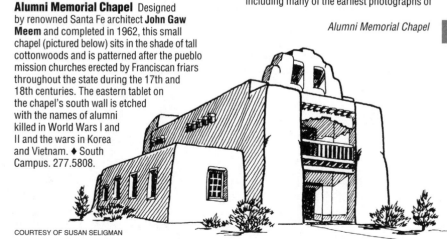

COURTESY OF SUSAN SELIGMAN

Images carved in Zimmerman Library ceiling beams

Southwest Pueblo and Navajo Indian peoples. The museum shop features high quality Native Amerian art, publications, and folk art from other indigenous peoples worldwide. ♦ Free. Daily. UNM Anthropology Building (University Blvd and Grand Ave NE). 277.4405

Zimmerman Library Another **John Gaw Meem** gem, this central campus facility was completed in 1938. **Meem**'s original core structure integrates murals and hand-carved wooden motifs into the Pueblo Revival design. Massive beams straddle library ceilings and feature abstract Native American images of birds and animals carved deeply into the surface. A four-panel mural in the lobby depicts the tricultural heritage of the region, while a stairwell mural runs up the library's four floors and charts the historical development of the alphabet. Named after former **UNM** president James Fulton Zimmerman, the original **Meem** library has undergone numerous additions through the years, and today houses more than a million books. ♦ Daily; call for summer hours. South Campus. 277.2003

Tamarind Institute Artists from around the world who want to learn the complex process of lithography are lured to this esteemed workshop and gallery run by the university. The staff of certified Master Printers is on hand to assist in the printmaking process, and the in-house gallery displays contemporary lithographs created by professional and novice artists alike. Free guided tours are held on the first Friday of the month. ♦ M-F. 108 Cornell Dr SE (at Central Ave SE). 277.3901

University Art Museum Since its establishment in 1963 as a department of the **UNM College of Fine Arts,** this attractive multilevel museum has amassed the largest fine arts collection in the state, with more than 23,000 paintings, drawings, prints, photographs, and sculptures. The permanent collection includes Spanish Colonial art, Old Master paintings and sculpture by such artists as Rembrandt, and works by 19th- and 20th-century American and European artists ranging from Picasso to O'Keeffe. The museum's collection of prints and photographs, including works by early pioneers in the field, is one of the most extensive in the country. Gallery talks are held Tuesday evening. ♦ Free. Daily. UNM Fine Arts Center (Redondo Dr and Cornell Dr NE, on southern edge of campus). 277.4001

Scholes Hall (UNM Administration Building) Listed on the National Register of Historic Places, this 1936 building (pictured below) was **John Gaw Meem**'s first campus project. The Pueblo Revival structure is named for the late France Scholes, one of the Southwest's leading historians and **UNM**'s first academic vice president. The east wing features a beautiful fresco, *Union of the Americas,* painted by Jesus Galvan in 1943. ♦ M-F. South Campus.

Scholes Hall

4 Salt of the Earth Books Situated in the hub of the university district, John Randall's bookstore is the area's most popular political and literary gathering place for **UNM** students and other Albuquerque intellectuals. Specializing in Southwest fiction and nonfiction, politics, and Chicano, Native American, and Latin American studies, Randall's intriguing selection includes both new and hard-to-find titles. His environmental, poetry, and children's book sections are equally fascinating, and the shop's frequent readings, book signings, and community forums are always lively events. ♦ Daily. 2128 Central Ave SE (at Yale Blvd). 842.1220

5 EJ's Coffee & Tea Co. ★★$ Coffee and customers are in constant flow at this popular coffeehouse. The high ceilings and hardwood decor create an inviting ambience for hard-working students as well as other confirmed coffee addicts. Besides more than 20 specialty coffees and teas, the establishment offers breakfast, lunch, and dinner, plus live poetry, music, and other esoteric entertainment. The menu leans toward healthy and vegetarian fare, with recommendations going to the scrambled tofu and enormous homemade bagels for breakfast, and the daily pasta or stir-fry specials at dinner. The eight different cheesecakes, in flavors like baklava and fuzzy navel, probably aren't so healthy, but they go great with a cup of fresh-roasted java. ♦ Health food/Cafe ♦ Daily breakfast, lunch, and dinner. 2201 Silver Ave SE (at Yale Blvd). 268.2233

6 The Quarters ★★$ One of the most popular spots for barbecue in the city, this casual restaurant serves heaping helpings of spicy ribs and chicken, plus huge sandwiches and fabulous fries. If you're not into barbecue, try the tender catfish, plump knockwurst, or classic Reuben sandwiches. Top it all off with a brew from the largest selection of imported beer in town. ♦ Barbecue ♦ M-Sa lunch and dinner. 801 Yale Blvd SE (at Coal Ave). 843.7505

7 El Patio ★★$ Since 1974 university students craving a home-cooked New Mexican meal have been flocking to this hot chile spot a half-block from campus. The New Mexican menu features plump *chile rellenos* (whole green chiles stuffed with cheese and deep-fried), tender *carne adovada* (pork marinated in red chiles), and possibly the best green-chile chicken enchiladas in town. Vegetarians opt for the tasty avocado burrito, and the red and green chiles can also be ordered without meat. Other draws include nightly guitar music and a pleasant enclosed patio, which is open year-round. The creamy flan is incredible. ♦ New Mexican ♦ Daily lunch and dinner. 142 Harvard Dr SE (at Silver Ave). 268.4245

OLYMPIA CAFE

8 Olympia Cafe ★$ The only Greek restaurant in the university area features little atmosphere, but a fabulous array of Greek specialties, including shish kebab, spanakopita (spinach and feta cheese in phyllo), moussaka (ground meat and eggplant), and hummus. The classic gyro, the tangy Greek salad, and the sweet-and-sticky baklava are established cafe favorites. And the large portions and low prices rank high with the college crowd. ♦ Greek ♦ M-Sa breakfast, lunch, and dinner. 2210 Central Ave SE (just east of Yale Blvd). 266.5222

FRONTIER

9 Frontier ★★$ Home of the famous Frontier sweet roll, a messy and moist mouthful of butter, cinnamon, and dough, this enormous barnlike building covers nearly an entire city block and has been a home-away-from-home to thousands of university denizens since 1971. Although it looks like a fast-food coffee shop, patrons here get real plates and utensils with their home-cooked meals and have their choice of seating for 325 amid a hodgepodge of Western art. Twenty-four hours a day, students spread their books out on tables and drink pots of coffee around meals of burgers, burritos, and old-fashioned bacon and eggs. Besides the sweet rolls, the *huevos rancheros* (fried eggs on corn tortillas smothered with chile salsa and topped with grated cheese), Western-style hash browns (potatoes topped with cheese and green chiles), and other New Mexican dishes are favorites here. And though you can ask for ketchup, chiles and salsa are the most popular condiments here; the management roasts 2,200 sacks of chile a year, and the salsa sits in a jug next to the sugar and cream. ♦ New Mexican ♦ Daily 24 hours. 2400 Central Ave SE (at Cornell Dr). 266.0550

10 Dartmouth Street Gallery Works by New Mexico artists, including Frank McCulloch, Angus Macpherson, and Joan Boyden, are spotlighted in this established contemporary art gallery. ♦ M-Sa 1-5PM or by appointment. 3011 Monte Vista Blvd NE (between Girard Blvd and Dartmouth Dr). 266.7751

11 Ralph Greene Gallery Owner Ralph Greene moved this contemporary art gallery to Nob Hill from SoHo after discovering the area's burgeoning arts scene. Besides the contemporary national and international artists he used to represent in New York City, Greene's collection now includes abstract and figurative paintings, prints, and sculpture by well-known New Mexico artists such as painter Charlie Hewitt, as well as international artists. ♦ M-Sa. 208 Dartmouth Dr NE (between Central Ave and Monte Vista Blvd). 266.1414

12 Fred's Bread & Bagel ★★$ This has to be the only bagelry in the world where green-chile bagels are as popular as pumpernickel or cinnamon raisin. Catering to some 600 to 700 bagel lovers, this always-bustling place is reputed to have the best bagel in town. The menu features more than a dozen bagel flavors, including oat bran, sourdough rye, and the popular green-chile cheese or green-chile blue corn. Bagel buyers also can choose from a host of "Fred's Spreads," creamy cream cheese spreads in flavors like garlic olive, honey nut, and, of course, green chile. But don't ask for Fred. Owner Aaron Hendron admits he just needed a name for his bakery that rhymes with bread. ♦ Bagels ♦ Daily breakfast, lunch, and dinner. 3009 Central Ave NE (between Dartmouth and Richmond Drs). 266.7323

13 Bow Wow Records Andy Horwitz's specialty record shop spins alternative sounds by independent labels only, and features an impressive selection of used records, CDs, and cassettes. A host of music accessories including books, videos, T-shirts, and posters also leans toward the alternative, and the back of the shop serves as an art-space for local artists. And even if you've never heard of the Butthole Surfers or the Dead Milkmen, the shop's staff will be more than helpful. ♦ Daily. 3103 Central Ave NE (between Richmond and Bryn Mawr Drs). 256.0928

13 Martha's Body Bueno Forget the gym. Lotions, potions, and sensual notions is Martha Doster's good body motto, which she translates into an aromatic selection of body oils, bath gels, lotions, soaps, shampoos, and more. Silky-skin lovers choose from either the Body Bueno brand of natural skin-care products, which come in chamomile, coconut, and a host of other tantalizing smells, or the standard Crabtree & Evelyn selection. Or if none of those scents suit your senses, staffers are on hand to mix body oils and other products to your taste. The shop also features shameless lingerie, unusual jewelry, and off-color, under-the-counter greeting cards. ♦ Daily. 3105 Central Ave NE (between Richmond and Bryn Mawr Drs). 255.1122

13 Peacecraft The politically aware patronize this nonprofit gallery, which sells handmade arts, crafts, and clothing from the Third World. The shop's emphasis is on traditional handicrafts of cultural significance, and the selection includes beautiful handwoven clothing, baskets, hats, and textiles from Mexico, Africa, and Guatemala; exquisite Peruvian pottery; and an unusual array of other ethnic, folk, and tribal arts. The shop is run by an all-volunteer staff, and all money goes back into purchasing more goods. ♦ M-Sa. 3107 Central Ave NE (between Richmond and Bryn Mawr Drs). 255.5229

14 Larry's Hats The old-time art of millinery lives on in Larry Koch's wonderful world of hats. An accomplished hat maker, Koch fashions old and new styles to fit the heads of teenagers and adults alike. His classic collection includes a number of antique hats, but mostly Koch custom-makes a fascinating range of shapes that tower overhead, sit low above the brow, or fall any-which-way the wearer wants. Just as fascinating is Koch's large selection of jewelry and accessories, which includes unusual costume jewelry, antique gloves, and old **Santo Domingo Pueblo** Indian pieces. The jewelry counter alone is worth a visit. ♦ M-Sa. 3102 Central Ave SE (between Richmond and Bryn Mawr Drs). 266.2095

14 In Crowd One of Nob Hill's most outrageous outfitters features funky fashions in natural materials and wild prints and colors; the great 1960s' go-go collection even makes polyeste look good. They also carry a wide array of unusual accessories. And it's probably the only place in town you'll find Doc Marten boots and shoes. ♦ M-Sa; Su noon-4PM. 3106 Central Ave SE (between Richmond and Bryn Mawr Drs). 268.3750

Lew Wallace, territorial governor of New Mexico during the mid-1800s, wrote much of his classic novel *Ben Hur* while visiting Albuquerque.

14 Off Broadway The largest vintage clothing store in the state is big on Western and formal vintage wear dating from the turn of the century to the 1960s. Especially notable is the 1940s sequined sweater collection, the vintage hats, and the funky hand-painted Mexican skirts. The shop also does a brisk rental business, just in case you left your Roaring '20s flapper fashions at home. ◆ M-Sa; Su noon-4PM. 3110 Central Ave SE (between Richmond and Bryn Mawr Drs). 268.1489

15 Sachs Appeal Boutique What appeals to shopkeeper Renee Sachs is an assortment of new and used clothing and accessories that ranges from garish skull-and-crossbones T-shirts to funky Spandex shapes to conservative business suits. The small but quality selection of handmade silver belts, bracelets, button covers, and rings gives a nod to Southwest style. ◆ M-Sa; Su noon-5PM. 3112 Central Ave SE (between Richmond and Bryn Mawr Drs). 266.1661

16 Monte Vista Fire Station ★★★$$ This fine restaurant served as local Fire Station No. 3 for 36 years before it started cooking some of the best contemporary American cuisine in town. Remodeled by owner Kerry Rayner to its original Pueblo Revival architectural style, the two-story restaurant today is also one of the city's outstanding examples of classic New Mexico adobe architecture—brass fire pole and all.

Chef Rosa Rajkovic explores an array of cuisines—from new Southwest to traditional French and Italian to new American—making for an exotic, ever-changing menu in a casual Art Deco atmosphere. Usual lunch and dinner features include pasta, grilled meats, poultry, and seafood. The crab cakes with goat cheese and the creamy wild-mushroom ravioli make frequent appearances as appetizers, and the silky white-chocolate mousse in a fudge crust is a must-eat for chocolate lovers. Upstairs—what was once the fire station's sleeping quarters—is one of the city's most popular indoor/outdoor bars. ◆ International ◆ M-F lunch and dinner; Sa-Su dinner. Bar daily. Reservations recommended. 3201 Central Ave NE (at Bryn Mawr Dr). 255.2424

17 CenterStage **Theatre-In-The-Making,** a local acting company, hits this Nob Hill stage every weekend for wonderful performances that range from off-Broadway to classical to experimental. Saturday afternoon performances are family oriented, and

original plays by New Mexico writers are staged regularly. This is some of the best theater in town. ◆ 3211 Central Ave NE (between Bryn Mawr and Wellesley Drs). 260.0331

17 Āja Eclectic natural-fiber clothing and one-of-a-kind handmade accessories give this affordable women's boutique an alternative appeal for women who like to create their own style. ◆ M-Sa. 3215 Central Ave NE (between Bryn Mawr and Wellesley Drs). 255.7804

18 Il Vicino ★★$ Owned by the same folks who run **Scalo Northern Italian Grill** (see below), this neighborhood pizzeria features fresh and fabulous European-style pizza baked in wood-fired ovens. Forget your run-of-the-mill pepperoni and try the pizza *rustica* (a buttery cornmeal crust topped with roasted garlic, artichoke hearts, calamata olives, capers, fresh tomato sauce, oregano, and mozzarella). The menu features 12 other house pizzas, and customers can create their own designer pies from a choice of 25 gourmet toppings. A few salads and pasta dishes are additional options, and wine comes by the bottle or glass. ◆ Pizza/Italian ◆ Daily lunch and dinner. 3403 Central Ave NE (at Tulane Dr). 266.7855

18 Guild Cinema Albuquerque's only art cinema screens art, independent, and foreign flicks, and serves popcorn drenched in real butter. ◆ 3405 Central Ave NE (between Tulane and Amherst Drs). 255.1848

Albuquerque resident and best-selling mystery author Tony Hillerman started his writing career penning commercials for Purina Pig Chow. He then went on to a career in journalism, and in the late 1960s, while teaching journalism at the University of New Mexico, wrote his first novel, *The Blessing Way*. It was the first in what would be a long line of mysteries set in the Navajo Indian reservation for which Hillerman has won worldwide acclaim. When he sent the original manuscript to his New York agent, she had this advice, "Just get rid of all the Indian stuff."

19 Double Rainbow ★★$ The famous San Francisco–based Double Rainbow ice cream is sold in this brightly lit place, which also offers great salads, sandwiches (try the grilled gouda and artichoke), and pastries. The chocolate-mousse cake is renowned as one of the most decadent desserts in town, while the huge selection of magazines includes New Age and Italian fashion rags that outsell *People* and *Time*. More than a thousand customers pass through here daily. Translation: The place is always packed. ◆ Ice cream/Cafe ◆ Daily breakfast, lunch, and dinner. 3416 Central Ave SE (between Tulane and Amherst Drs). 255.6633

19 Wargames West Adventure is the name of the game(s) in Wayne R. Godfrey's incredible specialty store. Brimming with an inventory of more than 6,000 different "games that make you think" and the accessories that go with them, Godfrey's collection is considered by his international clientele of avid adventure gamers to be one of the largest of its kind in the world. But Godfrey's games are not the typical department store kind; these brainy board puzzlers—you won't find any electronic gadgets here—are created to challenge the minds and imaginations of fantasy gamers. The selection ranges from the best-selling "Dungeons and Dragons" to science fiction to mystery and traditional war games. ◆ M-Sa. 3422 Central Ave SE (between Tulane and Amherst Drs). 256.1820, 800/SAY.GAME

20 Wear It! The style in Janet Moses's popular women's clothing store is contemporary and comfortable, and the service is as impeccable as the fine linen and silks you'll find here. She also carries a great selection of denim, cotton, and rayon, plus fun accessories and designer names. ◆ M-Sa; Su noon-5PM. 107 Amherst Dr SE (at Central Ave). 266.7764

21 P.T. Crow Trading Co. Walk into this custom cowboy boot shop, and chances are when you walk outside again, you'll be wearing a pair of shoes that are at least 20 years older than the ones you wore in. Specializing in vintage cowboy boots, shop owners Ron and Linda Linton have rummaged through flea markets, garage sales, and the closets of cowboy boot collectors to put you into a pair of Old West footwear—their extensive classic collection of vintage boots are well worn but well preserved. If you prefer a new pair, boots can be custom-made to look like vintage. Most popular are colorful reproductions of the flamboyant designs of the 1930s and 1940s worn by the likes of Tom Mix and Roy Rogers, but customers are free to conceive of creative designs to suit their own wild West style. ◆ M-Sa. 114 Amherst Dr SE (at Silver Ave). 256.1763, 800/657.0944

22 Nob Hill Business Center Built in 1947 as the city's first auto-oriented shopping center, this building is a streamlined architectural display of contemporary and regional design styles of the era. It is also the hub of the resurrected Nob Hill district, and is listed on the National Register of Historic Places. ◆ 3500 Central Ave SE (between Amherst Dr and Carlisle Blvd)

Within the Nob Hill Business Center:

The Corner Bookstore Every neighborhood has a favorite bookstore, and in Nob Hill, this is it. Situated on a busy neighborhood corner with cars whizzing by, this small shop offers a relaxed and cozy atmosphere and a well-rounded selection of titles that draw bookworms en masse. Especially popular is the shop's huge travel section, which, besides essays, guides, and other odes to wanderlust, includes more than 500 maps from around the world. The audio lending library features scores of books on tape. There's also a large selection of foreign language books that includes lessons in literally every language. ◆ Daily. 266.2044

Scalo Northern Italian Grill ★★★$$ The trendy Nob Hill set congregates at this informal but elegant Italian restaurant. The food is straightforward but solid, with good fresh pasta specials and meat, chicken, and fish entrées. Notable eatables include the *ravioli di magro al basilico* (filled with spinach and ricotta cheese in a basil cream sauce), the *agnello alla griglia splendido* (grilled lamb with red onions and garlic), and the *salmon a pesto e pumnate* (salmon fillet with pesto and sun-dried tomato cream sauce). The deep-dish pies are popular lunch picks, and the carpaccio appetizer, homemade desserts, and Italian wines are good anytime. ◆ Italian ◆ M-F lunch and dinner; Sa-Su dinner. 255.8782

Chez What? ★$ Live acoustic music plus excellent sandwiches and pasta are on order in this upbeat neighborhood bar with a casual bistro atmosphere. Sit outdoors on the patio and be on the pulse of the Nob Hill scene. ◆ Cafe ◆ Daily lunch and dinner. 262.1848

Restaurants/Clubs: Red   **Hotels:** Blue
Shops/ 🌳 Outdoors: Green   **Sights/Culture:** Black

Beeps With its huge selection of gifts for all personalities and occasions, this fun card and novelty store is the ultimate gift shop. Gifts here range from genuine to gag and include everything from silk ties to satin boxers to rubber cockroaches. The best-selling T-shirt selection is one of the largest in Albuquerque, and the one-of-a-kind greeting card line runs the gamut from the extremely tasteful to the completely tasteless. ♦ M-Sa; Su noon-6PM. 262.1900

American Indian Designer Collection
This is the bustling factory and showroom of renowned Pima Indian beadworker Melody Lightfeather, where workers busily stitch beads onto designer tennis shoes that bear her original designs. Lightfeather also produces designer beaded clothing for Continental Leather Corporation, as well as beaded jewelry. ♦ M-Sa. 268.6060

23 Cafe Zurich ★★$ Local European wanna-bes fill this dainty Deco corner cafe. Covered from floor to ceiling in checkerboard black-and-white, this small European-style establishment is best known for its wide selection of hot espresso drinks, cool Italian sodas, and wickedly luscious desserts. Chocoholics swear by the *caffè mocha* paired with a piece of the chocolate torte. Soups, salads, sandwiches, and great gourmet pizzas are also featured, with kudos going to the French onion soup and the pesto pizza. Regular art exhibits, specialty magazines, and hip hairdos round out the eclectic feel, but sidewalk seating on congested Central Avenue doesn't even come close to Paris. ♦ Cafe/Pizza ♦ Daily lunch and dinner. 3513 Central Ave NE (between Amherst Dr and Carlisle Blvd). 265.2556

23 Nirvana ★★$$ This Nob Hill eatery specializes in the vegetarian cuisine of southern India, a cooking style that is miles away from the tangy curries and grilled meats of the northern part of that country. Ravi

Goradi's cooking distinguishes itself by the absence of animal meats and animal by-products, substituted by the use of whole or powdered rice and lentils. But that hardly means bland. Try the huge *masala dosai* (a gram flour crepe filled with onions, potatoes, nuts, and tomatoes) or the *oothapam* (cashews, onions, green chile, green bell peppers, and raisins on a lentil sourdough pancake). Dishes come with moist wheat flatbreads plus a coconut-ginger chutney or a yogurt-based soup. The service is gracious but unhurried, which gives you time to relax amidst a tasteful decor of gray relief wall sculptures and to enjoy live Indian music and dance. ♦ Southern Indian ♦ M-Sa lunch and dinner; Su dinner. Reservations recommended for dinner. 3523 Central Ave NE (between Amherst Dr and Carlisle Blvd). 265.2172

24 University Lodge $ Situated six blocks east of **UNM** in the middle of Nob Hill, this 53-room hotel is clean and comfortable but average in every way. The pastel rooms are adequately sized with standard motel furnishings, and rooms for people with disabilities are also available. The food in the hotel's small restaurant is decent, and an outdoor swimming pool is open during the warmer months. ♦ 3711 Central Ave NE (between Hermosa and Solano Drs). 266.7663

25 Outpost Performance Space This funky storefront performance space is a popular venue for some of the best music, dance, readings, and other live performances in Albuquerque. Hosting roughly 80 events annually, the intimate space seats up to a hundred people—on folding chairs in an alcohol- and smoke-free environment—and is best known for its eclectic blend of musical events, including folk, jazz, and world beat by local, national, and international acts. ♦ Hours vary. 112 Morningside Dr SE (between Central and Silver Aves). 268.0044

26 Classic Century Square Three floors of antiques, arts and crafts, and collectibles by some 70 independent dealers are featured in this antiques extravaganza—a great spot to find old Indian collectibles and Western memorabilia. ♦ M-Sa; Su noon-5PM. 4616 Central Ave SE (at Jefferson St). 265.3161

Born in the dawn of geologic history, some 250 to 300 million years ago, New Mexico is a playground for amateur anthropologists and paleontologists. Indeed, people here are so hard-core about the state's past that the Museum of Natural History, located in Albuquerque, set up a Fossil Hot Line (505/841.8837) to assist those who are in pursuit of the prehistoric.

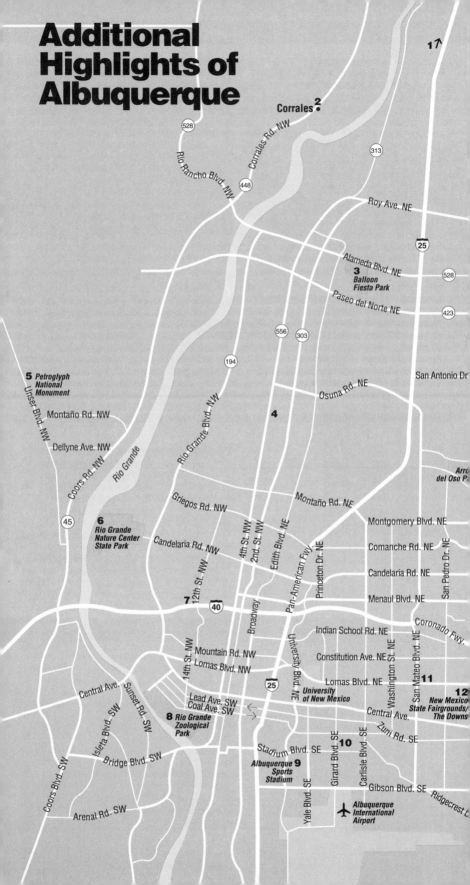

Additional Highlights of Albuquerque

1 ↗

Corrales 2

528

Rio Rancho Blvd. NW

Corrales Rd. NW

448

313

Roy Ave. NE

25

Alameda Blvd. NE

3 Balloon Fiesta Park

528

Paseo del Norte NE

423

556   303

San Antonio Dr

5 Petroglyph National Monument

Unser Blvd. NW

194

Montaño Rd. NW

Dellyne Ave. NW

Coors Rd. NW

Rio Grande

Rio Grande Blvd. NW

Osuna Rd. NE

4

Griegos Rd. NW

Montaño Rd. NE

Arro del Oso P

45

6 Rio Grande Nature Center State Park

Candelaria Rd. NW

Montgomery Blvd. NE

4th St. NW

2nd. St. NW

Edith Blvd. NE

Pan-American Fwy.

Princeton Dr. NE

Comanche Rd. NE

San Pedro Dr. NE

Candelaria Rd. NE

12th St. NW

7

Menaul Blvd. NE

40

Broadway

Coronado Fwy.

Indian School Rd. NE

14th St. NW

Mountain Rd. NW

Constitution Ave. NE

Washington St. NE

San Mateo Blvd. NE

11

Lomas Blvd. NW

University Blvd.

Lomas Blvd. NE

12 New Mexico State Fairgrounds/ The Downs

Central Ave.

Sunset Rd. SW

25

University of New Mexico

Central Ave.

Isleta Blvd. SW

Lead Ave. SW

Coal Ave. SW

Zuni Rd. SE

8 Rio Grande Zoological Park

Bridge Blvd. SW

Stadium Blvd. SE

Girard Blvd. SE

10

Carlisle Blvd. SE

Coors Blvd. SW

9 Albuquerque Sports Stadium

Yale Blvd. SE

Gibson Blvd. SE

Ridgecrest L

Arenal Rd. SW

✈ Albuquerque International Airport

There's a variety of interesting things to do and see beyond the borders of the three walking areas in Albuquerque that are highlighted in the earlier chapters. For glimpses into the city's fascinating history, the village of **Corrales** provides a feel for the region's pre-urban past, the **Spanish History Museum** explores New Mexico's deeply rooted Hispanic heritage, and the **Petroglyph National Monument** transports people back to prehistoric times. Nature lovers won't want to miss the lush **Rio Grande Nature Center State**

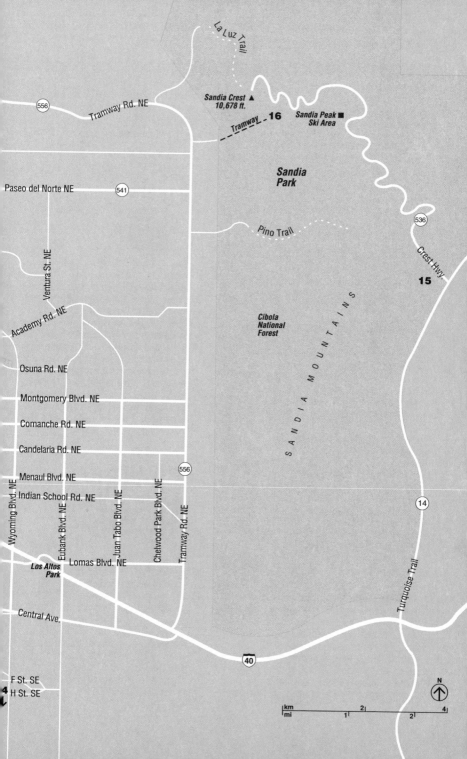

Park, nostalgia buffs will get a kick out of the memorabilia-filled **Ernie Pyle Memorial Library,** and those who are fascinated by Native American culture will want to visit the extraordinary **Indian Pueblo Cultural Center.** For the kids, there's the exotic **Rio Grande Zoological Park** and the wondrous **Tinkertown Museum.** To sample the best New Mexican food in town, visit the all-time favorite restaurant, **Sadie's.** And for the ultimate view of Albuquerque, take the thrilling 2.7-mile-long **Sandia Peak Aerial Tramway** to the city's highest point.

1 Prairie Star ★★★$$$ Sunset is prime time to take in the incredible view of Albuquerque's Sandia Mountains from the patio of this rambling 1940s adobe hacienda. Located approximately 15 minutes north of Albuquerque in the town of Bernalillo, the 6,000-square-foot Mission-style home sits on a rural site leased from the **Santa Ana Pueblo.** Outside, the Rio Grande meanders nearby as high plains stretch into the distance, while inside, diners are surrounded by regional art and traditional New Mexican architectural motifs: vigas with smaller *latillas* (peeled wooden poles) wedged in between, blazing kiva fireplaces, and *bancos* (small benches that gracefully emerge from thick adobe walls). The menu offers an exquisite range of New American, Southwestern, and classical cuisine, including a lightly breaded and fried appetizer of fresh green chile, a tender lamb loin, and a hearty Truchas trout with piñon nuts. Homemade bread and desserts are featured daily, and complimentary champagne accompanies Sunday brunch. The wine list is extensive, but the tangy margaritas are still the favorite for sipping as the sun slips behind the Sandias. ◆ American/Southwestern ◆ M-Sa dinner; Su brunch and dinner. Reservations recommended. 255 Prairie Star Rd, Bernalillo. Take I-25 north to Bernalillo exit 242, turn left on NM 44, cross the Rio Grande, turn right a half-mile past the river onto Jemez Dam Rd, and drive a half-mile north. 867.3327

2 Corrales A drive through this tiny village gives visitors a taste of what Santa Fe, Taos, and yes, even Albuquerque, were once like. A largely agricultural hamlet filled with farm fields, horse corrals, and ancient adobe homes, the area today is also an artists' haven and home to wonderful farmers' markets, specialty shops, restaurants, and other attractions sprinkled alongside Corrales

Road, the village's main thoroughfare.
◆ Take I-40 west to Coors Rd and continue north to Corrales
Within Corrales:

Los Colores Set slightly back from the road in the shade of a huge cottonwood, this unique regional museum is located in the historic **Alejandro Gonzales House** and is dedicated to the textile traditions of old Mexico and New Mexico. The museum's focal point is its collection of more than 200 antique Mexican serapes representing two centuries of weaving traditions. Changing exhibits of traditional and contemporary folk art and weaving are also featured.
◆ Donation requested. Tu-Su 1-4PM. 4499 Corrales Rd NW. 898.5077

The Desert Rose ★★$ This small cafe located next to **Los Colores** is a popular breakfast spot for bicyclists, balloonists, and other locals in the know. Try the Desert Rose steak (12 ounces of rib eye with lots of red or green chile, topped with melted cheddar cheese), or the *paparito* (potatoes, eggs, and chorizo in a flour tortilla smothered in red or green chile), another favorite. ◆ American/New Mexican ◆ Tu-Sa breakfast, lunch, and dinner; Su breakfast and lunch. 4515 Corrales Rd NW. 898.2269

Casa Vieja ★★★$$$ Classic French and Northern Italian cuisine is offered in the warm adobe setting of the oldest house in Corrales, built circa 1706. Daily specials feature poultry, beef, and seafood plus a selection of several wonderful pasta dishes; interesting seasonal entrées include sautéed soft-shell crab in the summer and wild boar in the fall. The back of the restaurant doubles as a gourmet pizzeria, where the unusual red-chile cheese pizza gets rave reviews. There's also an extensive selection of French and California wines, with a reserve wine list that predates World War II. ◆ Continental ◆ Tu-Su breakfast, lunch, and dinner. Reservations recommended. 4541 Corrales Rd NW. 898.7489

Las Nutrias Vineyard and Winery The grapes grown here have won numerous awards for this winery's distinctly New Mexican wines. Complimentary tastings let your own palate decide the quality of the vintage. The enchanting scenic rural setting surely deserves some awards, too. ◆ W-Su noon-6PM or by appointment. 4627 Corrales Rd NW. 897.7863

Old San Ysidro Church Once the center of Corrales, the original **San Ysidro Church,** named after the patron saint of agriculture, was washed away during the Rio Grande flood of 1868. Some of the original church timbers, however, were recovered and used in the beautiful adobe Mission-style structure seen today. ◆ Old Church Rd NW. Turn east off of northbound Corrales Rd and continue about three minutes east. No phone

3 Balloon Fiesta Park Every October the largest gathering of balloonists in the world convenes in this park for the Albuquerque International Balloon Fiesta. (For more information on this event, see "Fiesta in the Sky" on page 111.) It is also used year-round by local balloonists to launch flights. On sunny weekends, you can hear the dragonlike roar of hot-air balloons as they skim just above the rooftops of surrounding suburbs. ◆ Off Edith Blvd NE (between Paseo del Norte and Alameda Blvd)

4 Sadie's ★★★★$ This favorite North Valley restaurant serves the best New Mexican food in town—the servings are massive, and the chile is authentic and hot. Try the red-chile cheese enchiladas, the guaco chicken (guacamole and chicken) tacos, or the green-chile stew. Everything comes with chips and scorching salsa, crispy *papitas* (fried potatoes), and fresh fluffy sopaipillas made to drench in honey. There's usually a line, but it's worth the wait. ◆ New Mexican ◆ Daily lunch and dinner. 6230 Fourth St NW (at Solar Rd, 2 blocks north of Montaño Rd). 345.5339

Restaurants/Clubs: Red	Hotels: Blue
Shops/ 🌳 Outdoors: Green	Sights/Culture: Black

5 Petroglyph National Monument

A glimpse into the fascinating world of some of the area's earliest Indian inhabitants can be found along this ancient 17-mile stretch of volcanic rock on Albuquerque's West Mesa. Here on the site of five extinct volcanoes, more than 17,000 petroglyphs (prehistoric rock drawings) dating back as early as AD 1300 provide a record of Native American hunters who camped along the lava flows and etched their heritage into the dark basalt. For years, the area stood as a state park, but in 1990 Congress designated it the country's first site for the preservation of prehistoric rock art. Four hiking trails take visitors along the escarpment through miles of symbolic images of birds, horned serpents, shield bearers (see the illustration above), flute players, and more, while plaques tell observers whether they represent human, animal, or ceremonial forms. Though somewhat strenuous, the **Mesa Point Trail** provides some of the best viewing. ◆ Fee per vehicle. Daily. 6900 Unser Blvd NW. Take I-40 west to Coors Rd and follow the signs. 897.8814

6 Rio Grande Nature Center State Park
All manner of fauna and flora can be viewed year-round in this stunning sanctuary for birds and migratory fowl in western Albuquerque. Located in a cottonwood forest on the east bank of the Rio Grande, the beautiful space features two miles of riverside trails where roadrunners (New Mexico's state bird), pheasant, skunks, beavers, and more frolic in their natural habitats. Free guided trail walks are held every weekend. The unique **Antoine Predock**–designed visitors' center is built half-above and half-below ground, providing fascinating over- and under-the-surface views of the frogs, ducks, birds, and turtles that live in the center's three-acre pond. During migration months, the center is also a popular resting spot for fowl such as snow geese and sandhill cranes. ◆ Nominal admission; children under age 6 free. Daily. 2901 Candelaria Rd NW (at the Rio Grande; Candelaria dead ends in the park). 344.7240

7 Indian Pueblo Cultural Center The life and culture of the Native American peoples of New Mexico's 19 Indian pueblos are highlighted in this spectacular, two-story, open horseshoe structure. (It is said to be a contemporary interpretation of the design of **Pueblo Bonito,** the prehistoric ruin that is considered the high point of Chaco Canyon Indian architecture.) Jointly owned and operated by the pueblos as a nonprofit organization, the center is a short drive north of Old Town, but the mood is miles away from Albuquerque's bustling city life. Murals depicting traditional Indian life line the walls while drumbeats drone from a central courtyard where ceremonial dances are performed for visitors most weekends and holidays. (Unlike dances held at the pueblos, picture-taking is allowed here—and at no charge.) Downstairs, a permanent exhibit charts the evolution of the pueblos from prehistoric times to the present, while the center's upper level showcases the distinctive arts and crafts of the individual pueblos. Visitors can see videos of the late **San Ildefonso** potter Maria Martinez demonstrating her renowned black pottery technique, or read instructions on how to bake bread in a traditional Indian *horno* (mud oven). The gift shop features the largest collection of Indian arts and crafts in the Southwest and some of the best buys on authentic Indian jewelry, textiles, painting, sculpture, baskets, leather works, and pottery to be found anywhere. The center's small restaurant is also the best place to sample authentic Native American cuisine, including *posole* (corn-based stew), tamales, and fluffy Indian fry bread. ♦ Admission for museum. Daily. 2401 12th St NW (just north of I-40). 843.7270

8 Rio Grande Zoological Park Home to more than 1,300 animals from around the world, this 60-acre zoo sits amid ancient cottonwoods on a stretch of riverside *bosque* (wooded area) a short distance south of Downtown. Known for its lush native landscaping and spacious naturalistic exhibits, the zoo includes an Amazon rain forest and an African savanna, home to a fine collection of endangered hoofed African animals, including gerenuk, sable, and bongo. Apes, elephants, rhinos, and giraffes also live at the zoo, as well as peacocks, pink flamingos, polar bears, and an array of Southwestern snakes, reptiles, and other native species. Don't miss the endangered Mexican gray wolf exhibit or Moonshadow, a rare snow leopard from the Himalayas. In the summer, let the kids loose in the outdoor petting zoo. ♦ Admission. Daily. 903 10th St SW (just south of Coal Ave). 843.7413

9 Albuquerque Sports Stadium The only known sports stadium with a drive-in spectator area is home to the **Albuquerque Dukes,** the top Triple-A farm team of the **Los Angeles Dodgers.** Pitcher Orel Hershiser played here, and every April through September other **Dodger** hopefuls take on their **Pacific Coast League** rivals in the 30,000-seat, city-owned stadium. ♦ 1601 Stadium Blvd SE (between University and Yale Blvds). 243.1791

10 Ernie Pyle Memorial Library A bust of beloved World War II correspondent Ernie Pyle greets visitors to the memorabilia-filled home of the Pulitzer Prize–winning writer who won the loyalty of readers worldwide with his "Worm's Eye View" of the war overseas. Pyle moved with his wife, Jerry, to the little white clapboard house in 1940 and returned there between assignments until his death at the hands of a sniper on the Pacific island of Ie Shima on 18 April 1945. Today, the house is home to the smallest branch of the **Albuquerque Public Library** and is a tribute to his illustrious writing career. On display are Pyle's Stetson, his pewter mug, and his favorite chair, plus photos, Pyle's hand-written articles, and news clippings of his career and his death. ♦ Free. Tu-Sa. 900 Girard Blvd SE (between Central Ave and Gibson Blvd). 256.2065

11 Courtyard Restaurant ★★★★$$$ A beautiful outdoor dining terrace and a display kitchen where the three chefs prepare innovative New Southwestern dishes of fish, beef, seafood, pasta, and veal are the highlights of this restaurant's contemporary design. Menu choices include spicy breaded calamari with two dipping sauces (Thai-chile and cocktail), New Mexican cordon bleu chicken stuffed with Monterey Jack cheese, and piñon- and rosemary-dusted tuna with a roasted garlic beurre blanc sauce. The key lime pie is wonderful, and the special Sunday brunch is a town favorite. Try the eggs benedict with a red-chile béarnaise sauce. Happy Hour packs the place on Friday nights. ♦ Southwestern ♦ M-Sa lunch and dinner; Su brunch. Reservations recommended. 1100 San Mateo Blvd NE (in the Fashion Square Shopping Center, at Lomas Blvd). 268.5354

12 New Mexico State Fairgrounds/The Downs at Albuquerque This spot doubles as the site of the annual New Mexico State Fair, one of the state's largest events, and as home to horse racing at the **Downs at Albuquerque.** Every September the fair features two weeks of down-home entertainment and cuisine, including one of the top professional rodeos in the country, a carnival, cooking contests, and animal exhibits, plus displays of the arts and culture of the state's Native American and Hispanic populations. Be sure to sample the native foods in the fair's Spanish and Indian villages.

The fair also kicks off a "mini" horse racing season at the **Downs at Albuquerque,** where a $500,000 purse—the state's richest—attracts the best thoroughbred and quarter horse talent in the Southwest. The regular season lasts from January through June, with races every Wednesday, Friday, Saturday, and Sunday. The glass-enclosed, climate-controlled grandstand is ideal for watching the jockeys chase some $3 million in annual purses. ♦ Bounded by Lomas Blvd NE and Central Ave NE, and Louisiana Blvd NE and San Pedro Dr NE. 262.1188

13 Uptown Shopping If you absolutely *must* go to a mall, Albuquerque's two major shopping centers are located in the fast-paced Uptown business district on Louisiana Boulevard between I-40 and Menaul Boulevard. **Coronado Center,** the state's largest mall, houses more than 160 stores, including **The Gap** (883.4646), **Foley's** (883.3600), and **Victoria's Secret** (889.0922). Down the road at **Winrock Center, Dillard's** (880.0866) and **Montgomery Ward** (888.5500) mix with fast food, books, and sporting goods. ♦ Daily. Coronado Center: Louisiana and Menaul Blvds NE. 881.2700; Winrock Center: Louisiana Blvd NE (just north of I-40). 883.6132

14 National Atomic Museum This Kirtland Air Force Base museum traces the history of the nuclear age and New Mexico's role in it, beginning with the top-secret Los Alamos–based Manhattan Project of the 1940s through today's development of nuclear technology and the problems of nuclear waste. Exhibits include replicas of the "Fat Man" and "Little Boy" bombs, full-scale models of the B-52 and F105D bombers, and historic flying machines. The classic documentary *Ten Seconds that Shook the World* (on the World War II atomic bomb story) is shown daily, while other displays and films deal with fusion, alternative energy, and peaceful applications of nuclear technology. ♦ Free. Daily. Kirtland Air Force Base, Wyoming Blvd SE and K St SE. 845.6670

15 Tinkertown Museum Bob and Carla Ward own this marvelous miniature world of animated hand-carved figurines. Located 20 minutes east of Albuquerque on the winding road to Sandia Crest, the museum is the result of more than 30 years of collecting and carving by Bob, a fan of the traveling miniature circus shows of the 1950s, and Carla, who has been crafting her own functional pottery since 1975. Together, the two have amassed a delightful collection of more than 900 carved wooden characters, complete with a tiny Western town and a circus with trapeze artists, dancing bears, fire-eaters, and a merry-go-round. Other museum highlights include wedding cake couples; an eerie mechanical Boot Hill Cemetery, where lightning crackles as an angel and devil battle over poor lost souls; and the gift shop's selection of Carla Ward's hand-thrown stoneware. All is enclosed between walls constructed of more than 40,000 glass bottles, another Ward hobby honed long before recycling became fashionable. ♦ Daily Apr-Oct. Sandia Park, NM 536. Take exit 175 north from I-40. 281.5233

16 Sandia Peak Aerial Tramway The best view of Albuquerque is from atop the world's longest aerial tramway ride. The spectacular 2.7-mile trip to the top of 10,400-foot-high Sandia Peak climbs 4,000 feet from the northern outskirts of the city through four of the Earth's seven life zones, the equivalent of traveling from Mexico to Alaska in biological terms. The 20-minute ride features dramatic vistas of high desert flora, jagged granite outcroppings, and pine-covered peaks, where elk, bear, bighorn sheep, and golden eagles roam. The observation deck at the summit provides an 11,000-square-mile panoramic view of Santa Fe, Los Alamos, and other distant sites. In winter, the tram whisks skiers to the Sandia Peak ski area, which features six lifts and 25 miles of beginner and intermediate slopes. The Sandias are also popular for cross-country skiing, hiking, and mountain biking, with various trails accessible by tram or by car. ♦ Fee. Daily. 10 Tramway Loop NE. From I-40, take Tramway Rd exit 167 and head north approximately 9 miles; from I-25, take Tramway Rd exit 234 and head approximately 5 miles east. 298.8518, 296.9585

At Sandia Peak:

High Finance ★★$$$ Perched two miles above Albuquerque atop Sandia Peak, this restaurant offers a breathtaking view plus a good selection of beef, seafood, and pasta in an elegant but casual setting. The fettuccine alfredo, the Santa Fe chicken (with green chile, tomatoes, onions, and melted cheese), and the prime rib and scampi are sure to satisfy. Dinner reservations include a discount tramway ticket to the top. ♦ Continental ♦ Daily lunch and dinner. Reservations recommended. 243.9742

Firehouse Restaurant ★★$$$ Located at the base of the **Sandia Peak Tramway,** this casual restaurant also provides good city views from its outdoor deck, plus steaks and seafood cooked over a mesquite grill. An old steam-powered fire engine doubles as a bar, there's live music in the lounge. ♦ Steaks/Seafood ♦ Daily dinner; deck and bar noon-11PM. Reservations required. 38 Tramway Rd. 856.3473

Sandia Crest House Gift Shop and Restaurant ★$ Yet more wonderful views, plus gifts, burgers, sandwiches, and snacks are served in this restaurant at the top of Sandia Crest. This spot provides good access to hiking trails, too. ♦ Snacks ♦ Daily. Sandia Crest. From I-40, take exit 175 north, follow NM 14 north, and head east on NM 536 to the summit. 243.0605

Albuquerque Day Trips

Escape from urban Albuquerque to a meandering mountain road or a historic Indian pueblo is possible in anywhere from three minutes to three hours. Those who really want to get out of town quickly should hit the beautiful **Turquoise Trail**, which winds through some of the most scenic and eclectic towns in the state and eventually leads to Santa Fe. And don't miss some of the area's other natural and historic wonders that are farther afield.

Some of the most notable getaways include the ruins of the capital of the Anasazi people at **Chaco Culture National Historic Park**, the spectacular bird sanctuary at the **Bosque del Apache Wildlife Refuge**, the ancient lava-crusted landscapes of **El Malpais National Monument and Conservation Area**, the massive sandstone mesa at **El Morro National Monument**, and the **Fort Sumner State Monument**, where the infamous Billy the Kid was gunned down and buried. Finally, both ancient Indian ruins and the modern-day homes of 11 of the state's Pueblo Indian tribes are situated throughout the area. The stunning **Acoma Pueblo** and the 17th-century **Salinas National Monument** are prime recommendations, although a day trip to any of the surrounding Indian sites will undoubtedly be insightful and memorable.

1 Turquoise Trail If you prefer backroad scenery over freeway frenzy, this historic trail should be your route of choice to Santa Fe. Beginning at I-40's Cedar Crest exit on Albuquerque's east side, NM 14 meanders north some 46 miles to Santa Fe, snaking through the old mining towns of Golden, Madrid, and Cerrillos, where miners once coaxed mass quantities of gold, coal, silver, lead, zinc, and turquoise from nearby hills. When World War II sent these men to war, the mines went bust and the towns went to the ghosts. Then during the 1960s, the sleepy villages reawakened to a new

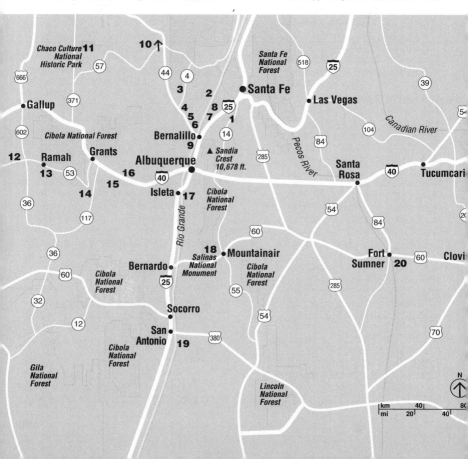

generation of residents—hippies, artists, writers, and the like—whose own frontier spirit has transformed the towns into historic centers steeped in a relaxed old-time atmosphere of art, music, theater, and more.

Winding through the shadows of Albuquerque's majestic Sandia Mountains, the trail makes its way past Cedar Crest and **Sandia Park** until the tiny village of **Golden** comes into view about 10 miles north. Once a bustling gold-mining town—and the site of the first gold rush west of the Mississippi in 1825—Golden sits on the northern edge of the San Pedro Mountains. Today a general store and a rock shop dot the highway along with a smattering of restored houses; most of the old homes, however, remain dilapidated and abandoned. Golden's architectural gem is the little church that rests on a hill at the edge of town. Built in the 1830s in honor of St. Francis of Assisi, the simple adobe mission hosts beautiful hand-carved statues and holds services twice yearly—the Feast of St. Peter on 29 June and the Feast of St. Francis on 4 October. **La Casita** (no phone), a gift shop on the village's northern end, serves as Golden's unofficial information center. Take your questions there, and if you want to see the interior of the **St. Francis Church,** ask Beatrice for the key.

About 12 miles north of Golden, in the mineral-rich Ortiz Mountains, is the renowned little coal town of **Madrid,** the only place in the country where hard (anthracite) and soft (bituminous) coal exist side by side. Once boasting a production of 500 tons of coal a day, Madrid was a thriving company town of about 2,500 people from 1893 to 1954. In the 1930s it was known worldwide as the "City of Lights" for its extraordinary annual Christmas display of more than 150,000 lights (the town owned the power company). Hillsides and streets were transformed into a giant toyland, a miniature Bethlehem, and other spectacular settings filled with Santa and scores of animated characters. So incredible was the spectacle that commercial airline pilots detoured through the area so their passengers could view it from above. In recent years, Madrid residents have begun lighting up the town again at Christmas, though on a much smaller scale than before.

Today Madrid is home to some 300 people who have converted old company stores and wooden houses into intriguing galleries, restaurants, and shops featuring works by local artisans, native foods, custom clothing, and imported goods. Recommended are **The Tapestry Gallery** (471.0194) for handwoven rugs and clothing; **Maya Jones** (473.3641) for Guatemalan imports; **Primitiva** (no phone) for local pottery, rugs, baskets, and folk art; and the **Madrid Supply Company** (471.9128) a local artists' showspace. Plan to stop for lunch at the **Mineshaft Tavern** (★★$; 473.0743), where the live entertainment and blue-cheese burger can't be beat. The **Old**

Coal Mine Museum (473.0743) features artifacts and memorabilia of Madrid's mining heyday. ♦ Museum: admission. Tours daily; museum daily. The **Engine House Theater** (473.0743) stages hilarious melodramas beneath the backdrop of an old steam locomotive. And in the summer, a superb series of outdoor concerts are held at Madrid's old ballpark.

A few more miles north is the still-sleepy village of **Cerrillos,** whose hills once bore some of the finest turquoise in the world, and whose boomtown-era residents once supported 21 saloons. The town retains an Old West ambience and has provided the setting for a number of Westerns, including the "Young Guns" and "Lonesome Dove" TV series. Highlights include the **Turquoise Trail Trading Post** (471.0629), where you can purchase miniature adobe bricks and tie-dyed T-shirts; and Casa Grande (471.2744), a rambling 21-room adobe that features a petting zoo, a turquoise-mining museum, and the What Not Shop, which carries antiques, old rocks, and Indian jewelry. From Cerrillos the trail continues another 15 miles to Santa Fe and I-25. ♦ NM 14, from I-40 at Tijeras Ave to I-25 in Santa Fe

2 Cochiti Pueblo

The famous pottery Storyteller figurine (pictured at right) originated here in the 1960s when pueblo potter Helen Cordero was inspired by memories of her grandfather spinning the ancient tales of the Cochiti tribe. Soon, other pueblo artists were creating their own versions of the openmouthed narrator whose lap is piled with listening youngsters, and the Storyteller became the distinctive symbol of the villagers' fine pottery skills. Craftspeople at this Keresan Indian pueblo are also praised for their traditional drums, which beat hypnotically each 14 July, when the tribe gathers for its annual feast day to perform the ceremonial Corn Dance in honor of their patron saint, San Buenaventura. The church erected in 1628 in honor of the saint still stands regally here amid squat modern pueblo homes.

Cochiti also is known for its prime recreational facilities, including Cochiti Dam, one of the largest earth and concrete dams in the country. The dam created Cochiti Lake, a beautiful seven-mile-long warm-water lake that is a windsurfer's wonderland and an angler's paradise, stocked with rainbow trout, bass, crappie, and pike. But don't bring a motor boat, as this is a no-wake lake. The pueblo's commercial center, tennis courts, and 18-hole championship golf course offer other alternatives. ♦ Free. Daily. Cameras, recorders, and sketch-books prohibited. Take I-25 north 45 miles to the Cochiti exit, then follow the signs west. 465.2244

3 Jemez Pueblo This picturesque pueblo, located northwest of Albuquerque in the foothills of the Jemez Mountains, became the state's sole Towa-speaking pueblo after **Pecos Pueblo** was abandoned in the 1830s. Today, the ceremonials of both pueblos are observed here; the Feast of Our Lady of the Angels, highlighted by the Old Pecos Bull Dance, is held on 2 August, while on 12 November the pueblo honors its patron saint, San Diego. Three miles north is the **Red Rock Scenic Area** (NM 44, no phone) where you can see and buy the pueblo's noted crafts—sculpture, pottery, jewelry, moccasins, drums, and baskets made from yucca fronds. The 88,000-acre reservation also includes fishing and hunting sites, permits for which must be purchased from the **Jemez Pueblo** game warden. ♦ Free. ♦ Daily. Photographs and sketches prohibited. Follow I-25 north 20 miles to Bernalillo, then go northwest about 20 miles along NM 44 and follow the signs to Jemez Pueblo. 834.7359

3 Jemez Springs/Jemez State Monument Twenty miles north of the pueblo, in the spectacular red sandstone Jemez Canyon, is Jemez Springs, an old resort town filled with bubbling hot mineral springs that attracts health-seekers from miles around. On the northern edge of the springs is **Jemez State Monument**, the site of the spectacular ruins of the prehistoric Jemez Indian pueblo of **Giusewa** (Place of the Boiling Waters). Also preserved here is the **San Jose de los Jemez Church** (no phone), a great stone structure built in 1622 as a place of worship and a fortress with eight-foot-thick rock walls and an octagonal bell tower. ♦ Jemez State Monument: admission; free for those under age 15. ♦ Daily. 20 miles north of Jemez Pueblo along NM 44. 829.3530

4 Zia Pueblo The ancient Zia sun sign (pictured above) that is the symbol of this small Keresan village is also the official emblem that appears on the New Mexico state flag and license plates. Likewise, the Zia bird and the double rainbow design both are distinctive **Zia Pueblo** symbols and figure prominently in the exquisite polychrome pottery created here. The pueblo is also known for its outstanding painters, some of whom are internationally recognized for their watercolors and oils. Located at its present site since the early 1300s, the people of Zia honor their patron saint, Our Lady of the Assumption, every 15 August with an all-day Corn Dance. Zia arts and crafts are sold at the tribe's **Cultural Center.** And two miles west of the village, Zia Lake offers fishing, with permits available at the site. ♦ Free. Daily. Photos, recorders, and sketchbooks prohibited. Take I-25 north 20 miles to Bernalillo, then go 17 miles northwest on NM 44. 867.3304

5 Santa Ana Pueblo The old village of this Keresan Indian pueblo houses few of its current tribal members; most of them live in modern stuccoed homes in nearby Bernalillo or surrounding farmlands. Nonetheless, the village comes alive each year when residents return for their annual 26 July feast day and pay homage to their patron saint, Santa Ana, with the day-long Corn Dance. Other ceremonial dances are held here on 1 and 6 January, Easter Sunday, 24 and 29 June, and 25-28 December. Visitors are encouraged to attend the ceremonials because that's the only time the ancient community opens to the public. Nearby, the new village of Santa Ana, however, bustles with activity year-round. At the **Ta Ma Myia Cooperative Association** (no phone), native crafts-people sell their fine woven belts and bold polychrome pottery, along with other arts and crafts. And the tribe's 27-hole Valle Grande Golf Course (Bernalillo, 867.9464) draws golfers from around the state. ♦ Free. The old pueblo is open during annual ceremonials only; contact the tribal governor's office for the best times to visit the new village. No photographs, recordings, or sketching permitted. Take I-25 north 20 miles to Bernalillo, then head northwest 8 miles on NM 44. 867.3301

6 Coronado State Monument and Park  Explorer Francisco Vásquez de Coronado wintered here in 1540 during the first

---

Restaurants/Clubs: Red   Hotels: Blue

Shops/ 🌳 Outdoors: Green   **Sights/Culture: Black**

exploration of the area by the Spanish as they searched for the elusive Seven Cities of Cibola, which were rumored to be made of gold. What they found instead was the ancient Tiwa-speaking people of Kuaua, whose awesome 1,200-room pueblo on the west banks of the Rio Grande represented the tribe's architectural sophistication. More than one thousand people once lived amid this maze of rooms and sacred underground kivas, which were painted with elaborate murals of ancient Indian symbols and plant and animal life. The pueblo was abandoned near the end of the 17th century, and its mud walls remained buried for 250 years until its excavation in 1935. The monument was created in 1940 to preserve the ruins, and today visitors can walk among the pueblo's crumbling rock walls and descend into an ancient kiva. A small archaeological museum displays ancient Kuaua murals and artifacts. Adjacent to the monument is the **Coronado State Park,** which features picnic shelters, campsites, and more Indian ruins. A good time to visit is during the fall; when the trees change to their glistening autumn hue, you might indeed think you've discovered cities of gold. ◆ Admission; children under age 6 free. Daily. Take I-25 north 20 miles to Bernalillo, then head northwest a few miles on NM 44. 867.5351

There's More to New Mexican Chow than Cheese and Chile

When people talk about eating Mexican food in this region of the country, they are not referring to the cuisine of Mexico, with its chicken mole and shrimp brochettes. The phrase is short for New Mexican food—and that is a very different kettle of chile.

New Mexican food is based on four ingredients: flour tortillas, corn tortillas, pinto beans, and chile pods. Toss in a little cheese, and these staples can be transformed into a surprising variety of delicious, hearty, and nourishing dishes. Chile pods are grown throughout the state and are typically processed into chopped green chile or red chile powder. (In New Mexico chile is always spelled with an e—the original Spanish spelling—not chili, which is Anglicized to reflect the pronunciation.) New Mexican chile has no resemblance to the mix of beef, beans, onions, and tomato sauce known as Texas chili. Many locals eat a bowl of plain green chile or with beans added in. More often the chile is served as a sauce over enchiladas, burritos, rellenos (chile pods stuffed with cheese), and other local dishes. Chile is an acquired taste, but once acquired it tends to become a lifetime predilection.

The style of New Mexican cuisine began to evolve centuries ago with the Pueblo Indians, who pounded corn into meal to make tortillas, which were a daily staple. Their diet was later blended with Navajo tastes, then spiced up by Spanish conquistadores and newcomers from Mexico. The resulting recipes are now served in the poorest New Mexican homes as well as a great many excellent restaurants.

A delicacy created in Northern New Mexico that might be unknown to most visitors is the sopaipilla (pronounced soap-a-pee-ya). These delicate, deep-fried puffy breads are served with most New Mexican meals as an alternative to tortillas. You break off a piece and put a few drops of honey inside. The sweet taste complements the chile and also reduces the burning sensation. Sopaipillas and honey may also serve as a substitute for dessert, and when they are light and fluffy, they are truly a

treat. Some of the best sopaipillas are served north of Santa Fe at the **Rancho de Chimayó** restaurant (see page 75) in Chimayó.

In recent years there has been an influx of upscale restaurants in Santa Fe that have attempted to merge New Mexican dishes with those of California, France, and Asia. This is known in New Mexico as Southwestern food and is served at such well-known restaurants as the **Coyote Cafe** (see page 36), **Santacafe** (see page 28), and **Anasazi** (see page 31). Basically, it's highbrow New Mexican food made with costlier and sometimes subtler ingredients. The lowly enchilada, which in traditional New Mexican cooking is filled with cheese, onions, chicken, or beef, may be stuffed with duck, shrimp, crab, rabbit, pheasant, or sea bass in a Southwestern restaurant. A chile relleno—a breaded, stuffed, fried chile pod that is a local joy—may be filled with a sweet-tasting goat cheese mixture instead of the traditional jack cheese. Some Southwestern food is superb, but all too often adding exotic ingredients to what is basically a simple, earthy kind of cooking results in an excess of richness. To sample true New Mexican food, go to a down-home New Mexican restaurant. You'll not only get the real thing, you'll get it at much lower prices.

7 San Felipe Pueblo One of the most traditional of the Rio Grande pueblos, this Keresan Indian community is renowned for its beautiful ceremonials. Most notable is the Green Corn Dance held on 1 May, when hundreds of men, women, and children honor their patron saint, San Felipe, singing ancient chants and dancing about in brilliant costumes on a central plaza that has been well-worn by generations of dancing feet. The craftspeople here are known for their exquisite beadwork and pottery; permission to walk around the village to talk to native artisans or other pueblo residents must be granted from the tribal office. ♦ Free. Call the tribal office for the best times to visit. No cameras, sketching, or recording permitted. Take I-25 north 20 miles to Bernalillo and follow the signs another 10 miles north. 867.3381

8 Santo Domingo Pueblo The largest of the eastern Keresan Indian pueblos is famous for its fine *heishi* (intricately ground shell, pronounced *he*-she), turquoise, and silver jewelry. Once a thriving farming community, it is now known for its marketing skills; more than 350 pueblo artisans sell their arts and crafts at roadside stands, on the **Palace of the Governor**'s portal in Santa Fe, and during the pueblo's annual Labor Day weekend arts-and-crafts fair. The community also performs one of the most dramatic Indian ceremonials in the area—more than 500 pueblo singers, dancers, and drummers participate in a colorful all-day Corn Dance on 4 August. The elaborate dance features "Koshare" clowns—nearly naked men who paint their bodies in black-and-white stripes and pester spectators—as well as men, women, and children tinged in orange and turquoise paint and clad in traditional ceremonial belts, animal skins, and headdresses. A small museum and **Tribal Cultural Center** are also located at the pueblo. ♦ Free; donations accepted. Daily. No photographs, sketching, and tape recording permitted. Take I-25 north 31 miles to Santo Domingo exit 259 and follow the signs. 465.2214

9 Sandia Pueblo Perhaps the most striking feature of this tiny Tiwa-speaking community is its huge "Las Vegas-style" bingo hall that's open round-the-clock. The pueblo's long history, however, is much more traditional: originally called Nafiat, the village was founded circa 1300. In 1540, after a visit by Spanish explorer Francisco Vásquez de Coronado, it was dubbed Sandia, which is Spanish for watermelon, the color of the surrounding mountains at sunset. The pueblo was abandoned after the 1680 Pueblo Revolt but tribal members returned to the village in later years—the ruins of the old pueblo are still visible near the present-day church.

The pueblo maintains a reputation as one of the most industrious in the state, with its bingo, horseback-riding stables, and the **Bien Mur Indian Market Center,** which includes arts and crafts from all of the New Mexico pueblos. The 40-acre Sandia Lakes Recreation Area also features fishing for bass, trout, and catfish; permits are available at the site. The pueblo's St. Anthony feast day is 13 June. Among other things, St. Anthony is the patron saint of good husbands, and on the annual feast day, pueblo mothers bring their single daughters in hopes the saint will find them a good match. ♦ Free. Daily. No photographs, sketching, or recording permitted. Follow I-25 north toward Bernalillo to tramway exit. Then head north on NM 313 for a few miles. 867.3317

10 Aztec Ruins National Monument The spectacular maze of rooms comprising these prehistoric communal dwellings were named incorrectly by 19th-century settlers who mistakenly believed they had been built by the Aztec Indians of Mexico. The ruins are actually the remnants of an ancient Anasazi pueblo that once bustled with activity. Built on a rise overlooking the turquoise waters of the Animas River, the ruins are highlighted by a two-acre U-shaped village, where visitors follow a self-guided trail to peer through decaying walls into underground kivas and crawl through tiny doorways. The 12th-century **Great Kiva,** which was restored to mint condition in 1934, features a timbered roof packed with mud and offers modern-day visitors a place to rest, listen to Navajo chants and contemplate the lives of the ancient ones. ♦ Admission. Daily. Follow I-25 north 20 miles to Bernalillo and head north 160 miles on NM 44 to Aztec. 334.6174

11 Chaco Culture National Historic Park Set in the heart of the flat San Juan Basin, Chaco Canyon was the site of the largest city (more than 5,000 people) in the Southwest during the Classic Anasazi period (about AD 1000-1200). The Chaco people also established "outlier" colonies across an area of more than 10,000 square miles of New Mexico and southern Colorado. These outposts were necessary because timber and food had to be brought into the arid San Juan Basin to support the city. Archaeologists debate endlessly about why the Anasazi chose to locate their capital in this place. One likely theory is that smoke from the city's signal fires, announcing the arrival of trade caravans from Mexico or heralding religious ceremonies, could be seen by lookouts for great distances across the San Juan Basin, as there were no mountains creating an obstruction. The extraordinary number and size of ceremonial kivas suggest Chaco Canyon was a spiritual center for the region. Pueblo Bonito, the largest of the several pueblo ruins within walking distance of one another in the canyon, contained more than 800 rooms at its heyday and is said to have been the largest residential building in the world in the 12th century. ♦ Admission. Daily. Fill the gas tank in Cuba; there is no gas, food service, or lodging in the park. Follow I-25 north to Bernalillo, then take NM 44 north 115 miles to Nageezi Trading Post and follow the unpaved park road west for about 29 miles. 786.7014, 988.6716

12 Zuni Pueblo Legends of the brilliant sunlit walls of the pueblo dwellings of Hawikuh, the ancient village of the Zuni Indians, are what prompted Francisco Vásquez de Coronado to begin an exploration of New Mexico in 1540 in search of the fabled Seven Cities of Cibola. When he arrived, however, he found no cities of gold, just the sophisticated Zuni Indian tribe. For more than a century, the Zunis grudgingly accepted the Spanish presence and the Christianity forced upon them, but after the 1680 Pueblo Revolt, Hawikuh was abandoned. In 1692 the Zuni resettled 12 miles north of Hawikuh.

With more than 8,000 members, this is the largest of the state's 19 pueblos and is renowned worldwide for its fine jewelers. Their unique inlay, overlay, and minute "needlepoint" styles combine silver with such rich stones as turquoise, black jet, coral, opal, lapis, and sugalite. Jewelry is for sale at the tribe's **Zuni Arts and Crafts Market.** The pueblo is also well known for its annual all-night Shalako Ceremony, during which dancers wear larger-than-life masks (such as the one illustrated above) that evoke the pantheon of Zuni gods. The ceremony takes place in late November or early December. ♦ Free. Daily. Photos, sketches, and recordings prohibited on feast days; cameras are allowed on other days for a fee. Take I-40 west about 120 miles to Gallup, then head 34 miles south on NM 602 to NM 53. Zuni Pueblo is several miles west on NM 53. 782.4481

13 El Morro National Monument For nearly a thousand years, New Mexico explorers, traders, soldiers, and settlers traveling an ancient Indian trade route couldn't resist taking a break in the shadow of a 200-foot-high sandstone mesa and etching their marks into its smooth surface. A portion of the pale cliff, known as Inscription Rock, is a virtual guest register of Southwest history with its prehistoric Indian petroglyphs and signatures of prominent passersby. When Juan de Oñate went through in 1605, he wrote: "Passed by here the Governor Don Juan de Oñate, from the discovery of the Sea of the South (the Gulf of California) on the 16th of April 1605." And Diego de Vargas, on his journey to reclaim the area after the 1680 Pueblo Revolt, noted: "Here was the General Don Diego de Vargas who conquered for our Holy Faith, and for the Royal Crown, all of New Mexico at his own expense, year of 1692." A natural water basin sits at the base of the towering mesa, while unexcavated Anasazi ruins, dating from the late 1300s, rest up top. The site also features a visitors' center, from which guided tours depart regularly, and a picnic area. ♦ Admission; children under 17 free. Daily. Follow I-40 west about 68 miles to Grants, then exit on NM 53 and continue about 40 miles west toward the village of Ramah. 783.4226

14 El Malpais National Monument and Conservation Area One of the most recent lava flows in North America—the remnants of five now-dormant volcanoes—is preserved at El Malpais, a 114,000-acre lava rock valley known as the Land of Fire and Ice. A succession of trails through the rugged lava beds leads to a number of volcanic wonders ranging from 700 to 50,000 years old, including volcanoes, ice caves, and the longest lava tube system in the world. The 7.5-mile **Zuni-Acoma Trail,** an ancient Indian trade route, crosses all five of the major lava flows, allowing visitors to walk on a chunky lava called "AA" and a ropelike lava known as pahoehoe. The lava is so hard that even though the trail has been in use for more than 800 years, there is little sign of wear (unlike the soles of your shoes when you're done with this walk). The five extinct volcanoes still loom overhead; visitors can peer down into the 800-foot-deep Bandera Crater, which last erupted one million years ago, or journey 75 feet below its jagged edge to a 31-degree ice cave, a freak of nature that early settlers used to store perishable foods. A must on any jaunt is La Ventana Natural Arch, located at the eastern end of the lava flow. The massive sandstone arch was formed after years of wind and water permeated the soft stone surface, creating a 125-foot-high by 165-foot-wide opening in the rock—a spectacular natural window to the world. Backcountry camping in the area is permitted, and a visitors' center is located 10 miles to the north in Grants at 620 East Santa Fe Avenue (285.4506). ♦ Free. Daily. Take I-40 about 58 miles west and exit south onto NM 117 at the Quemado exit. The lava flow area lines the west side of NM 117. Monument headquarters 285.4641

15 Acoma Pueblo Considered by many to be the most incredible of the state's 19 pueblos, **Acoma** sits 7,000 feet above sea level atop a 367-foot mesa—the Rock of Acuco—and provides a dreamy panoramic view of chamisa, juniper, red sandstone cliffs, and an endless azure sky. Appropriately called the "Sky City," the pueblo's Keresan residents are estimated to have lived here since AD 1075, making it the oldest continually inhabited city in the country. The village's multistory rock-walled dwellings occupy 70 acres of the mesa top, along with a magnificent mission church. Villagers once scaled the mesa by an ancient rock stairway and a system of handholds and toeholds chipped into the cliff. Both the pueblo and its mission are listed as National Historic Landmarks on the National Register of Historic Places.

While several thousand Indians once lived here, today the pueblo is home to about 50 residents who continue to live without water or electricity, hauling their daily necessities—even dirt for their cemetery—along a narrow road that leads from below. The other 4,000 pueblo members now live in the surrounding villages of Acomita, Anzac, and McCarty's. They return to the mesa for annual ceremonials, especially the elaborate San Esteban Feast Day held on 2 September, when residents of all ages don traditional garb and perform the Harvest Dance throughout the day. The jewel of the pueblo is the massive church, the **Mission of San Esteban del Rey,** erected in honor of the pueblo's patron saint. The church's whitewashed walls and dirt floor contrast beautifully with its 17th-century altar paintings and hand-carved wooden saints. The giant 40-foot-long ceiling beams that cross overhead were cut in the mountains 30 miles away and hauled back to the mesa upon the backs of the village men.

The only way to see the pueblo is by guided tours, which depart regularly from the visitors' center at the mesa's base. The center also includes a restaurant featuring native foods and a small museum, which gives the history of the pueblo and its prized thin-shelled pottery. Made from white clay, the pots are embellished with orange and black optical art line patterns and Mimbres (an ancient tribe that was a forerunner of the Pueblo people) designs and are valued by collectors worldwide. Pots are for sale in the visitors' center's crafts shop, at outdoor booths, and at the ancient pueblo.
♦ Admission. Tours daily; museum daily. Cameras are permitted only on non-feast days; there's a $5 fee. Take I-40 about 52 miles west to the Acoma exit, then head another 11 miles southwest on Indian Rd 23. 252.1139

16 Laguna Pueblo The largest of the Keresan Indian pueblos, it includes six villages scattered over thousands of acres: Old Laguna, Paguate, Mesita, Paraje, Encinal, and Seama. The pueblo is also one of the state's most enterprising, bringing income to its residents through such innovative economic development projects on the reservation as the prosperous Laguna Industries, which manufactures communications shelters for the US Army. The pueblo was also once the site of one of the world's richest uranium mines, and the ongoing Laguna Reclamation Project is dedicated to restoring the mine lands to again provide mining jobs for pueblo residents. Clay is also excavated on pueblo land, and the production of the pueblo's traditional polychrome pottery—which incorporates distinctive geometric and plant and animal designs—also provides income for pueblo artists.

While each of the Laguna villages celebrates its own feast day, the entire pueblo turns out at Old Laguna on 19 September to celebrate St. Joseph's Day with Corn, Buffalo, and Eagle dances and an arts-and-crafts fair. During fishing season, permits for the Paguate Reservoir can be purchased in that village.
♦ Free. Daily. Photography regulations vary in each community. Take I-40 west 46 miles, and follow the signs to the individual villages. 552.6654, 243.7616

17 Isleta Pueblo This 16th-century pueblo is the largest of the Tiwa-speaking pueblos and home to the **San Augustin Church,** one of the oldest missions in the US. Erected about 1613, the massive adobe facade boasts two towers, a small belfry in the center, and a smaller bell hanging just above the entrance. Tribal legend has it that Fray Juan Padilla, a Spanish priest who was buried in the sanctuary of the church, periodically leaves his cottonwood coffin and comes to the surface of the sanctuary to reveal his remains to the pueblo people, many of whom regard him as a saint. The tribe also holds two annual feast days in honor of its patron saint, San Augustin, on 28 August and 4 September.

Located on the west banks of the Rio Grande just south of Albuquerque, the original pueblo was abandoned during the 1680 Pueblo

Revolt. Villagers returned later and built a new Isleta, or "little island," which today has grown to some 3,000 residents scattered among several settlements. Pueblo artisans are known for their polychrome pottery—red and black on a white background—while the pueblo's large bingo hall and camping and fishing areas lure many visitors to the reservation. One of the largest of the state's pueblos, in 1986 Isleta became the first to elect a woman as tribal governor, although not without creating considerable controversy. Camping, fishing, and picnicking permits must be purchased on site. ♦ Free. Daily. Photographs are allowed (for free) except on feast days. Follow I-25 south 13 miles, then follow the signs west to Isleta. 869.3111

18 Salinas National Monument The ruins of three abandoned 17th-century Indian villages represent the classic encounter between European civilization and prehistoric Indian tribes. This 645-acre monument is the site of three magnificent villages—Quarai, Abo, and Gran Quivira—that were abandoned in the 1670s after the arrival of the Spanish. Each of the villages features the remains of spectacular earthen Spanish-style missions erected before their inhabitants left. The area was situated near a salt lake, which was an important source of salt for early residents and traders, and the pueblos in its vicinity became known as the Salinas (Spanish for saline) tribes. Today, the villages are located within a 25-mile radius of Mountainair.

The Quarai ruins, with red sandstone walls five feet thick and 40 feet high, are some of the most beautiful in the monument. There, the well-preserved 1630 church of **La Purisima Concepción de Cuarac** continues to tower 100 feet across and 40 feet above a grassy plain. Seventeen miles to the southwest at Abo, the 30-foot-high bright red sandstone mission of **San Gregorio** boasts stone buttresses that represent the tribe's sophisticated building techniques. Nearby, the Abo River flows past the ancient Indians' three-story rock-walled homes. Still farther south is the awesome village of Gran Quivira, once home to a thriving community of 1,500. Here, Indians farmed beans and squash, hunted bison, and fashioned pottery. In 1659 they built the massive mission of **San Buenaventura** atop a windswept mesa with 30-foot-high limestone walls standing six-feet-thick. The multilevel ruins also are scattered with underground kivas, where villagers worshiped their traditional gods. Self-guided tour pamphlets are available at the monument's visitors' center (847.2585) in the **Shaffer Hotel** ($; Hwy 60, 847.2888) in Mountainair or at the individual sites. ♦ Free. Daily. Take I-25 south 50 miles to Bernardino, then take Hwy 60 about 35 miles to Mountainair, at the junction of Hwy 60 and NM 55. Quarai is 10 miles north of Mountainair off NM 55. Abo is 7 miles west of

Mountainair on Hwy 60. Gran Quivira is 25 miles south of Mountainair on NM 55

19 Bosque del Apache Wildlife Refuge 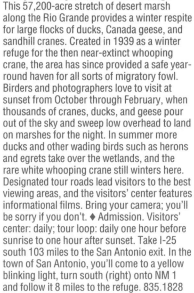 This 57,200-acre stretch of desert marsh along the Rio Grande provides a winter respite for large flocks of ducks, Canada geese, and sandhill cranes. Created in 1939 as a winter refuge for the then near-extinct whooping crane, the area has since provided a safe year-round haven for all sorts of migratory fowl. Birders and photographers love to visit at sunset from October through February, when thousands of cranes, ducks, and geese pour out of the sky and sweep low overhead to land on marshes for the night. In summer more ducks and other wading birds such as herons and egrets take over the wetlands, and the rare white whooping crane still winters here. Designated tour roads lead visitors to the best viewing areas, and the visitors' center features informational films. Bring your camera; you'll be sorry if you don't. ♦ Admission. Visitors' center: daily; tour loop: daily one hour before sunrise to one hour after sunset. Take I-25 south 103 miles to the San Antonio exit. In the town of San Antonio, you'll come to a yellow blinking light, turn south (right) onto NM 1 and follow it 8 miles to the refuge. 835.1828

20 Fort Sumner State Monument The crumbling ruins of **Fort Sumner's Bosque Redondo Reservation** are a harsh reminder of the incarceration of more than 9,000 Mescalero Apache and Navajo from 1863 to 1868 by the US Army. Moved from their homes in Canyon de Chelly, the Indians were forced to endure the infamous "Long Walk" to the site, as well as the wretched living conditions at the fort on the state's rugged eastern plains. When a treaty was signed five years later, those who had survived were allowed to return to Arizona. The fort was later sold and converted into a large ranch—the same ranch where Pat Garrett gunned down Billy the Kid after the infamous outlaw's escape from the Lincoln County Jail in 1881. The Kid was buried in the military cemetery nearby, but because the fugitive's fans keep trying to steal his tombstone, a chain link fence now surrounds the marker. Adjacent to the cemetery is the **Billy the Kid Museum** (355.2380), housing a collection of photographs and memorabilia of the state's most notorious outlaw. ♦ Admission. M, Th-Su. Follow I-40 east about 113 miles to Santa Rosa, then take Hwy 84 south for 45 miles and follow the signs. 355.2573

Art of the Ages: New Mexico's Hispanic Legacy

Traces of the Hispanic peoples who settled in New Mexico nearly 400 years ago can still be found in all areas of contemporary life—from the strains of *Varsovianas* and other traditional Spanish dances that echo through local clubs and dance halls to the plump tortillas and steaming bowls of beans and chile that grace dinner tables throughout the state. Yet perhaps nothing better expresses the vitality of the state's Hispanic culture than the traditional arts and crafts that have endured through generations of people and centuries of change.

During the 1600s, when the first Spaniards journeyed into what was then a remote northern region of the Mexican empire, they began using local materials to fashion practical goods and religious objects to adorn their homes and Catholic churches. At first, the work echoed the traditional motifs of Spain and Mexico. But in time, native artisans developed styles and techniques that diverged from these traditions and reflected instead the styles that were unique to Hispanic New Mexico. The result was a vibrant regional art form that was distinctively their own.

Today, the techniques and styles honed by the earliest New Mexico settlers are used to make respected arts and crafts. Created by local artists—many of whose families have been practicing the same methods for generations—such art works are still used by native New Mexicans for ornamental and religious purposes. They are also collected by museums, galleries, and art connoisseurs worldwide, whose regard for the heritage of the state's Hispanic population has encouraged the sustenance of traditional arts and crafts.

Some of the oldest of these art forms are *santos*. These depictions of religious figures are made in the form of *bultos* (three-dimensional carvings) or *retablos* (paintings on panels of wood). The artists who make the sacred icons are known as *santeros,* and most of them still use traditional methods, creating the icons with native materials such as aspen, pine, or cottonwood, and natural pigments derived from native vegetables, minerals, and clay.

The art of tinwork also harkens back to the days of the state's early Spanish pioneers, who created utilitarian objects as well as crosses, chalices, and other religious items from silver. When that precious metal ran short, tin was substituted, and new methods of cutting, punching, and stamping evolved. Today, tin is transformed by local tinsmiths into a number of decorative and sacred objects, including mirrors, crosses, candlesticks, and Christmas tree ornaments.

Besides tin, such metals as iron, silver, and gold are shaped into functional and decorative arts. With-standing the heat of a fiery forge, blacksmiths bend iron into tools, latches, and household objects such as candlestick holders. Goldsmiths and silversmiths shape those precious metals into delicate filigree jewelry, as well as objects like bowls, pitchers, and chalices made for daily or sacred use.

Hispanic weavers have also been practicing their unique textile traditions in New Mexico for generations. Weaving on massive looms with hand-spun and vegetable-dyed wools, they work in the distinctive Rio Grande style, combining Mexican "Saltillo" and "Vallero" design techniques with Pueblo and Navajo motifs and other New Mexico Hispanic and Anglo influences. The textiles usually take the shape of rugs, but are also transformed into clothing, place mats, and decorative items. The hand stitched "Colcha" style of embroidery seen on many rugs, quilts, and other ornamental textiles is also unique to the region. Rather than thread, artists use thick yarn to create colorful floral and animal motifs.

Traditional Spanish Colonial furniture is another distinctively New Mexican craft. Hand-carved from such native woods as juniper and ponderosa pine, the style is distinguished by the use of mortise and tenon joints in place of nails. Featuring such simple motifs as rosettes or flowers, the furniture, commonly chairs, tables, chests, and *trasteros* (cupboards), is known for its elegant simplicity.

The complex art of straw appliqué represents the innovative use of native materials to develop a truly unique New Mexican art form. Applying wheat straw to bare or painted wood, artists take advantage of the straw's natural sheen to create dazzling designs on chests, crosses, jewelry boxes, and other items.

And then there are the lesser-known traditional Spanish Colonial art forms such as *reatas* (lariats), *ramilletes* (cut paper garlands), pottery, and bone carving that still survive in contemporary Hispanic New Mexico. *Reatas* are woven from horse hair, utilitarian pottery—such as bowls, plates, and pitchers—are handmade from local micaceous clays and fired outdoors, and tool handles, rings, and neckerchief slides are carved from animal bone and polished to a glistening shine.

These Hispanic arts and crafts are exhibited and sold in galleries, shops, and museums throughout New Mexico. But perhaps the biggest champion of authentic Spanish Colonial art is the Santa Fe–based Spanish Colonial Arts Society. Founded in 1925 to encourage, promote, and educate the public about ancient Hispanic arts and crafts, it is the sponsor of the annual Traditional Spanish Market, the largest traditional Hispanic art market in the country, plus the smaller Winter Market, another Hispanic art showcase. Held in Santa Fe each year during the last full weekend in July and the first weekend in December, respectively, these markets are the best place for Hispanic art aficionados to meet and buy from local artists. The markets provide an opportunity to learn firsthand about the continuing traditions that are at the heart of New Mexico's Hispanic culture.

For more information on the traditional Hispanic arts and crafts of New Mexico, call the **Spanish Colonial Arts Society** (983.4038).

Index

C

D

Index

M

Index

Restaurants

Only restaurants with star ratings are listed below. All restaurants are listed alphabetically in the main (preceding) index. Always call in advance to ensure a restaurant has not closed, changed its hours, or booked its tables for a private party. The restaurant price ratings are based on the average cost of an entrée for one person, excluding tax and tip.

★★★★ An Extraordinary Experience

★★★ Excellent

★★ Very Good

★ Good

$$$$ Big Bucks ($20 and up)

$$$ Expensive ($15-$20)

$$ Reasonable ($10-$15)

$ The Price Is Right (less than $10)

Hotels

The hotels listed below are grouped according to their price ratings; they are also listed in the main index. The hotel price ratings reflect the base price of a standard room for two people for one night during the peak season.

$$$$ Big Bucks ($140 and up)

$$$ Expensive ($80-$140)

$$ Reasonable ($50-$80)

$ The Price Is Right (less than $50)

ACCESS® Guides

Order by phone, toll-free: 1-800-331-3761

Travel: Promo # RØØ111
WSJ: Promo # RØØ211

Name _____ Phone _____

Address _____

City _____ State _____ Zip _____

Please send me the following **ACCESS**® Guides:

☐ **BARCELONA**ACCESS® $17.00
0-06-277000-4

☐ **BOSTON**ACCESS® $18.00
0-06-277049-7

☐ **BUDGET EUROPE**ACCESS® $18.00
0-06-277120-5

☐ **CAPE COD**ACCESS® $18.00
0-06-277123-X

☐ **CARIBBEAN**ACCESS® $18.00
0-06-277128-0

☐ **CHICAGO**ACCESS® $18.00
0-06-277048-9

☐ **FLORENCE/VENICE/MILAN**ACCESS®
$17.00
0-06-277081-0

☐ **HAWAII**ACCESS® $18.00
0-06-277068-3

☐ **LAS VEGAS**ACCESS® $18.00
0-06-277055-1

☐ **LONDON**ACCESS® $18.00
0-06-277129-9

☐ **LOS ANGELES**ACCESS® $18.00
0-06-277131-0

☐ **MEXICO**ACCESS® $18.00
0-06-277127-2

☐ **MIAMI & SOUTH FLORIDA**ACCESS®
$18.00
0-06-277070-5

☐ **MONTREAL & QUEBEC CITY**ACCESS® $18.00
0-06-277079-9

☐ **NEW ORLEANS**ACCESS® $18.00
0-06-277118-3

☐ **NEW YORK CITY**ACCESS® $18.00
0-06-277124-8

☐ **ORLANDO & CENTRAL FLORIDA**ACCESS® $18.00
0-06-277069-1

☐ **PARIS**ACCESS® $18.00
0-06-277132-9

☐ **PHILADELPHIA**ACCESS® $18.00
0-06-277065-9

☐ **ROME**ACCESS® $18.00
0-06-277053-5

☐ **SAN DIEGO**ACCESS® $18.00
0-06-277004-7

☐ **SAN FRANCISCO**ACCESS® $18.00
0-06-277121-3

☐ **SANTA FE/TAOS/ ALBUQUERQUE**ACCESS® $18.00
0-06-277054-3

☐ **SEATTLE**ACCESS® $18.00
0-06-277050-0

☐ **SKI COUNTRY**ACCESS®
Eastern United States $18.00
0-06-277125-6

☐ **SKI COUNTRY**ACCESS®
Western United States $18.00
0-06-277066-7

☐ **THE WALL STREET JOURNAL**
Guide to Understanding Money & Markets
$13.95
0-06-772516-3

☐ **WASHINGTON DC**ACCESS® $18.00
0-06-277077-2

☐ **WINE COUNTRY**ACCESS®
Northern California $18.00
0-06-277122-1

Prices subject to change without notice.

Total for **ACCESS**® Guides:	$
Please add applicable sales tax:	
Add $4.00 for first book S&H, $1.00 per additional book:	
Total payment:	$

☐ Check or Money Order enclosed. Offer valid in the United States only.
Please make payable to HarperCollins*Publishers*.

☐ Charge my credit card   ☐ American Express   ☐ Visa   ☐ MasterCard

Card no. _____ Exp. date _____

Signature _____

Send orders to:
HarperCollins*Publishers*
P.O. Box 588
Dunmore, PA 18512-0588

Send correspondence to:
ACCESS®PRESS
10 East 53rd Street, 18th Floor
New York, NY 10022